YOUR COSMIC BLUEPRINT

YOUR COSMIC BLUEPRINT

Master the Art of Reading an Astrology Chart

MONTE FARBER & AMY ZERNER

MANDALA

SAN RAFAEL LOS ANGELES LONDON

CONTENTS

INTRODUCTION

Throughout recorded history, the wisest people of every culture have come to the same conclusion as to what is the most empowering advice to share with their fellow human beings to help them live their best life, each one a variation on The Oracle at Delphi's "Know thyself" and Shakespeare's "To thine own self, be true."

But how do we do it? How can each of us, seemingly alone and adrift in this sea of humanity, know the unique impact we can have on the world and on our daily life if we can somehow find a way to be true to ourselves and our authentic nature?

It is often said that people do not come with instruction manuals. My wife, award-winning artist, fashion designer, and fellow astrologer, Amy Zerner, and I say that people actually *do* come with instruction manuals—and, even better, with instruction manuals that are unique to them. We're talking about your astrological birth chart, the map of how the planets of our solar system lined up around your personal nativity scene like ten wise people offering you their unique gift of insightful guidance to help you live your best life, if you first take the time to learn how to hear what they're trying to tell you.

Around here, in the Enchanted World of Amy Zerner and Monte Farber, we call an astrological birth chart a cosmic blueprint, and this book will teach you how to read and gain valuable, practical information from your cosmic blueprint and everyone else's too.

We believe that you deserve to be the star of your own show and have written *Your Cosmic Blueprint* to help you do it. This book is designed to take you on an enjoyable journey from where you are now on your life's path and supercharge your self-understanding to a level enjoyed by astrologers like me and the people who are able to avail themselves of our services, which often cost a lot of money. For the price of lunch, why not find out who you're having dinner with—starting with you!

The goal of this book is to help you understand yourself so much better that you take better control of your life, realize your purpose, live your dreams, and make the rest of your life after *Your Cosmic Blueprint* a lot more fun and meaningful than it has been up until now. Learning to read our own cosmic blueprints did exactly that for both Amy and me. Happiness lasts longer if you share it. *Your Cosmic Blueprint* is our way of sharing our good fortune with you.

Your Cosmic Blueprint is the book my wife and I wish we had available to us many years ago when we were first learning astrology. Back in the day, astrology books were very hard to read, over-the-top sexist, and written for a time and a lifestyle that mercifully no longer exists as the norm. There were no books that taught you how to look at and read a chart, putting all its various components together to reveal a whole person—only books that taught the meanings of the individual planets in their signs and houses (a concept you will be learning soon). They, and almost all astrology books that followed right up until this one, were like badly written cookbooks that simply listed the ingredients but did not explain to you when and how to put the ingredients together to make the delicious dishes. Until now, after we have spent several years creating *Your Cosmic Blueprint*, there has never been a book that teaches you how to blend these ingredients in a way that produces a three-dimensional picture of the person whose chart you are observing.

Your Cosmic Blueprint is designed to take you on an exciting journey that will empower you with a skill you can use and enjoy for the rest of your life. Though it may sound like too much to promise, read on and you will soon find that knowing how to read an astrology chart is now possible for you because we have made learning this ancient practice easier than it has ever been in astrology's five-thousand-year-old history.

Virtually all musical compositions in the history of Western music have been created using variations of the same twelve notes. Similarly, the position of the planets in each of our unique-to-us cosmic blueprints, in combination with their position within the twelve signs of astrology's zodiac, are the themes rich with meaning that each of us expresses differently to create and respond to the unique opportunities and challenges of our life. Real astrology teaches respect and tolerance for others because we can see how alike we all are as much as we can see how different we all are. Knowledge is power, and knowledge of astrology is extremely empowering.

Just as a blueprint is a plan for the construction of a home, the astrological birth chart done for the day, place, and time of your birth contains the plan for the construction of your personality, your character, and the events of your life. Knowing how to read your cosmic blueprint—your astrological birth chart—can give you useful, profound, and in many cases vital information about how you look at and approach the world and, equally important, how the people of the world look back at you and how they are inclined to see you. Just knowing how others see you can often resolve important questions you have had your whole life.

When combined with astrology's take on your unique way of looking at, experiencing, and interacting with your world and the world at large, you will have an improved self-concept and understand why we tell people that astrology is not fortune-telling, but it can definitely help you make your fortune. In fact, one of America's first billionaires, J. P. Morgan, a client and student of astrologer Evangeline Adams, is famously quoted as saying, "Millionaires don't use astrology, billionaires do."

Though astrology has been around for five thousand years, I have dedicated my life to helping people see and learn its wisdom. I know I can make learning astrology easy and fun because I have done it before. My book and oracle card set, *Karma Cards*, first published in 1988 to immediate international success and still in print, has helped millions of people around the world learn the basics of astrology, but not how to read an astrological birth chart, as I do herein.

Karma Cards was an innovative and fun teaching game using oracle cards. *Your Cosmic Blueprint* is an astrology school in a book. It contains a lot more than the basic astrological insights I shared in my *Karma Cards* kit. It is also informed by what Amy and I have shared in our other successful astrological titles, *Sun Sign Secrets*, *Astrology for Wellness*, *Mindful Astrology*, and, of course, the couple of thousand chart readings I have done for clients over the past decades. It even contains a few tips that came through to Amy and me while working with astrologer chef John Okas on *Signs & Seasons: An Astrological Cookbook*.

I wrote *Your Cosmic Blueprint* to completely revolutionize the teaching of astrology and specifically how to read an astrological birth chart. Please know that you are in good hands. I have over forty years of experience as a counseling and teaching astrologer. I have innovated several new techniques for the twenty-first-century use of the five-thousand-year-old art of reading an astrological birth chart, all of which you will find in this book. Amy and I are living the life most people only dream about due in surprisingly large degree to our own journey in understanding how to read our own cosmic blueprints. There is no one in the world better equipped to help you live a life filled with love, light, and laughter. Using our time-tested, real-world-proven methods will enable you to realize how reading an astrology chart and gaining valuable insights from it can actually be something that everybody can learn—at least the way I teach it.

It ain't rocket science—it's the ancient wisdom of astrology!

If you read *Your Cosmic Blueprint* from cover to cover and, most importantly, in the order in which we have created it for you, you will then have the ability to read any astrology chart in which you are interested. You will learn enough about how to read an astrological birth chart that you will also be able to read the cosmic blueprints of other people you care about or who interest you, your pets, corporations, nations, organizations, and historical figures and events. You will be amazed at how many charts are available to you for free download from the internet—including yours! While you brainstorm and interpret, using what you have learned in this book, you will, using astrology as your guide, free up your ability to think and produce the spark that ignites the engine of your intuition—and that is exactly what we want when we read astrology charts.

I know this may sound like impossible hype, but reading charts has done exactly that for my wife, Amy, and me. For our more than fifty years together, we have been empowered by knowing how to read cosmic blueprints. Amy's award-winning sewn-fabric collage tapestries are the beautiful visuals we will see on our journey as we learn how to read astrological charts. *Your Cosmic Blueprint* has been created with the goal of empowering you to live your best life possible. What's worked for us can work for you!

When I first met Amy, she was studying astrology and I was studying Amy, and so I started studying astrology. I may have been skeptical, but I wasn't stupid. She was so fascinating to me on so many levels that my Brooklyn Technical High School scientific skepticism was replaced by amazement as she and her friend and college roommate at Pratt Institute, Rupert Smith, the artist and master printmaker for Andy Warhol, read my chart.

Back then, I was a professional musician playing and singing in bands. At the time, I knew astrology only as the daily horror-scope advice column illogically and unbelievably dividing up the human race into twelve signs and published in daily newspapers (remember them?) on the same pages as the cartoons—the "funny pages." It didn't make much sense to me because I didn't know that real astrology works because it is based on your unique birth chart, a map of the planets erected for the exact day, place, and (ideally) time of your birth. (We love that old-school tradition to say an astrological birth chart is erected, like a home is erected by builders following blueprints.)

Allow me to digress and share with you another important benefit of knowing how to read a cosmic blueprint. Being a musician was and still is a great way to simultaneously make a living and meet people. But as good as playing in a rock-and-roll band was for meeting and getting to know people, knowing how to read someone's astrology chart is ten times better. Why? Because you are focusing on the other person and helping them better know themselves—their strengths, their weaknesses, and even their secrets. You would not believe the things people share when they have faith in you to be a true helping counselor—a trust that should never be violated by sharing what you learn about a person whose cosmic blueprint you are reading with anyone else. (That was your first astrology lesson, by the way. The practice of astrology is empowering, but power must be used with tact and discretion. Professional confidentiality is not just for the other practices, those of doctors, lawyers, and religious counselors.)

I recall as if it was yesterday when Rupert said, "The music is fine for now, but you're going to really make it as a writer." I had never even dreamed of being a writer of anything else but songs and the occasional poem. More than three million copies of my books in print in eighteen languages later, I bless Rupert's memory for changing our lives so profoundly—it was he who got Amy into astrology—by opening our minds, hearts, and daily life to the power of real astrology.

Our good fortune continued when we started getting our cosmic blueprints read by our friend, the master astrologer Leor Warner, of blessed memory, who taught us a lot as he read our charts for us. He saw our astrological ability right there in our cosmic blueprints. He always encouraged me to do readings for other people, and so I did, finding that I enjoyed it as much as they did. I have been a professional practicing astrological counselor for decades, reading the cosmic blueprints of people, pets, projects, and anything else that has a time of birth—like businesses do for the day and time they first open their doors or sign the incorporation papers, and even for towns, cities, and nations. I know how to share with you the secrets that make it simple, easy, and fun to learn how to read your cosmic blueprint and that of the abovementioned entities.

NOTE: *In most books, editors have scrupulously removed before publication information unnecessarily repeated by their authors, but this is a teaching book, so there* **WILL** *be repetition if and when I believe repeating something will help you better learn and retain a particular fact or concept.*

Astrology is, in essence, a psychological language, a symbolic representation of many of the same aspects of personality that are explored in the various schools and methods of psychology and philosophy. Your cosmic blueprint symbolizes the many individual aspects of your personality, abilities, and fears and the things affecting your potential for happiness and success as you define them. Knowing it helps you define them more precisely and get to better know aspects of yourself you may have downplayed, avoided, or not been aware of—the very definition of life-changing knowledge.

If knowledge is power, then the self-knowledge gained from knowing how to read a cosmic blueprint conveys to you the power to change your life. As a legendary philosopher and military strategist, the Chinese general Sun Tzu, famously said, "He who overcomes others is great. He who overcomes himself is greatest."

I am working on overcoming myself too, but one thing I know beyond a doubt is that I know how to explain astrology to you simply and in a way in which you do not have to memorize anything. You can instead concentrate on the truly enjoyable practice of looking at your cosmic blueprint, your life, and Life in general through the lens of astrology. Once you understand the basic concepts, I will show you how to use them to interpret the astrological stories that are right there in each of our cosmic blueprints. We call our innovative method "Starry Telling." I would love to explain it to you now, but it can only be experienced at the time when your astrological knowledge has progressed to the point where it will make sense to you. Trust me! (Uh-oh!)

I know asking anyone to trust you at this point in history is a big ask. All I can say is that I have taught a lot of wonderful people how to read a cosmic blueprint in real time in online seminars and in real life. I have watched with delight as my teaching method allowed my students to go from not knowing anything about chart interpretation to being able to look at a natal chart and obtain useful information that helped them better understand themselves, their partners, their children, their family members, their friends, their coworkers, their bosses, their pets, and anyone else they were interested in whose birth information was available to them. A few of the people who took my classes even went on to become professional astrologers because my method focuses on the most important things necessary for people to get to know and like themselves and empower themselves to live their lives to the fullest.

NOTE: *This book contains information based on my decades of work as a counseling astrologer and my personal experience helping people understand their cosmic blueprint—their astrological birth chart. For legal reasons, I have to remind you that everything in this book should be understood to be for entertainment purposes only. I want to add that medical and legal issues are outside the scope of this book, and nothing in it should ever cause someone to ignore the advice of doctors, psychologists, other healers, or attorneys, who are licensed to practice and whom you have investigated and found to be honest, skilled, credible, attentive to your needs, and willing to represent you and/or involve you in your healing.*

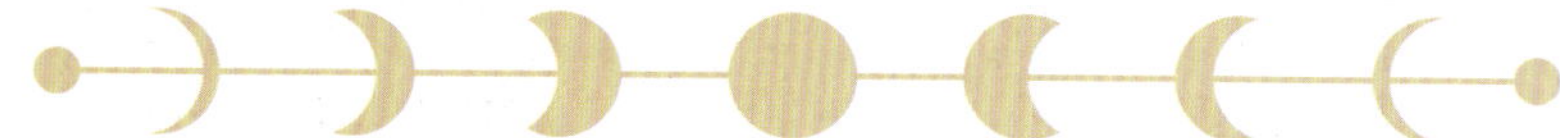

WHAT IS ASTROLOGY & HOW DOES IT WORK?

Astrology is the study of how planetary positions in space and as mapped on an astrological birth chart, which we call a cosmic blueprint, relate to an individual's character, as well as Earthly events. Its long and rich history, having been around for several thousand years, has resulted in a wealth of philosophical and psychological wisdom. As the Greek philosopher Heraclitus said, "Character is destiny." Who you are—complete with all of your goals, tendencies, habits, virtues, and vices—will determine how you act and react, and thereby create your life's story, your destiny.

I cannot stress enough that our free will is what we are empowering with astrology's ability to guide us. As the Egyptian astrologer Ptolemy famously said, "The stars incline, they do not compel." There is no "good" astrological indication in a person's cosmic blueprint that cannot be abused and thereby altered into an energy detrimental to that person's best interests. And there is no "bad" astrological indication whose energy cannot be used constructively to be supportive to that person's best interests.

The purpose of understanding astrology is so it can help you better know yourself and those you care about. You will then be better able to use your free will to shape your life to your liking. Astrology is designed to help you become fully yourself. It can point out your strengths and weaknesses so that you can better accept yourself as you are and use your strengths to compensate for your weaknesses. There is no such thing as a "bad" cosmic blueprint. It is up to each of us to get to know ourselves as best we can and make our charts work for us and not against us.

The practice of astrology results from millennia of observation during which astrologers noticed, again and again, meaningful coincidences between the positions of the planets in the heavens and events taking place on Earth. In ancient times, they were especially mindful of how these meaningful coincidences related to the cosmic blueprints made for the rulers of the nations because they felt that what happened to those rulers happened to their nations. When horoscopes started to be constructed for the rest of us and not just the nobility, the seeds of democracy were first sown.

Astrology has evolved into a language-like system that lets us "read" the map of the positions of the planets at the moment of our birth—the moment of our first breath, to be more precise. Amy and I visualize the taking of a baby's first breath as if it were breathing in a special kind of hologram formed by the matrix of energies caused by the interplay of the subtle gravitational and other energy waves emanating from the Sun, the Moon, and the rest of the planets in our solar system. Whatever our manner of birth and first-drawn breath, we can interpret the map of this frozen moment in time and space to gain valuable insights into our individuality.

There are quite a few scientific theories that explain why astrology works. Once again, we could just tell you that our evidence is empirical; we have seen it work too many times to deny that it works, and therefore, it works. Just trust us. However, in this age of fake news, no one should just take anyone's word for anything.

Our current favorite explanation for astrology's uncanny ability to give insight into a person's personality, and even its ability to forecast future events, is the chaos theory formulated by Benoit Mandelbrot (1924–2010). Mandelbrot coined the word *fractal* in 1975 for his newly formulated study of fractal geometry, which was expanded on by Edward Norton Lorenz (1917–2008). Lorenz coined the term *deterministic chaos*, which expresses the principle now known colloquially as chaos theory. Chaos theory concerns itself with nonlinear systems like the weather, brain function, or financial markets and seeks to help understand how the effect of small changes or events can dramatically affect the results of seemingly unrelated events.

The most widely known phrase used to explain chaos theory, "A butterfly flapping its wings in China can produce a tornado in Texas," was proven to be a startlingly apt analogy at the time of the COVID-19 global pandemic. The proven power of this butterfly effect, the total interrelatedness of things, is a serious reminder to us all to be mindful of our thoughts and deeds and to recognize that actions have consequences.

The theory of synchronicity, by pioneering Swiss psychologist Carl Jung, is a second explanation for how the energy patterns formed by planetary placements in space and symbolized in one's astrological birth chart (see page 21) can influence a person here on Earth. Jung's theory states that things occurring at the same moment form a relationship of significance, not actual causality. When you are born, you are a mirror of the energy patterns present at the time and place of your birth, including the energy patterns formed by the subtle gravitational waves given off by the Sun, the Moon, and the planets of our solar system. This pattern, symbolically represented by the map of their placement in your astrology chart, can be read in a manner similar to the way a First Peoples shaman can look at the clouds in the sky or the movement of the leaves in the trees or the animals on a prairie and read from these images signs of things to come and answers to questions.

A third explanation for how we can be influenced by the stars, whose chemicals we are all made from, is based on Albert Einstein's theory of relativity ($E = mc^2$), which at its heart proves that all matter is made of the same thing—that is, energy. If we, and everything else in the universe, are all made of the same energy, then at a most basic level, we are all connected, a part of one great whole.

The ancient seers conceived of an infinitely vast library containing the total sum of all the knowledge of the universe, past, present, and future, naming it the Akashic Records. Today's seers, also known as quantum physicists, use the same concept and call it the quantum field. Is it also possible that this quantum field of infinite knowledge can be accessed by a sincere seeker, like an astrologer reading a client's chart in order to help them navigate the challenges of their life more successfully? We think it is very possible, indeed.

Perhaps this is the level that allows us to read not only an astrological birth chart but also other people's minds, effecting spiritual communications, and can be an explanation for psychic phenomena and even the prediction of future events!

Astrology can even be used to predict themes and events one can expect to encounter in one's future. I do it for my clients all the time. I am not infallible, but I am correct in my predictions much more than chance would allow. However, before you can try making predictions using astrology, you need to thoroughly understand what is contained in the following pages, which will offer you a way of tapping into the magic that astrology (meaning "the logic of the stars," from the Greek words *aster*, meaning "star," and *logos*, meaning "reason") has to offer.

FIRST THINGS FIRST: DOWNLOAD YOUR COSMIC BLUEPRINT

Speaking of star logic, to read your astrology chart, it is first necessary that you have it in your possession. Fortunately for all of us, this process, once laborious and difficult, is now as easy as going online and entering your birth information into a form.

Back in the days when computers or even sophisticated calculators were used only by scientists, Amy and I had to go totally old-school and laboriously do the math to calculate the position of the planets in a person's birth chart and then draw each chart by hand! You can imagine how grateful we are that, here in the twenty-first century, obtaining a person's birth chart is as easy as going online to one of the many astrology websites that offer free birth charts.

For the purposes of this book, I recommend you obtain the free chart you can get from the website AstroGraph.com. The free birth chart it provides looks the way I prefer it to look for teaching purposes—like a round pizza with twelve equally sized slices! (I told you this was going to be fun!)

When you reach AstroGraph.com's main page, click on Birth Charts. Ideally, you will be able to input your birthday, the place where you were born, and the time you were born, if you know it. Most people will be able to ascertain the date, place, and time of their birth from a birth certificate, a family member, a hospital record, or the office of the clerk in the jurisdiction in which they were born. Since the 1930s, it has been the law in the United States and other countries around the world that all babies' birth times must be recorded. If it is not on your birth certificate, you may have to contact the county clerk's office where you were born to obtain a copy of what is called your vault birth certificate—the one you need to obtain a passport or conduct business internationally.

I have done many charts for people who for a variety of reasons cannot obtain a record of their birth time, their precise birthday, or their place of birth, and if you are one of them, fear not! Follow the instructions below.

IF YOU DO NOT KNOW YOUR BIRTH TIME

Where it asks you to input the time of your birth on AstroGraph.com, you will be able to move the slider to "Unknown (use sunrise)" to indicate you do not know your birth time. The website will erect your birth chart as if you were born at sunrise. I will show you how to get a lot of useful information out of that chart while you do a bit of sleuthing to find out your actual birth time. I will also give hints throughout this book that will help you figure out an approximate time.

IF YOU DO NOT KNOW YOUR DATE OR PLACE OF BIRTH

Go to AstroGraph.com and do as I said for unknown birth time: Move the slider next to "Unknown (use sunrise)" using your best guess as to your place or date of birth. If you have an approximate date of birth, use that date and run a couple of extra charts based on a day before that date and a day after. If you have no idea of your date of birth, you can still learn astrology and erect the charts of people you care about, which may lead you to become such a skilled astrologer that you use the process known as rectification using important dates in your life and/or get an intuitive hit on your birthday and/or place of birth. It's not magic, it's astrology, and it works!

Before we move on, please go to AstroGraph.com and get your free astrology birth chart. Please do so even if you have had your astrology chart printed out for you previously by another website or astrologer. If your cosmic blueprint does not look like a pizza with twelve equal slices, my instructions are not going to do you much good.

Welcome back. The center of your astrological birth chart, though it may be partially filled with colored lines, really symbolizes the specific place on Earth where you were born. As I said, this is why we astrologers call a birth chart a natal chart and why the person for whom the chart was drawn up is often referred to by astrologers and astrology books as the native. A birth or natal chart is cast for the moment of your personal nativity scene.

Another word used in place of "cosmic blueprint," "astrology chart," "birth chart," or "natal chart" is *horoscope*, a word derived from the Greek words *hōra*, the source of the word *hour*, and *skopos*, from which the final syllable in *telescope* is derived, which when put together mean "to watch the hour."

An astrology chart is a unique kind of map. Your cosmic blueprint is a symbolic recreation of what an ancient astrologer would see in the night sky sitting outside in the northern hemisphere, where astrology originated. The astrologer's feet would be pointed to the south, and Earth's turning would cause the sky to seem to revolve, with the planets rising on the astrologer's left, to the east, watching the hour—preferably the minute—and waiting for the baby to be born so they could erect the child's natal horoscope. (Fun fact: An astrology chart is the only map you will ever see where east is on the left and south is at the top.)

As you look at your pizzalike astrology chart, you will see that there are a bunch of unfamiliar symbols with numbers on some but not all the slices. You can think of them as the toppings on this astrological pizza. It is important for you to note that in almost every person's chart, the toppings are not distributed evenly the way an experienced pizza maker would do it. Almost every person's chart has slices that do not have any toppings on them! Do not be concerned with the empty slices in your chart.

Although an astrological chart looks like a twelve-slice pizza with unevenly distributed toppings, it is a precisely calculated symbolic space map based on the same astronomical measurements astronomers use to plot the positions of the planets. Every birth chart is a frozen-in-time snapshot of how the planets lined up around you when you were born.

(Please note that the Sun and the Moon, as well as the known planets, are included when I use the term *planets* in the context of an astrology chart.)

The horizontal line you see in a chart bisecting the pizza into six slices of an upper half and six slices of a lower half represents the surface of the Earth stretching from your place of birth in the center of the pizza to the horizons—the horizon east and the horizon west.

That means that the "toppings," or planets—which could include the Sun and/or the Moon—in the six slices below the horizontal line were out in space behind the Earth (from your point of view) when you were born. The toppings in the six slices above the horizontal line represent the planets—and that could include the Sun and/or the Moon—that were up in the sky when you were born. Whether it was day or night or cloudy or foggy or whatever, they were up there.

So the main toppings are the ten planets of astrology: the Sun, the Moon, Mercury, Venus, Mars, Jupiter, Saturn, Uranus, Neptune, and Pluto. (Yes, to us astrologers, Pluto always was and is definitely a planet!) Conspicuous by its absence is the Earth because an astrology chart is a map of how the planets, including the Sun and our Moon, lined up around you as you drew your first breath here on planet Earth.

NOTE: *Your cosmic blueprint is, ideally, erected not for the moment you are born but for the moment you take your first breath, which is why astrology works for those born by Caesarean section.*

And as for the twelve individual slices of this astrological pizza, they are called the houses of the chart because the planets occupy them the way we live in our homes. Each slice represents a slice of life—twelve areas of personal experience common to us all.

There's a house dedicated to you and your personal experience of your uniqueness. Opposite that house is a house dedicated to your experience of committed partnership. There's a house dedicated to the nurturing caregiver(s) who love unconditionally, and opposite that house is the one for the caregiver(s) who wanted you to know the cold, hard facts of life so you would not be naive and taken advantage of.

Don't concern yourself with houses yet. We will do a deep-dish dive into the twelve slices/houses of your astrological birth chart pizza later on, after you have a solid grounding in the meanings of the planets and the signs. But before we do, I am going to show you that there is a lot of information you can glean from your cosmic blueprint right now!

THE FIVE DISTRIBUTION PATTERNS & THEIR MEANINGS

You can read a bit about your astrology chart right now. The first thing every experienced astrologer looks at when they begin to read a birth chart is the overall picture created by the distribution pattern of the various planets and important chart points, which I have referred to as the toppings on the twelve slices of the pizzalike astrology chart. This is because there are a few important and helpful facts about y/our personality that can be derived just from observing the distribution pattern of the toppings and answering the following questions about it:

- Are they spread out all over the pizza?
- Are the planets all or mostly in the six slices above or mostly in the six slices below the horizontal horizon line that bisects a chart into upper (in the sky above you) and lower (behind the Earth) halves?
- Are they all or mostly on the six slices to the left (rising in the east) or mostly on the six slices on the right side (setting on the western side) of the vertical line that goes from the bottom of the chart to the top of it?

Each of those distribution patterns of the planet/toppings means something to astrologers like me and you.

NOTE: *Although they look like the other toppings, do not include in your estimation of the distribution pattern the ones that look like headphones worn on your head or like earbuds worn under your chin. They are not planets; they are sensitive points of a chart, called by astrologers the North and South Nodes of the Moon (and astronomers the ascending and descending nodes), whose definitions you will find on page 72, and they are always exactly opposite each other. We also do not count the topping that is a circle with an x inside of it, which is called the Part of Fortune and is a sensitive point whose meaning I will explain when we reach page 275, nor do we count the topping that looks like an upright key for a lock, the comet Chiron, which I will explain when we get to page 297.*

Here, briefly, is the meaning of the five basic distribution patterns of the planet/toppings that are revealed to us by looking at the twelve-slice pizza of an astrology chart.

Spread out: Characteristic of a person having various and often conflicting interests, skills, and ideas about life in general and the living of their life. This person may change careers several times or at the very least more often than most people. In their youth, this person is uncomfortable with the question "What do you want to be when you grow up?"

Mostly above the horizon: Characteristic of a person more comfortable with interests, skills, and ideas about the things in life connected to their relationship to the people, places, and groups out in the world outside of their family. In their youth, this person is uncomfortable with the question "Why do you care so much about what other people think of you?"

Mostly below the horizon: Characteristic of a person more comfortable with interests, skills, and ideas about the aspects of life that are personal to them, their family, and the worlds they create for themselves wherever they go. In their youth, this person is uncomfortable with the question "Why don't you go outside more and make friends with the other children?"

Mostly to the left of the vertical line: Characteristic of a person more comfortable with being self-sufficient and independent and being the initiator of actions meant to improve, strengthen, and defend their position in life. In their youth, this person is uncomfortable with the question "Why do you resent and resist me and other people when we are just trying to help you?"

Mostly to the right of the vertical line: Characteristic of a person more comfortable with teamwork, learning from the experiences of others, and allowing things to happen at their own pace and in their own time. In their youth, this person is uncomfortable with the question "Why are you so willing to give in to other people and afraid to stand up for yourself?"

NOTE: *No astrologer can, from just looking at a toppings/planet distribution pattern, determine whether a specific person absolutely loves, is just OK with, or is bothered in one or more ways by the character traits I have ascribed to the preceding five distribution patterns. Only you know how you feel about your type of distribution pattern at this point in your life. When reading for other people, if you feel like sharing this distribution pattern or any astrological advice, give them the space to process this potentially new and impactful information and to access their feelings about what you have shared with them.*

THE TWELVE SUN SIGNS OF THE ASTROLOGICAL ZODIAC

It is time to learn about the twelve "cheeses" of the astrology pizza, the twelve Sun signs of the zodiac.

We started our journey to becoming an astrologer with the easy-to-spot pattern distributions of the various toppings of the chart, which you now know are the symbols for the planets. And when I say *planets*, recall that we astrologers include both the Sun and the Moon when we talk about the planets of a chart, though we know they are a star and Earth's satellite, respectively. I include you when I say "we astrologers" because now you already know more about real astrology than most people.

If you are reading this book, you most likely know your Sun sign, the sign of the zodiac you tell people when they ask you, "What's your sign?" You probably know the Sun sign of your family members, friends, and coworkers, and maybe even those of your pet(s) and a few famous people. (We astrologers call it the Sun sign because it is the sign of the zodiac in which the Sun, as viewed from Earth, appeared to be passing through when a person was born.)

The zodiac is a narrow, circular band of space through which the Sun, the Moon, and the planets appear, as viewed from Earth, to pass through as they orbit the Sun. Even though the Earth is spinning, the view of the Sun from Earth shows it as appearing to be "in" a particular sign of the zodiac "wheel" that both astrologers and astronomers use to help them place the positions of the planets in space.

The word *zodiac* comes from the Greek term *kyklos zodiakos*, meaning "circle of animals." Though there are, indeed, animals (Aries's Ram, Taurus's Bull, Leo's Lion), zodiac symbols include people (Gemini's Twins, Virgo's Maiden with a shaft of wheat, Aquarius's Water-Bearer pouring water from a jug for all to drink), fish (Pisces's Fishes, one swimming upstream and the other down), a crustacean (Cancer's Crab, which carries its home with it), an arachnid (Scorpio's Scorpion), a couple of mythological hybrids (Sagittarius's Centaur a half-man, half-horse, and Capricorn's Goat with a fish's tail), and the "inanimate" but ever-moving balance Scales of Libra.

I have been calling the planets of your astrology chart the toppings to help you get used to the fact that they are distributed on the various slices of your chart like the toppings on a pizza. The word *planet* is derived from the Greek word for "wanderer," derived from the notion that the stars in the night sky seemed to be stationary in terms of their relative position to each other, but the celestial bodies our ancient forebears saw and called planets seemed to slowly change their position in the night sky relative to the infinitely more numerous fixed stars.

When a planet—and that includes the Sun and Moon—passes through a sign of the zodiac, that sign adds its unique flavor to that planet just the way a cheese gives its unique flavor to each pizza topping.

THE SUN ☉

The Sun gives light and life to an individual astrology chart the same way it does to everyone on Earth. The Sun's immense size and power make it the first planet we astrologers look at.

When you read any cosmic blueprint, it is easy to spot the planetary symbol, also known as a glyph, that describes where the Sun was at the time of birth, whether that birth is of a person, an animal, a business, or a nation. The glyph symbol for the Sun is a circle with a dot in the center of it.

The glyph for the Sun obviously represents the Sun's position of being in the center of the solar system with all the planets orbiting around it, but like all the other glyphs, the meaning of the planet represented is contained within this little picture, if you know how to look at it.

Through the ages—and astrology has been around for over five thousand years—a circle has always represented completion, especially the complete totality of the Great Spirit, or what we can also call All-There-Is. The dot in the center of the circle represents our individual existence in the middle of All-There-Is. We are each at the center of our personal life just as the Sun is at the center of the solar system. Astrology can easily be seen as having led to the science of what we now call astronomy, the way alchemy preserved the science of chemistry during the Dark Ages.

Our cosmic blueprint gives us clues to our individual personalities because it can be viewed as a language, one that is most like the language of psychology. In that language, the dot in the center of that circle represents our ego, the apparent reality that we exist separately and act independently and that we are at the center of our existence, our personal solar system, with everyone and everything else in our life seemingly existing around us. We even use the expression "in our circle" to describe people we are connected to in some way.

In addition to one's ego, the Sun in an astrology chart can give us clues to *our vital force, our purpose, how we identify our unique being, and how we experience our personal reality.* We navigate the course of our lives on Earth just as Earth courses around the Sun, navigating the vastness of existence the way the Sun is actually moving through space as a single part of our spiraling Milky Way galaxy, one of millions of its stars in one of billions of galaxies in our expanding universe. It is both humbling and exhilarating to learn how our cosmic blueprint links us to such unimaginable vastness.

THE MEANING OF THE SUN IN THE TWELVE SIGNS OF THE ZODIAC

This is not the kind of astrology book you may have read before. I have thought about this subject continually during the many decades I have been a practicing astrological counselor, and I have come to some conclusions that make my readings more valuable to my clients and that I believe will help you become a much better reader yourself.

I pride myself on being an innovator. Experience has taught me a hard lesson: If you share some of the major conclusions I am about to share with you with other astrologers, they may push back quite strongly on one or more of these ways of looking at chart readings or astrological interpretations. That is why I strongly advise you not to have those kinds of discussions with anyone, whether they be astrologers or the uninitiated, until you have read the entire book and become comfortable with my way of doing things.

The truth is not afraid of questions, and neither am I. When you are first learning astrology or any subject, it is all too easy to become confused and otherwise influenced by others, especially by those you have reason to respect, and to thereby have your learning process derailed when people disagree with you. There is an old joke: "Put two astrologers in a room and you get three opinions." As with so many clichés, it came to be one because of how often it is true.

Here is one of my many push-backable personal beliefs about astrology I am excited to share with you: Although it is true that our Sun sign offers insightful information about our ego, our purpose, our vital energy, how we identify ourselves, and what motivates us to be ourselves, we do not come into this world as perfect examples of each sign's various meanings and associations. We are here to discover, explore, expand, and add new definitions to the following meanings and associations of the Sun, Moon, and planets through the signs of the zodiac.

PRO TIP: *The dates given in this chapter (and in every astrology book or column you see) for the Sun entering and leaving every sign are approximate, not exact. For example, the first day of the spring equinox in the northern hemisphere, which is the first day of fall in the southern hemisphere, and which is also both the beginning of the astrological New Year and the 1st degree of Aries, the first sign of western astrology, can be March 20 or March 21, and the change to the next sign, Taurus, can occur on either April 19 or April 20.*

For convenience, we refer here, for example, to March 21–April 20 as being the time of Aries, but please remember, as all astrologers must do, that this date and all the sign-change dates of this chapter and in virtually every astrology book or column ever written are approximate and specific to the year you are working with. If you or the person whose chart you are interested in are born near the cusp, or the borderline, of two signs, you must pay particular attention to having a fairly accurate time of birth to make sure you know in which sign the Sun was when the native of this cosmic blueprint was born.

The Sun in a chart gives us not only a clue to the ego of the native whose chart we are looking at but also some insight into this being's purpose in life. As you will see, every Sun sign has a plan and a mission. That mission has a spectrum of meanings—another one of my astrological beliefs I have observed in my decades of astrological study.

Savor the following meanings of the Sun in the twelve signs of the zodiac. Take these meanings to heart because getting the essence of the meanings of the twelve signs of the zodiac is a crucial part of learning how to read your cosmic blueprint.

NOTE: *You will find a list of keywords at the end of each Sun sign's description. Using these keywords is a vital part of my method of teaching you how to decode your cosmic blueprint. I will give you three examples of how to use some listed keywords and concepts found in the body of the text for each sign at the end of each Sun sign's description. Using these, you will begin to see for yourself how our cosmic blueprints are written in the stars!*

Aries ♈

March 21–April 20

ARIES KEYWORDS

bravery, initiate, pioneer, "be the first," challenge, fight, willpower, child-like, adventure, explore, daring, courage, honesty, competition, "bossy action," aggression, energy, spontaneity, "without hesitation," "first impulse," "fight, flight, or freeze," "only afraid of feeling afraid"

KEYWORD-USE EXAMPLES FOR THE SUN IN ARIES:

Ego (the Sun) needs to feel brave (Aries). Purpose (the Sun) is to initiate without hesitation (Aries). Fight, flight, or freeze response (Aries) can affect their vitality (the Sun).

People born during the time of Aries are here to learn about being brave. They must be brave enough to endure the patience required by the difficult parts of their chosen courses of action. They are not comfortable with fixed or long-range plans and prefer to initiate various quick, precise, and focused actions to accomplish their goals without much forethought or, seemingly, concern for the consequences of their actions.

The spectrum of meanings for their unrivaled ability to overcome opposition can range from heroically putting themselves first and alone in a battle to being a self-actualized pioneer in some way and all the way to putting, to the detriment of other people, themselves and their interests first.

Aries prove their strength to themselves by going on their first impulse and not second-guessing, thereby avoiding the only thing they fear: fear itself, or opposition from within themselves that saps their strength. Because fear so rarely intrudes into their consciousness, they have a highly developed fight, flight, or freeze reflex and can sometimes experience panic attacks if they sense fear within themselves. They feel insecure when people question their spontaneous and instinctual way of being and push back strongly and fearlessly. Surprisingly, though they will usually stand up to anyone anytime and anyplace, they will strategically withdraw if they feel they are losing a battle.

Aries are always ready, willing, and able to start a project without delay. They can be exemplary successes born of go-it-alone bravery that saves the day, the set-them-and-forget-them trusted worker who always gets the job done as quickly as possible, or the bossy or overly aggressive loner. They are usually too self-involved to bother anyone who doesn't antagonize them but can sometimes be pushed beyond endurance and, like the Ram, their zodiac symbol, butt heads with a perceived opponent. They thrive when they are in charge of a project or working alone.

Arians must remember that fear and self-doubt are not signs of weakness or losing control, nor are they a guarantee of failure. If an

Aries feels even slightly afraid, the emotion makes them either lash out or panic. Rams must stay spontaneous and not let their fear cause self-defeating behavior or paralyze them into inaction, causing even more self-doubt. The faintest whiff of fear can stop them in their tracks, giving Aries the reputation of starting but not finishing what they start.

Taurus ♉

April 21–May 21

TAURUS KEYWORDS

strong, slow, steady, stubborn, values, money, luxury, acquire, nature, prosperity, caution, control, security, tenacity, "can cope with anything," beauty, habits, possessions, kindness, calmness, harmony, sensuality, organization

KEYWORD-USE EXAMPLES FOR THE SUN IN TAURUS:

Ego (the Sun) needs to feel strong enough to cope with any challenge (Taurus). Purpose (the Sun) can be to tenaciously acquire possessions (Taurus). Level of prosperity (Taurus) can affect their vitality (the Sun).

People born during the time of Taurus are here to learn about being strong enough to endure the difficulties that are part of their plan to achieve a goal so they can then fully enjoy the fruits of their labors. They are not comfortable with impetuous people, situations requiring immediate responsive actions, or being part of a group that is deviating from the plan or, even worse, proceeding in an unplanned or erratic manner.

The spectrum of meanings for their unrivaled ability to cope can range from heroic demonstrations of strength used to overcome what would thwart anyone else to being a consistent and dependable cornerstone of a family or other group, and all the way to harmful acts born of selfishness, stubbornness, or the release of pent-up anger born of frustrations from continuing their struggles with situations that are beyond hope of being resolved successfully.

They prove their strength to themselves by staying the course, sticking to the plan, and never giving up unless forced to. They have a highly developed appreciation for the best life has to offer and will work hard to get it and then take the time to savor their pleasures. They are made insecure by lazy people wasting time looking for shortcuts, risky ways of doing things, or giving up the fight because they consider these things to be weaknesses of character. Because they are here to prove their strength, most Taurus natives would deny, even to themselves, that these kinds of thoughts ever occurred to them.

Taureans are willing to pull their weight and even do the work of others if it will help them get what they want. They can be exemplary successes born of superior strength, the unsung plodding workers who are proud of their hard work, or the most infuriatingly stubborn obstacles to needed changes. They are usually unflappable and patient but can sometimes, like the Bull, their zodiac symbol, be pushed beyond endurance and erupt. They thrive when they are allowed to operate at their own chosen pace.

Taureans value a middle-of-the-road approach to life. Not likely to get caught up in the latest trend, they believe in being themselves. Taureans need to understand that being true to their values does not mean they should be afraid to change course sometimes. They need luxury and the finer things in life, not stress. Anger or poverty can make them sick.

Gemini ♊

May 21–June 20

GEMINI KEYWORDS

changeable, multitask, quick, logic, "socially adept," "communications field," mischievous, restless, gossip, versatile, curiosity, precocious, "rumor mill," advertising, witty, talkative, salesmanship, "media savvy," flexibility, informed, "boredom adverse," "cannot be pinned down to one idea," "can hold both sides of an argument"

KEYWORD-USE EXAMPLES FOR THE SUN IN GEMINI:

Informed, curious, and versatile (Gemini) is how they ego identify (the Sun). Purpose (the Sun) is to communicate (Gemini). Feeling free to change their minds (Gemini) can affect their vitality (the Sun).

People born during the time of Gemini are here to learn about everything and everyone. They use their innate communication skills to implement a self-directed education, even if they follow traditional educational pathways. They strive to be flexible enough to see all sides of any matter and endure the difficulties that can occur when inflexible people misjudge them as vacillating, unprincipled, or two-faced.

The spectrum of meanings for their unrivaled ability to multitask can range from heroic demonstrations of the power of words and ideas to save the day to being a comprehensive clearinghouse for the communication of the latest information and all the way to harmful gossip or acts born of double-dealing, vacillation, or allowing their fear of sameness or boredom to stop them from attending to crucial details.

They prove their strength to themselves by keeping an open mind, knowing a little about everything, and being as mentally agile as possible. They are never boring. In fact, boredom is anathema to a Gemini. They have a highly developed appreciation for the infinite possibilities life has to offer and believe they could know everything there is to know if they had the time and the information available to them. They are made insecure by people wanting them to be the exact same person with the same opinions, beliefs, and facts as they were previously.

Geminis are willing to work tirelessly at anything that piques their curiosity and allows them to learn something. They can be exemplary successes in the arts of communications and information sharing, the networkers and word-of-mouth influencers on which every enterprise depends, or the undependable, ever-restless freelancers incapable of loyalty to anyone or anything. They are usually surprisingly conventional despite knowing the latest trends and fashions but can sometimes become so experimental with a new concept that they appear to be two separate people, like their zodiac symbol, the Twins. They thrive when they are allowed to freely change their focus and their opinions.

Geminis want to experience life fully and in as many ways as they can. They may even go so far as to live something of a double life. They have two opinions about everything—more if they have actually studied a particular subject in depth. They are experts in making connections and may make their living in the communications field.

Cancer ♋

June 21–July 22

CANCER KEYWORDS

nurturing, helpful, fertile, clairvoyant, caring, protective, emotions, moods, feelings, intuitions, "wax and wane," reflect, respond, adapt, habits, cycles, mother, "unconditional love," overbearing, "our past," sensitive, oversensitive, "home cooking," homemaking, conditioning, forgiving, enabling

KEYWORD-USE EXAMPLES FOR THE SUN IN CANCER:

Ego (the Sun) needs to feel that they are protective, caring, and loving unconditionally (Cancer). Purpose (the Sun) can be to nurture family, friends, groups, and entities of all kinds (Cancer). Level of sensitivity and especially oversensitivity (Cancer) can affect their vitality (the Sun).

People born during the time of Cancer are here to learn about being strong enough to endure the difficulties that are part of nurturing and training individuals, families, groups, businesses, and even loosely organized movements so those they have chosen to mother can function well on their own and succeed to the best of their abilities. They are also challenged to know when and how to let those in their care fend for themselves.

The spectrum of meanings for their unique, instinctual caring abilities can range from heroic demonstrations of intuiting and anticipating problems in time for them to be addressed to being a constant source of support and cohesion for an individual, family, or other group and all the way to harmful acts born of the failure to see the dangers posed by ignoring or enabling negative traits of those whom they care about unconditionally.

Cancer natives prove their strength to themselves by forgiving but not forgetting the transgressions of those they are nurturing so they can help them become better. They have a highly developed appreciation for the difficulties of everyday life and will rise above their own limitations to help any living creature in need of aid. They are made insecure by people who never express appreciation for the sacrifices made by the Cancerian on their behalf and never reciprocate the offering of assistance the Cancerian so readily offered to them.

Cancerians are willing to work hard for anything that makes them feel part of a family. They can be the honored, blessed, and respected matriarch or patriarch, the unsung dependable parent or caregiver on which every family and nation depends, or the oversensitive, self-protective, overbearing busybody whose hurtful words and deeds create lasting problems. They are usually kind and understanding but can sometimes be pushed beyond endurance and, like the Crab, their zodiac symbol, either pull in and hide or act aggressively when they feel threatened. They thrive when they are treated with kindness, thoughtfulness, and appreciation.

Cancerians are driven to be focused by feelings and intuition more than the other signs. A surprising amount of their decisions are based on them. While highly sensitive in the way they behave toward others, Cancerians are usually most sensitive when it comes to their own feelings. They are easily hurt by actions or attitudes that other signs are likely to dismiss or not even notice.

Leo ♌

July 23–August 22

LEO KEYWORDS

self-assertive, creativity, recognition, loving, theatrical, leadership, romance, pleasures, fun, hospitality, appreciation, playfulness, entertainment, children, gambling, sports, games, performance, drama, prideful, "take a chance," invest, affection

KEYWORD-USE EXAMPLES FOR THE SUN IN LEO:

Ego (the Sun) needs to show others how to live a successful life (Leo). Purpose (the Sun) is leadership (Leo). Level of being recognized, admired, and shown affection (Leo) can affect their vitality (the Sun).

People born during the time of Leo are here to learn about being strong enough to endure the difficulties of their plan to boldly lead by example and act out the changes they want to see in the people of their world. Their lack of shyness and willingness to engage with others requires that they learn to cope with drama in daily life without becoming a drama queen. They show us all how life is to be lived, a trait that produces the blowback of no one ever feeling sorry for them.

The spectrum of meanings for their unrivaled ability to inspire loyalty in people and organize them so they can best accomplish tasks can range from heroic actions that rally others and achieve victory to being the symbolic leader for a chosen cause and all the way to harmful acts born of wounded pride or unbridled egomania.

Leos prove their strength to themselves by displaying their abilities in such a way that others notice and respond. They like an audience and are comfortable with being the center of attention, speaking in public, or even celebrity and notoriety. They have a unique ability to act as if a situation is real and are therefore natural-born actors and captivating storytellers. Leos can be the generous benefactor who subtly makes it plain that they want appreciation for their actions to being quite demonstrative about how they want things to be done to harmful acts from megalomaniacal, my-way-or-the-highway, dictatorial behavior. They are made insecure by people ridiculing, diminishing, or especially ignoring their influence and achievements.

Prideful Leos take responsibility for their decisions and actions. They are usually affectionate, demonstrative, and creative, but, like the Lion, their zodiac symbol, can sometimes be lazy and overly expectant of privileges. They thrive when they are encouraged to run the show as they see fit.

Many Leos find it difficult to be a team player, especially if they are not proud of the team. At times, Leos need to fall back on the

fake-it-till-you-make-it strategy, which can lead to suffering from imposter syndrome, the fear that they are not as worthy of praise and support as they wish they were, and that people who matter to them will discover this fact. Sometimes, even the best of leaders must put on an act to get the job done.

Virgo ♍

August 23–September 22

VIRGO KEYWORDS

think, overthink, analyze, overanalyze, discriminate, "divide into component parts," criticize, reason, logic, "connect the dots," worry, perfectionism, procrastinate, "critical-path analysis," "make by hand," craft, form, "zoom in," detail, predict, calculate, order, cleanliness

KEYWORD-USE EXAMPLES FOR THE SUN IN VIRGO:

Ego (the Sun) needs perfect order and cleanliness to avoid worry (Virgo). Purpose (the Sun) is attention to details (Virgo). Level of worry about small details and outcomes (Virgo) can affect their vitality (the Sun).

People born during the time of Virgo are here to learn about being strong enough to endure the difficulties that are part of working hard to be of service, focusing one's concentration on the little things that are so vitally important in life, and developing a useful collection of abilities.

The spectrum of meanings for their unrivaled attention to detail can range from problem-solving and flaw detection that saves the day to being a skilled and focused worker and all the way to harmful acts born of small-mindedness, miscalculations, and misunderstandings caused by being overly critical or failing to see the big picture.

Virgos prove their strength to themselves by devoting themselves fully to a task, dividing it up into as many small pieces as possible while trying to ensure a thorough overview and a successful outcome, and by denying themselves the pleasure of achievement after any project ends by focusing on what went wrong and what could have been done better. They have a highly developed appreciation for the ideas, talents, and skills of those who have achieved success and stood the test of time. They are made insecure by people who want them to act before they have mapped out and evaluated all the possibilities of a specific situation.

Virgos are willing to do what it takes to do everything correctly. They can be exemplary successes born of unique and impressively attained skills, the unsung, dependable workers who attend to the crucial details, or the people who cause problems by virtue of their ceaseless worry, criticism, and procrastination due to illogical overthinking and perfectionism. They are usually shy and self-effacing but can sometimes be pushed beyond endurance by worrying about everything, especially how the purity of their actions will be judged—wanting, like the symbol for their zodiac sign, to be innocent and virginal. They thrive when they feel accepted and useful.

Virgos are driven by a search for perfection. This is apparent in everything they do or say—and especially in what they don't

do or say. In fact, they would rather do nothing than do the wrong thing, which often leads others to misinterpret their behavior as laziness-based procrastination. But at the heart of the typical Virgo is the hardest worker you've ever met—ready, willing, and able to help anyone deemed worthy of their devoted service.

Libra ♎

September 23–October 22

LIBRA KEYWORDS

union, "committed partnership," refinement, sophistication, infinity, midpoints, "contract law," balance, cooperation, fairness, marriage, harmony, commitment, romantic, indecisive, "public relations," diplomacy, "good manners"

KEYWORD-USE EXAMPLES FOR THE SUN IN LIBRA:

Ego (the Sun) needs to feel on the side of fairness, justice, and harmony (Libra). Purpose (the Sun) is finding a balanced, beautiful life in a world of duality (Libra). Feeling angry or indecisive (Libra) can affect their vitality (the Sun).

People born during the time of Libra are here to learn about being strong enough to endure the difficulties that are part of their plan to advance the cause of balance, beauty, and harmony, avoiding extremes and living the Middle Way of Buddhism. The balance scale used as the sign's symbol is the only inanimate object representing a zodiac sign, a reminder that the perfection Libras seek is beyond the abilities of living beings and their organizations.

The spectrum of meanings for their unrivaled ability to seek harmony can range from heroic demonstrations of commitment and well-reasoned decisions used to save the day to being a fair and impartial voice when rational judgments are needed and all the way to harmful acts born of indecisiveness, pretense, or delays meant to help avoid unpleasant situations.

Librans prove their strength to themselves by honoring their commitments and being as fair as they can be as they try to make the world more beautiful in some way, according to their definition of beauty. They are made insecure by people pressuring them to make decisions when they are still uncommitted, weighing both sides of an issue.

Librans can be exemplary successes born of their natural abilities in negotiation, the middle class on which every society depends, or the people who refuse to decide or pick a side when that is what is needed the most. They are usually peace loving but can sometimes be pushed beyond endurance and fight fiercely for justice and fairness. They thrive when they are allowed to have a bit of wiggle room in their decisions.

Libras can be driven to extreme actions if their desire to bring beauty and harmony to their world and the world at large meets too much resistance. They have refined tastes and may recoil from or act against people or things that are unrefined, disharmonious, or hateful. Other people may misinterpret this attitude as snobbishness. A Libra may give the impression of being a pushover because of

an unwillingness to argue or cause a disturbance. They will, however, fight for justice and the underdog, despite the unpleasantness that often brings.

Scorpio ♏

October 23–November 21

SCORPIO KEYWORDS

passionate, intense, secretive, silent, profound, intuitive, mysterious, misunderstood, "good detective," transform, power, transcend, resurrect, regenerate, absolute, conscience, control, obsession, judge, purify, "death and rebirth," "black or white," "Phoenix rising from the ashes of its former self," vengeance

KEYWORD-USE EXAMPLES FOR THE SUN IN SCORPIO:

Ego (the Sun) needs to feel powerful (Scorpio). Purpose (the Sun) is to transform themselves, everyone, and everything they care about (Scorpio). Their vitality (the Sun) can be affected when their passionate and mysterious way of being causes them to be misunderstood (Scorpio).

People born during the time of Scorpio are here to learn about being strong enough to endure the difficulties that are part of their plan to live life as intensely and passionately as is humanly possible. They are also here to remind us that there are many aspects of life that are beyond words, indescribable, and can only be experienced, not explained.

The spectrum of meanings for their unrivaled ability to endure can range from heroic demonstrations of overwhelming or seemingly magical power used to transform a person, situation, or thing to a degree that saves the day to being a crucial but hidden influence that steers a situation the way they want it to go and all the way to harmful acts born of cruel judgments, life-or-death power struggles, and extreme or underhanded actions.

Scorpios prove their strength to themselves by keeping their own counsel and never compromising. They have an experientially developed appreciation for the highest, lowest, and most extreme version of just about any aspect of existence. They are made insecure by people who somehow seem to have uncovered their secrets or weaknesses they believe they, themselves, have but will never reveal.

Scorpios often work like secret agents or special-operations soldiers dropped behind enemy lines. They can be exemplary successes who rise to the top with little fanfare, the unsung agents of change, renewal, or detection that make things happen, or the people who work selfishly to possess or destroy what other people have, desire, or enjoy. They are usually silent and secretive but can sometimes be pushed beyond endurance and, like the Scorpion, their zodiac symbol, say or do things that sting. They thrive when they are allowed to be in a position where they have no one telling them what they are and are not supposed to be or do.

Scorpios are keen students of psychology and always want to know what makes people do the things they do. Compulsions and strange behavior do not faze them. Undeveloped Scorpios can use their intimate understanding of human motivations for ruthless manipulation cunningly designed to attain selfish goals. While Scorpios are constantly trying to uncover the secrets of others, they guard their own privacy with almost manic intensity. They can be vengeful.

Sagittarius ♐

November 22–December 21

SAGITTARIUS KEYWORDS

freedom, teaching, learning, spiritual, travel, philosophical, open, expand, enlarge, increase, develop, achieve, integrate, encourage, prosper, jovial, "positive outlook," luck, wealth, generosity, bounty, "broad perspective," "higher education," law, philosophy, religion, broadcasting, publishing

KEYWORD-USE EXAMPLES FOR THE SUN IN SAGITTARIUS:

Ego (the Sun) needs to show you that they know the absolute truth of everything (Sagittarius). Purpose (the Sun) is learning the ways of the world and sharing them (Sagittarius). Level of feeling confident about the efficacy of their philosophy and how it is received by others (Sagittarius) can affect their vitality (the Sun).

People born during the time of Sagittarius are here to learn about being strong enough to endure the difficulties that are part of their devotion to learning, understanding, and speaking the truth. They are drawn to nature and to understanding all things that are considered natural and wise by various cultures.

The spectrum of meanings for their unrivaled ability to be brutally honest can range from heroic demonstrations of acting courageously and speaking truth to power to save the day to being the person who knows how things work and the best way to do something and all the way to harmful acts born of too much said and done at the wrong time.

Sagittarians prove their strength to themselves by staying true to their beliefs, while at the same time seeking and being open to new beliefs they might adopt as their own. They have a highly developed appreciation for the best the world has to offer and will travel, read, or get involved with anything that brings the world to them or brings them to the world. They are made insecure by people who cannot handle their truth.

Sagittarians are willing to work hard to develop a philosophy they can believe in and live by. They can be exemplary successes born of both knowledge and the wisdom to apply it, the unsung philosophers among us who help us navigate daily life, or the intemperate know-it-alls who speak when it would be best if they stayed silent. They are usually gentle when speaking their truth but can sometimes be pushed beyond endurance and, like the Archer, their zodiac symbol, let loose pointed barbs. They thrive when they are allowed to act and speak their mind without restraint.

Capricorn ♑

December 22–January 19

CAPRICORN KEYWORDS

authoritative, serious, organized, responsible, structure, career-oriented, permanent, traditional, conservative, mature, fears, cautious, realistic, "define and understand rules and limits," "authority figures," "material success," discipline, concern, taciturn, teach, test, "dark humor," focus, concentrate, "endure restriction"

KEYWORD-USE EXAMPLES FOR THE SUN IN CAPRICORN:

Ego (the Sun) needs to be respected by those the native respects (Capricorn). Purpose (the Sun) is to achieve authority and success (Capricorn). Level of being respected and taken seriously (Capricorn) can affect their vitality (the Sun).

People born during the time of Capricorn are here to learn about being strong enough to endure the difficulties that are part of their plan to achieve authority, self-respect, and the respect of those whom they, themselves, respect. They see their jobs as part of a career plan.

The spectrum of meanings for their unrivaled ability to do what must be done can range from heroic demonstrations of willpower used to save the day to conserving and preserving what has deservedly stood the test of time and all the way to harmful acts born of slavish adherence to outmoded ways requiring unquestioning submission to an authority or a tradition now unsuitable for the time or place they live in.

Capricorns prove their strength to themselves by being disciplined, playing by the rules, and gaining authority even if it means playing the long game. They have a highly developed appreciation for the ironies and dark humor the harsh realities of life have to offer, and surprisingly deep sensual needs. They are made insecure by unserious people wasting time figuring out shortcuts, because it is a weakness that so rarely intrudes into their consciousness.

Capricorns are willing to work long and hard to achieve tangible things that last. They can be exemplary successes born of unwavering dedication and self-denial, the unsung dependable workers on which every enterprise depends, or the inflexible traditionalist holdovers in a situation where things have changed drastically. They usually suffer in silence or just mull things over and over but can sometimes be pushed beyond endurance to throw caution to the wind and, like the Goat, their zodiac symbol, do risky things. They thrive when they are allowed to achieve the series of goals they have set in the manner and the order they have set them.

Aquarius ♒

January 20–February 18

AQUARIUS KEYWORDS

humanitarian, inventive, friendly but detached, idealistic, altruistic, progressive, "technically proficient," eccentric, genius, futuristic, original, free-thinker, unusual, disruptive, explosive, excite, absent-minded, upset, revolutionize, reform, rebel, unemotional, enlighten, liberate, freedom

KEYWORD-USE EXAMPLES FOR THE SUN IN AQUARIUS:

Ego (the Sun) needs to feel part of a movement to create a better future for humanity (Aquarius). Purpose (the Sun) is to revolutionize (Aquarius). Their vitality (the Sun) is proportional to how much freedom they have to innovate and rebel (Aquarius).

People born during the time of Aquarius are here to learn about being strong enough to endure the difficulties that are part of their plan to use unusual methods to make the future very different from the past and present.

The spectrum of meanings for their unrivaled ability to bring sooner-than-expected change can range from brilliant inventions, methods, and concepts that save the day to being the person who questions and makes small changes to the status quo and all the way to harmful acts born of unneeded disruption and rebelliousness for its own sake.

Aquarians prove their strength to themselves by daring to be and do the unusual, fearlessly questioning everything, and thinking outside of the box. They have a highly developed appreciation for timelessly good ideas from the past that can be modified and applied to the creation of a better future. They are made insecure by people who cannot follow their freewheeling thought process and try to slow it, and them, down.

Aquarians are willing to think and go to extremes to test the efficacy and practicality of their theories. They can be exemplary successes born of visionary invention, the people who can improvise and improve just about anything, or the unfeeling barbarian whose ill-conceived "improvement" cruelly imposes a new way of thinking or doing that fails to incorporate time-honored facts. They are usually friendly and good in a crisis, but after the danger has passed, they can suddenly erupt. They thrive when they are allowed total freedom.

Pisces ♓

February 19–March 20

PISCES KEYWORDS

sensitive, spiritual, psychic, emotional, receptive, moody, vague, otherworldly, inspirational, faith, idealize, fantasize, imagination, dreams, confuse, illusion, deceive, weaken, dissolve, sacrifice, surrender, suffer, martyrdom, escape, "drug addiction and alcoholism"

KEYWORD-USE EXAMPLES FOR THE SUN IN PISCES:

Ego (the Sun) needs to show others how to live according to the tenets of a spiritual practice (Pisces). Purpose (the Sun) is feeling oneness with all (Pisces). Sensitivity to the situation, feelings, and suffering of others (Pisces) can affect their vitality (the Sun).

People born during the time of Pisces are here to learn about being strong enough to endure the difficulties that are part of their plan to achieve a more compassionate, comfortable, and equitable lifestyle for themselves and others.

The spectrum of meanings for their unrivaled ability to empathize can range from heroic demonstrations of charity and sacrifice used to help the less fortunate to working to take care of the needs of other beings and all the way to harmful acts born of self-destructive tendencies, especially the escape from the harsh realities of life into addiction and deception or the subjugating of one's own identity and needs to that of a supposedly more worthy being, cause, or cult.

Pisceans prove their strength to themselves by being aware of others as fellow beings, charitable acts, and self-denial for a higher purpose. They have a highly developed appreciation for facts and theories about the multidimensional nature of conscious life and must guard against taking on the emotions of others. They are made insecure by people who are selfish or harsh or who insist on a strictly materialistic view of existence.

Pisceans are willing to put into practice utopian concepts, even if these concepts have never succeeded in past circumstances. They can be exemplary successes born of seemingly psychic intuition, the salt-of-the-Earth people who exemplify true spirituality, or those who give up on life and lose themselves in fantasies of their own making. They are usually kind and quiet but can sometimes be pushed beyond endurance and lash out or, like their zodiac symbol, two Fishes—one swimming upstream and the other downstream—become directionless. They thrive when they are continuously encouraged and never ridiculed.

USING KEYWORDS: THE SECRET TO YOUR SUCCESS

Using my keyword technique will enable you to decipher the meaning of every planet in every sign and in every house without having to look up the meanings of said planet, sign, and house. I use it all the time. Using keywords generates the spark of ideas regarding what a particular aspect of your cosmic blueprint can tell you. That spark can be fanned by your logical mind and intuition to create mental constructs that offer you insights into that aspect.

The way the keyword technique works is, you take the basic meaning of the planet—in this case, the Sun—which for this example we will say is identity, ego, vitality, or purpose, and combine it with any of the keywords you can either recall or look up for the sign of the zodiac in which the Sun resides in the chart you are looking at.

For example, the Sun in Pisces would be "Purpose (or identity or ego or vitality) is ____." Fill in the blank with one or more of the keywords (adapted for grammatical sense) for Pisces: *sensitive, spiritual, psychic, emotional, receptive, moody, vague, otherworldly, inspirational, faith, idealize, fantasize, imagination, dreams, confuse, illusion, deceive, weaken, dissolve, sacrifice, surrender, suffer, martyrdom, escape, "drug addiction and alcoholism."*

Obviously, there are positive, neutral, and negative keywords associated with the Sun sign Pisces, and this is true of all the signs, planets, and houses (the twelve pizza slices!) of your astrology chart. I will be showing you when and how to apply the more negative keywords later on.

(Explaining how they work would, at this point, be more confusing and harmful than helpful. I know you are likely going to use the tough and negative keywords anyway—this isn't my first rodeo—so when you do so, do it on an experimental basis. Don't make the rookie mistake of thinking they definitively explain problematic aspects in the astrology chart you are looking at and personality traits in you and others.)

At this point, our goal is to get you comfortable with making keyword sentences or sentence fragments. Many of the ones you create will be spot-on, and that is the feeling we are going to try to experience again and again. Trust me, however, that taking the keyword statements you explore as gospel at this point is not the way to go. Just have fun with them.

To get the most out of the keyword technique, have fun playing around with the possible combinations and how they can be interpreted. For example: "Purpose is sensitive" could mean that it is important to this Pisces Sun person to be sensitive or to examine what it means to be sensitive. But don't forget that you can arrange the keywords in any order. For example, you might have "sensitive purpose," which could mean that their purpose in life is somehow connected to a subject that is sensitive at this time in world history or even that they might feel that their purpose is somehow connected to the sensitivities of one or more people with whom they are close or care about. It could also mean that they are sensitive about some aspect of learning their purpose in life and so you should be careful if you feel it necessary to discuss that subject. You may see one or more additional interpretations in "sensitive purpose" or any of the other keyword combinations—and, if so, congratulations! You are an astrologer! Keep up the great work.

Of course, some keyword combinations make more immediate sense than others. *Purpose is spiritual. Ego is sensitive. Identity (identifies as) is martyrdom.* Use them any way that makes sense to you, and use them a lot. Why? Because keyword combinations give you a good jumping-off point from which to explore the meaning of the Sun and, in future chapters, every planet in any sign. Using my keyword process helps free you up from your mind's desire to rigidly classify and "know" the meaning of a particular part of an astrological chart. It is infinitely better than laboriously memorizing a couple of Sun sign meanings.

Although, as I said previously, the definition of the word *astrology*, a combination of *astro* ("star") and *logos* ("wisdom"), does not differentiate between "wisdoms"; the similarity between *logos* and *logic*, which derives from it, implies the emphasis of the use of one's logical mind to learn about the stars—actually, the wandering planets.

However, the best readers combine the fact-based logical part of their brain with the use of their intuitive abilities, which we all have but which need to be acknowledged and developed to be used properly. The maximum use of our creative faculties results in the best possible readings of a cosmic blueprint.

You will get even more keyword-based "stories" when we get to the meaning of the houses, at which point you will be able to make a full sentence—hence, an admittedly short story—composed of the keywords mixed with the meanings of the planet, the sign, and the house. Applying the keyword technique to an actual astrology chart is what makes you a real astrologer. First, however, we need to up your astrological game a bit before we move on to delineating the Moon in the twelve signs. Before we go to the Moon, you need to know about the Four Elements of astrology.

THE FOUR ELEMENTS

NOTE: *You must understand the following before you move on to the Moon.*

In the previous section, we delineated the meanings of the Sun in all twelve signs of the zodiac. The reason we say the Sun "moves" through the signs is not because the Sun actually moves through space to traverse the twelve signs. We astrologers—and that now includes you!—say the Sun is moving through the twelve signs because it can be seen this way when plotted against the backdrop of the zodiac and its fixed stars, seen from our home planet Earth to pass through the twelve unique signs of the zodiac, thereby defining the passage of one year.

Speaking of one year, the astrological New Year starts on the spring solstice in the northern hemisphere, the first day of spring and the 1st degree of Aries, when the Sun returns to that 1st degree. In fact, the expression "Many happy returns" refers to the apparent return of the Sun to the degree of the zodiac it was on when you were born. Each sign has 30 degrees, and all twelve combine to make 360 degrees of the zodiac circle.

Now it is time to introduce you to an additional and equally crucial layer of meaning that can be added to each of the twelve signs: the concept of the Four Elements. It should be much easier for you to understand now that you have learned the meaning of the Sun in the twelve signs.

You may have noticed that there were certain similarities in the meanings of some signs. Astrology has classified the twelve signs of the zodiac into Four Elements: Fire, Air, Water, and Earth. If you look at the upper left portion of the chart you obtained from AstroGraph.com, you will notice the Four Elements, and each of them will either have a number beside it or no number. No number indicates that there are no components of your cosmic blueprint in that particular element.

Each element has three zodiac signs associated with it. Knowing which element a sign belongs to is very helpful for increasing your understanding of that sign and for helping you remember its meaning.

Fire △

Aries, Leo, and Sagittarius are all Fire signs because, since ancient days, the metaphysical (beyond the physical) meaning of Fire has been similar to the many keywords associated with the word *fiery*: *active, impetuous, hotheaded, vibrant, intense, bright, brilliant, spicy, hot, burning, red-hot, excitable, irritable,* and *vivid.*

Fire signs burn brightly with the passionate desire particular to this astrological element.

When you see Aries, Leo, or Sagittarius in a person's cosmic blueprint—and not just the Sun but any planet in a Fire sign—you know that this person is at the very least interested in or attracted to action-oriented and passionate people and causes, though much more likely to be the kind of person who initiates action rather than passively watches and waits for it. Fire signs do not like to wait for anything or anyone. Aries, Leo, and Sagittarius are impulsive, energetic, quick to anger, and quick to forgive. People with Fire signs in their cosmic blueprints are usually found in occupations connected with getting things moving, recognition for their achievements, passionate causes, and adventure.

Air △

Gemini, Libra, and Aquarius are all Air signs because they are each concerned with the realm of ideas, which the ancients symbolized as being carried over the air millennia before radio, TV, and other over-the-air broadcasts came into being and were supplanted by the internet.

Air signs are all committed to exploring the power of ideas. Some keywords I associate with the word *idea* that can add to your understanding of the nature of Gemini, Libra, and Aquarius are *learning, understanding, solution, method, theory, suspicion, hunch, plan, recommendation, proposition, interpretation, sentiment, doctrine, concept, surmise, inkling, approximation, estimation, abstraction, impression,* and *judgment.*

When you see Gemini, Libra, or Aquarius in a chart—and not just the Sun but any planet in an Air sign—you know that this person is at the very least interested in or attracted to mental pursuits, philosophy, invention, and communication in some form, especially reading about or conversing with people skilled in those areas or writing about what they know. Gemini, Libra, and Aquarius are usually polite and diplomatic unless their theories are disrespected. People with Air signs in their cosmic blueprints are usually found in occupations connected with information, the mind, and the intellectual aspects of life.

Water 

Cancer, Scorpio, and Pisces are all Water signs because they are each concerned with the realm of emotions, which the ancients symbolized as being like the rising and falling oceans and great lakes that connect the landmasses and enable us to travel around the world but can also easily overwhelm anyone who fails to take them and the tides of emotions seriously. Some keywords I associate with the word *emotion* that can add to your understanding of the Water signs are *intuition, feeling, fervor, ardor, instinct, sensation, soft-hearted, tenderness, "gut feeling," vehement, agitation, excitement,* and *sentimental.*

When you see Cancer, Scorpio, or Pisces in a chart—and not just the Sun but any planet in a Water sign—you know that this person is at the very least interested in or attracted to experiencing their feelings and the feelings of others, as well as the things that support, sustain, and connect us all, like active caring, compassion, intuition, and extrasensory perception (ESP). People with the Water signs prominent in their astrology charts are sensitive, feeling types and need employment where they can be connected and imaginative, and can deal with the emotional side of life. They have to make sure that what they are feeling is actually what *they* are feeling and that they are not picking up on what someone else in the room or even in the next room or apartment is feeling.

Earth 

Taurus, Virgo, and Capricorn are all Earth signs because they are each concerned with the realm of matter, especially practical matters and all objects and concepts related to surviving and thriving in our daily lives here in the material world. Some keywords I associate with the word *material* that can add to your understanding of the Earth signs are *body*, *possessions*, *"movable property," stuff*, *"things you can touch," own*, *fabric*, *"subject matter," papers*, *tangible*, *corporeal*, *palpable*, *elements*, *pieces*, *substance*, *"physical properties," appearances*, *articles*, *items*, *necessities*, *holdable*, *practical*, *belongings*, *"personal property," goods*, *effects*, and *paraphernalia*.

When you see Taurus, Virgo, or Capricorn in a chart—and not just the Sun but any planet in an Earth sign—you know that this person is at the very least interested in or attracted to everyone and anything that can offer them practical and useful advice or help them in some way have a richer, more secure, and materially comfortable experience of life. They concern themselves with everything related to health, food, work, achievement, and recognition. Earth signs respond to the world through their five senses: what they see, hear, taste, touch, and smell. They are attracted to occupations that allow them to feel secure enough to enjoy themselves.

IF A PERSON HAS NONE OF A PARTICULAR ELEMENT IN THEIR CHART

A person who has none of a particular element in their astrology chart will experience the things related to that element very differently than people who do have one or more planets in that element. Keep in mind that a person without a particular element in their astrology chart may manifest this as being strongly attracted to people who do have a lot of the missing element in their astrology charts. Or they may have difficulty relating to people with a lot of the element that they themselves are missing.

No Fire

Not having any Fire can incline a person to have issues with or be less driven to achieve or to not need to be passionate about how they approach life, including their love life. Or they can try to get things going with a passion that seems inappropriate for what they are trying to achieve. They can seem strangely attracted to or sometimes repelled by people whose charts have a lot of planets in Fire signs.

No Air

Not having any Air can incline a person to have issues with originating, formulating, or communicating ideas or with being interested in coming up with new ways of doing things. Or they can always seem to be at the idea stage, constantly trying to acquire more and more information and never actually committing to a plan. They can seem strangely attracted to or sometimes repelled by people whose charts have a lot of planets in Air signs.

No Water

Not having any Water can incline a person to have issues with being compassionate to the feelings of other people, including the people they believe they love. This obviously makes it difficult for them to have lasting relationships with people who want their partner to care a lot about them. They can seem strangely attracted to or sometimes repelled by people whose charts have a lot of planets in Water signs.

No Earth

Not having any Earth can incline a person to have issues with or do surprising things in order to fulfill what they consider to be critical practical needs they have to address. They may take jobs that they do not like or for which they are overqualified if it brings them "guaranteed" security. They can seem strangely attracted to or sometimes repelled by people whose charts have a lot of planets in Earth signs.

Speaking of no Earth, it's time for us to go to the Moon!

THE MOON THROUGH THE TWELVE SIGNS OF THE ZODIAC

We have delineated the meanings of the Sun through the zodiac signs and learned how the position of the Sun in your cosmic blueprint can give you strong clues as to your ego, purpose, vitality, how you identify, and more. We have also learned about astrology's Four Elements and their associated concepts: Fire (action), Air (ideas), Water (emotions), and Earth (practical matters). Now let's do the same for the Moon, and we'll add each sign's element to help reinforce your understanding of how each sign is either Fire, Air, Water, or Earth.

The symbol or glyph for the Moon in astrology shows a waxing crescent Moon. The image is so familiar that it is easy to spot as one of the toppings on your chart/pizza. I want to point out again that the meaning of the various planets is contained within their glyphs, but only if you know how to look at each glyph's component parts. It's a bit like reading your cosmic blueprint. The Moon glyph can be seen to be made up of two semicircles—the full-circle glyph for the Sun cut in two pieces, symbolizing the division of the Great Spirit or All-There-Is into individual "souls." The Moon represents the emotional half of the individualized soul (the other half of the spirit circle, which you will see is used in the glyphs for the planets Mercury, Saturn, Jupiter, and Uranus, symbolizes the purely mental half). The symbol for the Moon can be seen as a parabolic mirror used to reflect, collect, and concentrate energy emanating from an external source the way the Moon reflects the Sun's light, or, on its side, a bowl to contain and nourish.

In astrology, not only is the Moon considered one of the planets, but because of its proximity to and many strong and demonstrable influences on the Earth, in addition, its importance is second only to the Sun in a person's horoscope chart. In fact, your own astrological practice may reveal to you enough evidence for you to join me in my belief that the Moon is at least the equal and may be the most important planet to look at in the chart of those who identify as women.

The Moon's gravitational pull produces the ebb and flow of the tides. The astrologers of old associated that connection along with the Moon's rapid passage through the zodiac (12 to 15 degrees during each twenty-four-hour period and traversing the entire zodiac in about twenty-eight days) with the often-rapid ebb and flow of our emotions. For comparison, the Sun, the second fastest of astrology's planets, moves 1 degree a day.

NOTE: *I believe the Moon in an astrology chart can be seen to relate to our emotional intelligence (our ability to successfully experience, process, and derive benefit from our emotions), our intuition, and the communication of all three of these things.*

The Moon was the first calendar and was used to predict the return of the seasons and the animals hunted by our ancestors, a matter of life or death. In fact, *month* is derived from *moon*. Many cultures around the world still use a lunar calendar in addition to the solar-based Gregorian calendar: the Buddhist, Burmese, Chinese, Hebrew, Hindu, Igbo (of West Africa), Islamic, Korean, Somali, Thai, and Vietnamese peoples.

The relatively swift and monthly regularity of the passage of the Moon through the twelve signs of the zodiac explains why astrologers view it as closely related to our habits. (I cannot overstate that all aspects of your cosmic blueprint have a spectrum of possible meanings. Using our free will to emphasize or diminish in our thoughts and actions these various possible meanings is what makes a person's character.)

Looking at astrology as a psychological language makes it so helpful for personal development, and being able to zoom in on a person's habits can help them answer questions about themselves whose answers have long evaded them. *There are habits that heal and habits that hurt.* Let that sink in for a minute, and you will see one of the main reasons knowing a person's Moon sign is often a key to their self-understanding.

The Moon changes shape from new to full and back again, taking 27.3 days to complete a revolution—the Moon rotates but we do not perceive it because it always faces the Earth—and 29.5 days to change from new Moon to new Moon. It is a schedule very close to that of a woman's menstrual cycle, and that informs the Moon's keyword associations: *women, fertility, feeding, planting, childbirth, mothering, nurturing in general, "emotional intelligence," cycles, habits, "unconditional love," protective, reflective, reflexive,* and *regular*.

The meteor-scarred surface of the Moon gives silent testimony to its protective nature as it revolves around the Earth with its "face"

continually facing our vulnerable planet like a mother watching over a child. It also rules the relationship between a child or person needing care and a nurturing caregiver, which in the past represented the idealized version of a mother but now can be anyone who is a nurturing, caring, forgiving, and protective caregiver to children or anyone else, just as the Moon watches over Earth.

THE NORTH AND SOUTH NODES OF THE MOON

The two nodes of the Moon in our astrology charts are the "toppings" that look like old-school headphones worn over your head, the North Node, or earbuds worn under your chin, the South Node. They can provide insights into how our inner life can help guide us to succeed or fail. The nodes are not regular planets, though they do move on a daily basis through the zodiac. They are the points where the imaginary line described by the Moon's orbit intersects the ecliptic,

the imaginary line described by the apparent yearly path of the Sun through the stars of the zodiac.

I realize that sounds like a lot of imaginary lines, but the nodes are very important. Both astronomers and astrologers know that the only time eclipses occur is when either a new Moon or a full Moon happens close to either of the nodes. If it's a new Moon that occurs near a node, then we here on Earth see a solar eclipse because the Moon gets between our planet and the Sun. And if it's a full Moon that occurs near a node, then we here on Earth see a lunar eclipse because our planet gets between the Sun and the Moon.

Astrologers through the ages have found that the nodes are sensitive points in understanding a cosmic blueprint. We can explain the nodes by looking at the Hindu concepts of karma and dharma. The South Node has to do with our karma, a concept similar to the Golden Rule of cause and effect (i.e., what goes around comes around). I named my *Karma Cards* based on Edgar Cayce's description of karma as "meeting yourself," which is what astrology is all about. The North Node has to do with your dharma, your work in the world that helps you balance your karma. The North and South Nodes are always directly opposite each other.

The circumstances and quality of our individual lives are determined by the causes and effects, both good and bad, that we accumulate (through our thoughts, words, and actions) at each moment. The law of cause and effect affirms that we each have personal responsibility for our own destiny. We create our destiny, and we have the power to change it.

The North Node is an ever-changing point of intersection between the paths the Moon and the Earth are moving in. Its symbol shows the two planets connected by a shared path, and that path is pointed up. The North Node symbolizes the best way our inner emotional life can help us succeed with our long-term goals.

If we are not emotionally fulfilled inside of ourselves, no amount of outward love or success will make us feel good about the world or ourselves. The North Node symbolizes being in harmony with what we should be doing to reach the place in our lives we have decided will make us feel emotionally fulfilled. It is the method by which we can shake off any ill feelings about our past actions and be reborn.

It is the Big Green Stoplight—it is the "good" node, the big *yes*! If you think that it also looks like a lucky horseshoe, you're right! You have good luck in the house where it lands in your birth chart—you can breathe easily in the area of life where the North Node lands. You are doing what you should be doing. You have earned your reward through efforts in this or other lifetimes. The North Node represents your dharma—your work in the world to mitigate your karma. *Dharma* means "to hold" or "to support." It signifies the path of righteousness—"the right way of living."

The South Node, which looks like earbuds worn under the chin, is the Big Red Stoplight. Its symbol shows the two planets connected by a shared path, and that path is pointed down. Where it lands in your birth chart, stop, look, listen, and remember. The Hindu concept of karma is very close to the meaning of the South Node. It symbolizes past actions we have made that we are not satisfied with. These past actions produce discomforting consequences we must deal with to learn why we did what we did.

Like astrology, itself, the South Node shows how similar, yet how different, we all are. Everyone has the South Node in their chart, just like everyone has done things they are not proud of. However, everyone's South Node is in a different place relative to the position of all the other planets in their chart, symbolizing that what we must learn and how we must learn it are very different for all of us.

Some astrologers say that the South Node represents bad karma, but that is a limited and fairly negative view. Karma is more than bad things happening to you because of what you've done. Karma is the work you have decided you must do in order to feel good about yourself. The South Node is a reminder that you may be going against what you know are your own best interests in the areas that the house it is in rules. When it is time to learn about the twelve houses of a cosmic blueprint, you will be able to see what you can learn from the difficulties you have encountered in the area of life symbolized by the astrological house the South Node is in.

In the pages ahead, I will outline the basic meanings of the Moon as it moves through the twelve signs of the zodiac and blends its meaning, emotions, and our emotional intelligence quotient with each sign's individual flavor, plus the Four Elements: Fire, Earth, Air, and Water. I will also add to each Moon sign's delineation a couple of habits that heal and habits that hurt. As with all our personality traits, whether they can hurt us or heal us is dependent on their being used appropriately, at the right time and in the right place, used in a manner in balance and harmony with our moral code and value system. To allow our emotions to rule our behavior without limit can weaken even the best qualities of any chart.

You will probably have your own opinions about my example habits that heal and habits that hurt, and that is a good thing. I hope you will have your own opinions about everything you read from this point on. Now that you have a strong grounding in the basic meanings of the twelve signs of the zodiac, you are encouraged to join me and our fellow astrologers on the lifelong-learning experience that is the practice of astrology. The purpose of this book is to help you read your cosmic blueprint, of course, but just as important is attaining the ability to think for yourself in the application of the information and techniques I am sharing with you herein and all information you encounter.

Moon in Aries ♈

Element: Fire

KEYWORDS

headstrong, bossy, "cannot be told what to do," power, sharp, impulsive, noisy, independent, self-confident, aggressive, combative, "able to work alone," active, "at the head of a group"

USING MOON IN ARIES KEYWORDS:

Feelings can cause them to be . . .

Emotions are stimulated by . . .

HABITS THAT HEAL:

self-reliant, brave, independent

HABITS THAT HURT:

combative, uncooperative, impulsive

No one can tell someone with their Moon in Aries what to do. They are brave, a fighter when feelings are involved. They are independent and do not care whether others are too. Others may try to get to them through their feelings because they instinctually know people with this Moon placement will act before they think. People with an Aries Moon must be on guard against being manipulated through their fiery temperament and reactive nature.

They are intelligent, quick-tempered, and courageous. They are self-reliant, and their job may take them from place to place. They are much better at directing others than at being able to stick to details and routine. They need to work hard to be sure that they have mastered their own techniques so that they will be qualified to be "the boss" or to work for themselves, alone, or at least unsupervised.

The direct way in which they talk and the efficiency with which they come to their own conclusions enable them to be good leaders. They could be a proficient teacher or a pioneering inventor. They are usually too energetic to tie themselves down to one job forever, unless they work for themselves. Their basic instinct is to want variety, new territory to claim and explore—and they often manage to get it in work as well as in love. It takes a quick-moving and quick-witted person to keep up with the energy, dynamism, and speed of someone with their Moon in Aries.

Moon in Taurus ♉

Element: Earth

KEYWORDS

"system oriented," plan, persevering, stubborn, careful, unstoppable, lazy, indolent, calm, "resistant to change," "good position for obtaining possessions," "talent for music, especially singing," "kind and compliant but always sensuous"

USING MOON IN TAURUS KEYWORDS:

Feelings can cause them to be . . .

Emotions are stimulated by . . .

HABITS THAT HEAL:

calm, patient, music loving

HABITS THAT HURT:

resistant to change, furious when pushed too far

People with their Moon in Taurus need comfort and security, preferring that things in their life do not change. They are loving and affectionate, and they, in turn, need affection. They want the best life has to offer. They are calm and patient but can find inertia a problem—it is hard for them to get going. But once they do, they are very hard to stop. They sometimes find themselves still trying to keep a relationship, job, or other situation going when they would be better off moving on and ending their struggles. They do not rush or change their feelings.

The placement of the Moon in Taurus indicates an even temperament. They are determined, ambitious, and independent. They like to stay in one place or in a place they own, and this desire prompts them to invest in real estate. They like to own houses, land, and other material objects. They like music and often have a melodious voice. They become rather fixed in their habits and have difficulty deviating from their established ways and their system of doing things. They are challenged to become even more independent.

They know what they want and why they want it. They have the courage to demand their rights because they seldom impose on others. When they accept a favor, they reciprocate in full. Their close friends know how generous and kind-hearted they are, but acquaintances can see them as self-centered.

Moon in Gemini ♊

Element: Air

KEYWORDS

progressive, curious, study, "emotional intellectual," movable, changeable, irresolute, travel, walking, visiting, handy, capable, speaker, double, "hard to pin down," multitasker

USING MOON IN GEMINI KEYWORDS:

Feelings can cause them to be . . .

Emotions are stimulated by . . .

HABITS THAT HEAL:

multitasking, curious, studious

HABITS THAT HURT:

scattered, noncommittal, boredom averse

People with their Moon in Gemini are desirous of experiencing life like no other Moon sign. They communicate their feelings—all of them—to others, but also to themselves, which can at times be emotionally exhausting. They want to know everything they can about how they feel and why they feel that way. Their emotions change so rapidly that they can become bored and restless with anyone or anything that does not engage their curiosity. They are usually cool in a crisis and often see it coming before anyone else. Moon in Gemini people need to be careful not to talk too much about themselves and how they feel.

Moon in Gemini natives have a flexible nature. They are candid, sincere, and progressive about what touches them on an emotional level. They are always busy, even when they seem to be at rest, because they are hungry to feel as much as possible. They can formulate more ideas about something that touches their emotions than a dozen others put together (unless there is another Moon in Gemini person among them). Their occupation will depend on their environment because they are hardwired be able to do almost anything that interests them.

Gemini Moons are known to have a daily schedule so arduous and so varied that it keeps others guessing how they manage to find time to sleep. They usually bounce back or recuperate very quickly from setbacks. Even when they appear to be doing too much multitasking and going at full speed, if they are enjoying and relaxing into riding the wave of their project, you can rest assured that they are more reposed than you would expect.

Moon in Cancer ♋

Element: Water

KEYWORDS

emotional, caring, intuitive, nurturing, economical, psychic, sensitive, home, family, mother, kind, "pleasant but changeable in friendships," "liable to imitate others," nostalgic, "living in the past," homesick

USING MOON IN CANCER KEYWORDS:

Feelings can cause them to be . . .

Emotions are stimulated by . . .

HABITS THAT HEAL:

caring, supportive, forgiving

HABITS THAT HURT:

smothering, oversensitive, too forgiving

NOTE: *Each of the twelve signs of the zodiac has a planet so sympatico with that sign that the planet is said to rule that sign: The Moon rules Cancer. The Moon in Cancer is an indication of a person who can be so intuitive or in tune with the emotions of others as to be thought psychic by those who know them.*

People with their Moon in Cancer can often display more emotional intelligence than the other Moon signs. They have the gift of being aware of their own emotions and that of other people and being able to appropriately deal with them. Cancer Moon is the archetypal mother or one who nurtures those they care about. They can forgive those who are trying to grow, though they will not forget the event's particulars.

Moon in Cancer people have a gently changeable, emotional nature like the ebb and flow of the tides. They usually like to stick close to home. They take family obligations seriously and have a very close relationship with their mother or the person who filled that role in their early life. They have great tenacity of purpose.

Cancer Moon's very tenderness and emotional delicacy makes them quite vulnerable to the barbs of jealousy and treachery, so they must never expose themselves to anyone whose character does not include the invaluable quality of loyalty. When they love, they do so genuinely. They want and can attract the same romantic devotion, but the desire to take care of those trying to grow can sometimes lead to relationships with emotionally needy or immature people.

Moon in Leo ♌

Element: Fire

KEYWORDS

noble, responsible, prideful, show-off, faithful, honest, generous, kind, imperious, appreciative, demonstrative, leadership, political, loving, languorous, romantic, actor, playful, exhibitionist, praise, risk-taker

USING MOON IN LEO KEYWORDS:

Feelings can cause them to be . . .

Emotions are stimulated by . . .

HABITS THAT HEAL:
affectionate, playful

HABITS THAT HURT:
show-off, imperious

People with their Moon in Leo need to feel proud of themselves and of everyone and everything that they consider important and with which they identify. They are very demonstrative of their feelings. When they like someone, they tell them, and they want the same from those who like them. They are usually playful. It is important for them to have their feelings acknowledged. They especially need to be aware of their need to share what makes them feel important and of what they are willing to do to attract attention to themselves. Exaggeration can be a weakness.

Leo Moons are noble and strong-willed. There is usually nothing cheap, petty, or underhanded in their nature. They are candid, proud, able, connected, and popular. They can be wonderful public speakers, first-class executives, or legendary managers. They command the respect of their associates, who come to trust their judgment implicitly. They can walk the line, thinking for themselves and for others at the same time.

Moon in Leo people are willing to endure a lot to show their love. When stressed, however, those accustomed to having their own way are not as thoughtful as they should be. When they are themselves, few Moon signs can be more generous, gracious, and noble than those with Moon in Leo. They need to be self-reliant without being imperious. Like Aries Moon people, when they're in a mood, it is very difficult to get them to do what they are told.

Moon in Virgo ♍

Element: Earth

KEYWORDS

competence, intellect, discriminating, analysis, worry, discerning, business, serious, service, self-deprecating, detail, work, artisan, critical, perfectionist, narrow-minded, "people pleaser"

USING MOON IN VIRGO KEYWORDS:

Feelings can cause them to be . . .

Emotions are stimulated by . . .

HABITS THAT HEAL:

discerning, detail oriented

HABITS THAT HURT:

perfectionism, self-deprecating

People with their Moon in Virgo are an unusual blend of happy and serious. They have developed skills because they like to be useful, neat, and orderly, and they do what it takes to make that happen. They are careful to avoid letting their personal feelings get in the way of any situation in which they find themselves.

Moon in Virgo people seem to not show their emotions unless one knows how to look for their way of doing so. They immediately get to the business of analyzing their emotions as soon as they become aware that they have an emotion to analyze, often worrying about its appropriateness to the point of believing they are being judged or disliked for being who they are.

Virgo Moons are polite, reserved, and practical. They can adapt themselves to circumstances. Critical analysis comes naturally to them, and they can use this trait to earn a living. If they can avoid perfectionism, they work well with others. They can detect a lie a mile away. They have a great memory that is unusually retentive and reliable. When they know something, they can prove it.

Moon in Libra ♎

Element: Air

KEYWORDS

harmony, beauty, kind, affectionate, committed, indecisive, naive, lazy, pleasant, artistic, dependable, courteous, agreeable, cooperative, partnership, fair, "seeking balance and harmony," "avoid confrontation"

USING MOON IN LIBRA KEYWORDS:

Feelings can cause them to be . . .

Emotions are stimulated by . . .

HABITS THAT HEAL:

seeking balance, cooperative

HABITS THAT HURT:

naive, overly agreeable

People with their Moon in Libra want to feel in harmony with their world and avoid discord, chaos, and feeling out of control. They feel deeply that everyone is beautiful in their own way. They are more than willing to use their refined sense of taste to improve everything and everyone. They are willing to fight for peace and justice. Their desire for peace at any cost can cause them to be taken advantage of or to give in when they should stand up for their beliefs.

Moon in Libra people are usually clear-thinking and warm-hearted. They are faithful, loyal, dependable, and courteous. They have wonderful manners and will go out of their way to not offend anyone, though they can be brave, bold, and aggressive when they believe it is necessary. They are partnership oriented and always seek to understand the emotions of others. They need to make an effort to understand people who prefer to be alone.

Libra Moons examine their emotions as they ebb and flow even more than many other Moon signs, and so it is often difficult for them to express how they feel at a particular moment because they know all too well how transitory their feelings are. The exception is that once they give their heart or their word, that is that. They know how to commit and will work hard to uphold their end of an agreement.

Moon in Scorpio ♏

Element: Water

KEYWORDS

passionate, secretive, definitive, persistent, self-confident, constant, mysterious, sensual, arrogant, authentic, energetic, stubborn, vengeful, rude, sexual, compulsive, investigative, stinging, extreme, brooding

USING MOON IN SCORPIO KEYWORDS:

Feelings can cause them to be . . .

Emotions are stimulated by . . .

HABITS THAT HEAL:

passionate, authentic

HABITS THAT HURT:

vengeful, brooding

People with their Moon in Scorpio are passionate beyond words, and they want to live their life in a more pure and intense way than others. It is difficult for them to put into words exactly how they are feeling. They are emotionally complex, often being as mystified as to how they are feeling about something as are those around them. This helps them to be good detectives because they are used to unraveling the puzzle of their inner life.

Moon in Scorpio people like to feel that they have secret powers and most of them do, in some way. They have an innate fascination with sex that can work for or against them. They can be jealous and quite vengeful if they feel insulted. They rarely forgive and never forget, so it is very important for them to be sure that what sets them off is not just an innocent misunderstanding or totally in their head.

Although they are inclined to keep themselves to themselves and hide, Scorpio Moons can be quite courageous and display extraordinary stamina and willpower when their emotions have been aroused by something or someone. People who are not as powerful or motivated may misunderstand this as them being compulsive, stubborn, or self-centered. It is important that they associate with people who appreciate their fearless qualities and unflagging energy for enterprises others would avoid.

Moon in Sagittarius ♐

Element: Fire

KEYWORDS

philosophical, sincere, broad-minded, honest, talkative, optimistic, glib, voluble, travel, "lifelong learning," knowledgeable, unreserved, "overly truthful," "too much information," dismissive, "nature lover"

USING MOON IN SAGITTARIUS KEYWORDS:

Feelings can cause them to be . . .

Emotions are stimulated by . . .

HABITS THAT HEAL:

honest, broad-minded

HABITS THAT HURT:

overly truthful, dismissive

People with their Moon in Sagittarius are philosophical and usually optimistic, sometimes to the point of being idealists. They feel things deeply and are more than willing to tell you about how they really feel, often going against their best interests while being so candidly honest. Their sincerity can lead to being disappointed when they see others are unable to accept them as they are or unwilling to be as forthcoming and honest in turn.

Moon in Sagittarius people are born travelers and often find that they have a strong affinity for one or more parts of the world they have never visited. When traveling in their rich inner world of feelings, they can sometimes get intuitive information that turns out to be true to a surprising degree. They are social and work well with others, though often better at mental occupations rather than physical ones. They can be surprisingly dismissive of the opinions of others.

Sagittarius Moons take things as they come. When things do not go as planned, they do not waste time regretting but use the time of defeat as the best time to plant the seeds of future successes. They have an innate affinity for animals and natural settings, both of which can restore their spiritual equilibrium when times are tough. They are instinctive hunters and can find what other people cannot begin to seek.

Moon in Capricorn ♑

Element: Earth

KEYWORDS

responsible, reserved, taciturn, saturnine, cautious, serious, hardworking, perseverance, frugal, ambitious, unemotional, determined, callous, negative, self-involved

USING MOON IN CAPRICORN KEYWORDS:

Feelings can cause them to be . . .

Emotions are stimulated by . . .

HABITS THAT HEAL:

perseverance, determined

HABITS THAT HURT:

self-involved, negative

People with their Moon in Capricorn are often made uncomfortable by their feelings. They are serious and cautious and judge harshly anyone who makes a mistake or causes them to feel ashamed, especially themselves. They are practical and ambitious, willing to work hard to feel valuable and respected. They usually seem older than they are and are often given too many adult responsibilities while they are young. Many are not comfortable being children and long for adulthood.

Moon in Capricorn people desire to do great things and be recognized by those they respect. They are prudent, economical, and good administrators. They are quite reserved in showing or discussing their feelings and are made uncomfortable by those who do so. They are no-nonsense, all-business kinds of people and want to get the job done as quickly and efficiently as possible so they can move on to the next task.

Capricorn Moons take pride in being dependable. When they agree to take on a responsibility, they will do anything and everything to make sure it is done and done correctly, even if it means inconveniencing themselves to do so. Their reputation is indivisible from their self-identity. This admirable trait brings them many appreciative and devoted friends, as well as career advancement and economic rewards. However, if their reputation suffers, so do they.

Moon in Aquarius ♒

Element: Air

KEYWORDS

unemotional, clinical, scientific, futuristic, humanitarian, cold, eccentric, "good in a crisis," perspective, fatalistic, unafraid, extreme, humane, independent, "uncomfortable with emotions," erratic

USING MOON IN AQUARIUS KEYWORDS:

Feelings can cause them to be . . .

Emotions are stimulated by . . .

HABITS THAT HEAL:

good in a crisis, humanitarian

HABITS THAT HURT:

emotionally cold, erratic

People with their Moon in Aquarius view their emotions the way a scientist would, at arm's length and detached from themselves in order to facilitate examination. They need to feel free to be themselves and to experiment, and so they can see emotions as a hindrance to this essential aspect of their being. They control their emotions so well that many people mistakenly believe them to be emotionless or even robotic.

Moon in Aquarius people like to shake things up, and so they will reveal their emotional side at odd times and in odd ways so as to disrupt people and situations that dissatisfy them in some way. They obtain emotional security by being detached from the effects of having uncontrollable emotions, but sometimes this results in surprising outbursts. This makes them wonderful in a crisis, but afterward, they can get upset about the same event even though it is now past.

Aquarius Moons are friendly and helpful, though they will surprise new or casual acquaintances by not allowing untested people to get too close to them on an emotional level. They rarely give up on anything or anyone once they have decided to support them. They are tolerant and will help everyone dedicated to freeing people and institutions from outmoded ways of living, thinking, and doing.

Moon in Pisces ♓

Element: Water

KEYWORDS

receptive, sensitive, calm, reserved, depressed, fantasy, caring, escape, psychic, dreamy, "in another world," caring, spiritual, philanthropic, quiet, naive, overwhelmed, subservient, oversensitive

USING MOON IN TAURUS KEYWORDS:

Feelings can cause them to be . . .

Emotions are stimulated by . . .

HABITS THAT HEAL:

spiritual, philanthropic

HABITS THAT HURT:

escapist, oversensitive

People with their Moon in Pisces are usually kind, sensitive, and compassionate. If they can prevent themselves from being overly influenced by their emotions and the emotions of those around them and keep things in perspective, they can receive useful information through their strong intuitive sense. Their inclination to be helpful to the point of self-sacrifice or otherwise overextending themselves is something they wrestle with their whole lives.

Moon in Pisces people are usually attentive, composed, and peaceful. They need to limit their time around negative or upset people because they will absorb these emotions like sponges. Strife and discord can affect their health. They need quiet alone time every day to examine their feelings unencumbered. They are naturally inclined to see the connections and common humanity of all people.

Pisces Moons are dreamers and can see how everyone is a sensitive artist in some way. Their intimate relationship with their emotions gives them an ability to express their complexity more easily than other Moon signs and therefore create art in all its forms. Some channel this ability to express the creative into service work, medicine, or spirituality. When they are tuned in to their psychic imagination, they can be seen by others as odd, distracted, or worried.

THE BENEFIT OF KNOWING YOUR MOON SIGN

As you have just learned, knowing the meaning of your Moon sign can be a revelation. Interpreting a cosmic blueprint's Moon sign offers an explanation as to why the native's feelings and their emotional intelligence quotient (their ability to successfully experience, process, and derive benefit from their emotions) are the way they are.

Over the course of my career reading people's cosmic blueprints, I have had several clients whose initial sessions focused primarily on the implications of their Moon sign in their lives. Until then, they had thought of themselves in terms of their Sun sign and were perplexed by how different they were from their Sun sign. We did not need to go much further in the reading because this was the area where the client had the most issues and we were able to get to the bottom of them quickly.

I mention this because we all have questions and issues we would like to know more about. At this point, it is a good idea for you to formulate a list of questions you have about yourself and your interactions with others. For those of you considering a career as a counseling astrologer, I would strongly suggest that you ask every client to also formulate a list of questions they would want answered, if possible, as a result of your interaction with them in regard to their cosmic blueprint. To put their minds at ease, you can tell them you have done it for yourself.

Using my keyword technique with both the Sun and the Moon and using your ability to free-associate with the combinations formed by the keywords will give you a powerful boost in the answering of questions. Have fun with the sentence fragments you can form with the keywords, allowing your intuition to offer concepts and solutions that may be valuable to addressing those questions and issues.

Although it may seem like an oversimplification, please trust me when I say that there will be times, when reading for someone who does not know astrology, that you will not need to go any further into a chart than the revelations of the Sun and Moon signs to offer useful, practical guidance. Being an astrological counselor means addressing your client's questions and issues, not demonstrating to them or to yourself how much you know and how clever you are.

RECAP: *Let's take another look at your cosmic blueprint, the whole pizza, and recap a bit as we move forward with some new information to increase your understanding of astrology. If you are reading this book in a state of relaxed concentration, you are absorbing this new way of looking at the world in the best possible way.*

Your cosmic blueprint most certainly does look like a pizza, but the slice lines could also be seen to be spokes of a wheel, which is why some astrologers refer to them as chart wheels. The center of the wheel symbolizes the specific place you were born, your personal nativity scene, which is why we also call a birth chart a natal chart, and the person for whom the chart was drawn up is sometimes called the native. The chart is cast for the moment you were born and took your first breath, thereby ingesting what I like to think of as a hologram of the subtle energies emanating from the Sun, the Moon, and even the other planets of our solar system, whether they were in the sky above you or behind the Earth when you were born.

As previously mentioned, another term commonly used in place of "cosmic blueprint," "astrology chart," "birth chart," or "natal chart" is *horoscope*, derived from the Greek words *hora*, meaning "hour," and *skopos*, meaning "to watch"—to watch the hour.

An astrology chart is a map, a symbolic recreation of an ancient astrologer sitting outside at night as the Earth's turning causes the sky to seem to revolve, watching the hour and waiting for the baby to be born so they could erect the child's natal horoscope. Astrologers not only were astronomers, but they also had to be skilled mathematicians to calculate a child's birth chart with any accuracy.

NOTE: *Western astrology evolved in the northern hemisphere, and so an astrologer watching the Sun, Moon, and planets rising and setting as the Earth turned would be facing south, which would put the direction east on her or his left. This is important to keep in mind because we are so used to seeing the direction east on the right side of every other kind of map.*

Now that you know the astrological meaning of the Sun, the Moon, the signs of the zodiac, the Four Elements, and the origin of the chart design, the art of learning how to read your cosmic blueprint can begin in earnest.

CAPRICORN
SAGITTARIUS
SCORPIO
LIBRA
VIRGO
LEO
CANCER
GEMINI
TAURUS
ARIES
PISCES
AQUARIUS

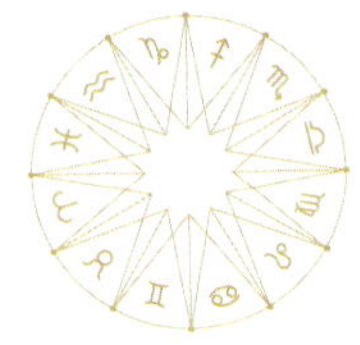

THE TWELVE HOUSES OF AN ASTROLOGY CHART

Everybody needs a place to live. The planets, the toppings on our astrological pizza, are no exception. It's interesting to note that wilderness-survival experts teach that finding shelter is priority number one, ahead of finding food and water.

When you look at your astrology chart, the planets, and the signs that they are in are symbolized by their respective glyphs. Each planet has its own glyph, and so does each of the twelve signs of the zodiac.

You now know the glyphs for the Sun—the circle with a dot in its center—and the crescent-moon glyph. You may also see in your cosmic blueprint the symbol for man, the circle with the arrow pointing from it, also the symbol for Mars, and the symbol for woman, the cross with a circle on top, also the symbol for Venus. You saw the glyphs for the twelve signs when I delineated the meanings of the Sun and Moon through the signs. We will learn the rest of the planetary symbol glyphs later.

The numbers 0 to 29 you see placed after each planet's glyph represent the degree of the sign of the zodiac in which that planet was at the time of birth or first breath. Each sign of the zodiac has 30 degrees, and 30 x 12 = 360. The number after the glyph representing that sign represents the minutes of that degree. There are 30 degrees in each sign and 60 minutes in each degree.

The twelve slices of a chart are known as the twelve houses of an astrology chart. They are called houses because these slices are where the planets live in your astrology chart, where they are active, where they do their thing and have their basic meaning flavored by both the zodiac sign (the cheese!) and the specific meanings associated with the particular house in which they are living, working, and acting.

In our cosmic pizza, each slice has a different flavor. Each of the twelve slices represents a slice of life. Knowing which house of your horoscope a particular planet is residing in and operating from is as important as knowing in which cheese slice/zodiac sign that planet is passing through and tells you a lot about how that planet's energies are going to manifest in your life.

The best thing I can do for you at this point in your astrological educational process is to tell you the meanings of the twelve houses. In my method of thinking and teaching, I have a unique way of explaining the meaning of the houses, but be prepared, because I do not go in numerical house order (i.e., First House, Second House, Third House, etc.).

Doing it my way will give you the most logically sound explanation for the distinct meanings of each of the twelve houses, allowing you to fully understand them and take their meanings to heart without the necessity of memorization. It will give you the best opportunity of having a deeper understanding of the planets and signs too.

I could just list the meanings of the Sun, the Moon, and the planets in each of the twelve houses of an astrology chart, but that would be giving you the fish instead of teaching you how to fish. My goal in this book is to empower you as a fellow astrologer and enable you to read your cosmic blueprint and those of people you care about, not to just be someone who knows a bit about astrology and how to look up meanings but doesn't know how to synthesize the various planets in a particular sign and house.

I will teach you how to put it all together and get useful, practical information out of any chart—information that will often surprise you even when it is about you yourself—because astrology enables us to step out of our habitual ways of thinking and see things from a new, different, and enlightening perspective. A large part of your astrological education is learning and understanding the meaning of the twelve houses of your cosmic blueprint.

THE CROSS OF MATTER

To know the meaning of the twelve houses of your cosmic blueprint, we must start with the basic cross that is the foundation for all the twelve house meanings. In every cosmic blueprint, this cross is the fundamental structure in the chart's circle, which you may recall is the ancient symbol for the soul, but here the circle represents the zodiac. (You'll recall that that word is derived from a Greek phrase denoting a circle of animals.)

This fusing of the two symbols, the cross in the circle, is the foundation of the astrological twelve-house system. On first glance, it looks like what you see if you look through a rifle's sight. A better and more fitting analogy is that this symbol looks like what you would see if you were in a submarine and looked at the surface of the sea through its periscope.

In that analogy, the horizonal line is the surface of the sea. Below this horizontal line is the sea, and above the horizontal line is the sky.

This analogy is also apt because, just as a submarine's periscope enables it to zero in on another ship, a cosmic blueprint allows us to zero in on a person's personality, character, strengths, weaknesses, and a lot more.

NOTE: *Where the horizontal and vertical lines intersect on an astrology chart symbolizes the precise place where the native is being born, right there in the middle of the chart, as if the whole world and the heavens above are turning around that spot. It is easy to understand how this seems to be true from your newborn point of view and that of your parent(s) at the time of your birth.*

Visualizing in your mind's eye how the planets lined up around you in the sky above you and below the surface of the Earth when you were born is an important part of learning to read your chart. It will help you understand what is going on when we get to the part of this book where we explore which houses of your chart the planets are living in. It is the house positions and the angles between the planets that, when added to the meaning of each planet in its sign of the zodiac, personalizes each planet's specific meanings to your cosmic blueprint.

"The angles between the planets?" I hear you exclaim. Be patient. In this book, we are not going to consider the angles between planets until I have given you a thorough grounding in the meanings of the planets, signs, and houses. I find that introducing the angles before achieving a solid grounding and understanding of the fundamentals of astrology can easily confuse and delay the proficiency of even the most dedicated student. I mention the angles only because many of you reading this book know a little about them, and I want you to know that we are going to cover them—just not yet.

As noted on page 27, the first thing we can see in a chart is whether the toppings are spread out around the pizza or concentrated in one or more halves or on a particular slice of the chart. At this point in your astrological education, you can understand that if the toppings are mainly on the left (eastern) side of your chart's vertical line, that means those planets were rising from behind the Earth, going over the horizontal horizon line and into the sky when you were born. If they are on the right (western) side of your chart's vertical line, they were setting or below the horizontal horizon line when you were born. If they're above the horizon line in your chart, that means they were in the sky when you were born, whether you could see them or not. All the planets below the horizon line were behind the Earth at the time of your birth and not visible from your birthplace location.

NOTE: *Look at the point that is furthest east, on the left of the horizontal line symbolizing the horizon. This would be the place where the Sun rises if you were born at sunrise. The sign of the zodiac precisely on the horizon at the moment you are born is what's known as your Rising Sign.*

THE RISING SIGN

A person's Rising Sign describes how they appear to other people *whether they want to appear to them that way or not.* Knowing your Rising Sign is as important as knowing your Sun and Moon signs, which I hope you remember are the signs the Sun and Moon were in (passing through) when you were born. Amy and I call your combination of Sun, Moon, and Rising Sign your Celestial Trilogy. Knowing how to interpret a chart's Celestial Trilogy is an important part of being an astrologer. By itself, it can provide a treasure trove of useful information. It is an essential step forward in learning how to read your cosmic blueprint.

RECAP: *Your Rising Sign is the sign of the zodiac that was on the eastern horizon, at the extreme left of the horizontal line dividing your chart into above and below the Earth, at the moment you breathed in the hologram of the subtle planetary energies. Your Rising Sign can give you a lot of otherwise impossible-to-know information about how you or the person whose cosmic blueprint you are reading appear to other people.*

If you have ever wondered why some people just do not seem to get you or if this is an issue for the person whose chart you are reading, knowing the chart's Rising Sign can help with understanding the problem better so it can be successfully dealt with.

If you have a copy of an astrology chart in front of you right now, you can easily identify the Rising Sign. It should be spelled out for you right there on the chart. It may be listed as Ascendant, or *ASC* for short, because the Rising Sign is the degree of the zodiac that is ascending into the sky on the eastern horizon when you were born.

If a person does not know their Rising Sign, it is very possible they do not know how other people are seeing them. This can explain a lot of the misunderstandings in our lives, including problems interacting with family members, friends, coworkers, bosses, authority figures, and everyone else.

PRO TIP: *As an astrologer, you have the ability to help people help themselves to better understand themselves and others. The importance of this ability cannot be overstated. However, you should never offer astrological advice to someone who has not requested it. You may be tempted, but do not do it, even for the most altruistic of reasons.*

If this seems unreasonable or overcautious to you, please remember that if you do choose to answer their questions, you will be saying things to them that they might remember for the rest of their lives, long after you have forgotten you said anything at all. You may seriously regret saying anything and have that regret sooner than you might think.

I am speaking to you from decades of experience—mine, and that of many professional astrologers. A lot of people cannot handle the truth, especially if you touch on an aspect of their personality that is a sore spot with them or a person close to them.

This is why I prefer to do readings over Zoom, and suggest you also confine your readings for others to remote videoconferencing. It is not necessary to be in the same place as a person you are reading for. Using Zoom also enables you to record the session's audio and video, and even obtain a transcript of the session enabled by artificial intelligence.

It is gratifying to Amy and me that because of the success of our previous books, more people than ever know a bit about us and the basics of astrology too. A person may know their Sun sign and perhaps even their Moon sign.

However, in my experience with people who do not know their Rising Sign, it's as if they get dressed in the dark every day and never look in a mirror. Another way to look at it is that they're wearing clothing that is not in fashion or age appropriate. They may know who they are and what they are trying to do, but they do not know how they appear to other people while they are trying to do it, and that is an important part of the personal interaction equation.

Knowing how you appear to other people adds a valuable dimension to your interactions. In some cases, an astrologer can spend a whole session focusing on a person's Celestial Trilogy—their Sun, Moon, and Rising Signs—and supply them with useful information that may provide answers to the questions or concerns that brought them to the reading.

PRO TIP: *I cannot overstress the fact that our job as astrologers is to help people help themselves, to respond to the questions that brought them to you, not to prove astrology works or dazzle them with your knowledge of it. This is why I strongly suggest you not read for anyone else until you feel completely comfortable with and knowledgeable about astrology. Your intuition will be strengthened by the time you have read this book cover to cover and will be able to help you judge whether family members, friends, and even potential clients are ready to have their cosmic blueprints read.*

The Earth turns, and all 360 degrees of the zodiac's twelve signs are on the horizon for four minutes every day. So here at the left (eastern) side of the horizontal line of your cosmic blueprint dividing Earth from sky is where the zodiacal sign that is your Rising Sign is found.

RECAP: *The Rising Sign is also called your Ascendant, abbreviated ASC, because it is the sign of the zodiac that is ascending, rising in the east, at your birth.*

It also bears repeating that a person's Rising Sign is how they appear to other people *whether they want to appear to them that way or not.* This is yet another reason to be kind to people—they may not how they are presenting themselves to you and to other people.

Always remember, when it comes to people you do not know well, that you're seeing their Rising Sign, their personality. (That term is derived from *persona*, the Latin word for "mask.") Adding this dimension to your experience of everyone in your daily life is eye-opening.

This might also be true for you and how you present yourself to others. In an ideal world, other people would give you the benefit of the doubt if they did not understand the reasons you are acting a certain way and you would do the same for them. If we astrologers remember to do this, we are being the change we want to see—the only way real change can occur.

There are twelve signs of the zodiac, so if you are born at sunrise, the Sun is right there on the horizon. We astrologers describe that as the Sun being conjunct your Rising Sign. If you were born at sunrise, when the Sun was conjunct the horizon and, consequently, conjunct your Rising Sign, then you are said to be a double Aries, Taurus, Gemini, or whatever sign your Sun is in, and what we see is what we get.

These double-sign individuals present themselves to the world as unique but identifiable ambassadors of one or more traits associated with that sign of the zodiac. Most people are not born at sunrise, however, so the odds are that your Sun sign and your Rising Sign are different.

Our Rising Sign/Ascendant is one of the most important things we will ever know about ourselves and is a concept exclusive to astrology. It is how our spirit has chosen to project ourselves into physical reality—that is why it is how others see us!

NOTE: *Your Rising Sign is more important than your Sun sign in early life because you can't speak. How you are perceived by your caregivers determines how they care for you. It is of crucial importance for parents and caregivers to know the Rising Sign of their preverbal or nonverbal children. From birth and even once the child can communicate clearly (and remember that there are many children who never can do so), the parents and caregivers can apply their knowledge of the child's Rising Sign and can therefore know how a child approaches, understands, and filters what they say/need/do.*

For example, you may be the shyest Cancer in the world, but if you have the zodiac sign Aries Rising, the world is going to perceive you as fiery, bossy, aggressive, or even combative, a very direct person at the very least. You may be the sexiest Scorpio alive in how you approach life, but if you have Virgo Rising, you're going to be perceived as being noncommittal about your attitude toward sex, or maybe worried about it or overly detail oriented about it.

You cannot be sure that all of what you are sending out as "This is who I am and this is what I want to say to you" is being perceived correctly unless you know your Rising Sign/Ascendant! When you do know your Rising Sign, you are empowered. When you are aware that no matter what you do, you are seen through the lens of your Rising Sign, you can learn to make that work for you and not against you.

Using my own cosmic blueprint as an example in true Leo Rising fashion, I have the Sun in Aquarius, a sign that typically can easily detach from emotions in order to dispassionately examine a problem and become aware of ways of innovating solutions. My Rising Sign, however, is Leo, the zodiac sign directly opposite Aquarius on the zodiac wheel.

Leo is the sign of showy display, showing others how life is lived, which is how it connects to the arts—especially the dramatic arts—and leadership. I know that my Leo Rising gives others the impression that I am dramatically committed to a particular aspect of what I am saying to them. I have to avoid seeming to make a big show of my commitment to a particular aspect or theory, while, in my mind, I am dispassionately examining an issue as thoroughly as I can, knowing that truth needs to prove itself in the real world, not just in my mind.

To those who do not know me and only see my Leo Rising, I can seem to care more about the situation than I actually do. Knowing my Rising Sign and its traits, I try to make sure that others know when I am turning something over in my mind and when I have concluded my deliberations and have arrived at a confidence level I can stand behind. It sounds like a small thing, and it is only one aspect of my Sun/Rising Sign combination, but it has made life better for me and those I interact with. I am not a fan of drama in personal interactions.

Now would be a good time to take another look at your chart and remind yourself what your Rising Sign is and what you know, as well as how you feel, about that sign of the zodiac. Be as honest with yourself as you can be.

When in doubt about the meanings of a particular Rising Sign, just add, "Looks like a _____," "Gives the appearance of being a _____," or "Seems to display the strengths and weaknesses of a ______" and fill in the blank with one or more keywords from the person's Rising Sign. At this point, you should have a pretty good idea of the meaning of the twelve signs of the zodiac and also how they are divided up into the Four Elements of astrology.

RECAP:

Fiery signs: Aries, Leo, Sagittarius
Earthy signs: Taurus, Virgo, Capricorn
Airy signs: Gemini, Libra, Aquarius
Watery signs: Cancer, Scorpio, Pisces

But wait—there's more, as the infomercials say. To properly understand the twelve signs of the zodiac, you need to add to your knowledge an understanding of the Three Qualities. Knowing about the Three Qualities will help you better understand the twelve Rising Signs.

THE THREE QUALITIES

The Three Qualities are known as Cardinal, Fixed, and Mutable. They are derived from each particular sign's position in the change of seasons.

The Cardinal Signs

The Cardinal signs are the signs of the zodiac that correspond to the four angles of the basic cross that we saw in our discussion of the Rising Sign. The word *cardinal* means "fundamental" or "of primary importance." While no sign is more important than any other sign, each of the four Cardinal signs—Aries, Cancer, Libra, and Capricorn—heralds the change of season: The first day of Aries is the first day of spring. The first day of Cancer is the first day of summer, Libra begins on the first day of fall, and Capricorn starts when winter begins.

As we do in so many other teachings about astrology, when it comes to the Three Qualities, the first one being the Cardinal signs, we start with Aries, the first sign of the zodiac. The 1st degree of the 30 degrees of the astrological sign Aries starts at the precise moment when spring in the northern hemisphere starts. That day is the astrological New Year's Day for we astrologers. The 1st degree of Aries, especially, as well as of the other three Cardinal signs, is considered quite powerful and important energetically and is sometimes referred to as a world point.

Cardinal Fire sign Aries is like the first flowers of spring poking their heads up through the snow, unstoppable in their passion to renew life despite winter's barren landscape. Cardinal Water sign Cancer is always going forward, nurturing and protecting either themselves or those they care about and doing so with an emphasis on the emotional level. Cardinal Air sign Libra is always striving to initiate, understand, and balance various ideas on an intellectual level. And Cardinal Earth sign Capricorn works hard to be respected on a practical, worldly level.

Each of the four Cardinal signs is inclined to always be initiating or otherwise going forward in a unique way that corresponds to one or more of the meanings of that particular sign with its unique element (Aries/Fire, Cancer/Water, Libra/Air, or Capricorn/Earth). The four Cardinal signs are always trying to move things along, usually with great vitality. They are goal oriented, active, enthusiastic, motivated, and ambitious. They initiate change and get things started the way they start the four seasons.

The Fixed Signs

Once the Cardinal signs have begun each season and started things moving toward a goal, the next stage is to take action to solidify or fix in place the gains that have been made coming out of the previous season. This is the basic meaning of the four astrological signs that we call Fixed signs: Taurus, Leo, Scorpio, and Aquarius.

All four Fixed signs are stubborn, stable in their unique way, and resolute. They want to fix—to anchor or make real and as lasting as possible—the gains achieved by the actions initiated by the goal-oriented Cardinal signs, who often move on once they have gotten things started. The Fixed signs understand the material world as a game to be played and enjoyed—especially the winnings.

Taurus is the Fixed Earth sign, so it wants to enjoy the best tangible, touchable, sensuous, valuable experiences possible. Taurus wants to be comfortable and as undisturbed as possible when savoring its enjoyment. Most of all, Taurus wants the good things in life to be theirs and for as long as possible.

Leo is the Fixed Fire sign, so its fiery passion burns with a more self-aware and sometimes selfish flame satisfying its desires than Cardinal Fire Aries, which is so goal oriented as to not give much attention to actually enjoying what its pioneering actions have produced and to not care how others see, feel, or think about their Arian actions. Fixed Fire Leo, the sign whose definition of stage fright is the fear of not being seen on the world stage, cares a great deal about what others think.

Scorpio is the Fixed Water sign, so its emotional intensity and connection to its fiercely private inner life are much more constant and focused on maintaining the power it derives from understanding and mastering its emotions and manipulating those of other people, especially that of anyone on whom Scorpio fixes its attention, much more so than that of the other two Water signs, Cardinal sign Cancer and Pisces.

Aquarius is the Fixed Air sign, an apparent contradiction in terms when one thinks of the winds and their constant shifting of direction and intensity. Yet this incessant, restless, and often sudden gusting of ideas exactly reflects Aquarius's dedication to letting ideas—especially those of an inventive, problem-solving nature—take them where they take them, irrespective of how disruptive they may be to established norms or conventional wisdom and customs, or regardless of the emotional impact the implementation of their futuristic thinking might have on anyone and everyone, even themselves.

The Mutable Signs

Between the stubborn Fixed signs (Taurus, Leo, Scorpio, and Aquarius) and the goal-oriented Cardinal signs (Aries, Cancer, Libra, and Capricorn) are the Mutable signs, flexible enough to act as a bridge between the two: Gemini, Virgo, Sagittarius, and Pisces.

Mutable sign Gemini comes after Fixed sign Taurus and before Cardinal sign Cancer. Mutable sign Virgo comes between Fixed sign Leo and Cardinal sign Libra. Mutable sign Sagittarius comes between Fixed sign Scorpio and Cardinal sign Capricorn. Mutable sign Pisces comes between Fixed sign Aquarius and Cardinal sign Aries.

Gemini is the Mutable Air sign, so you can always depend on someone with the Sun, Moon, Rising Sign, or prominently placed planets in Gemini to be able to use their ability to rapidly see both sides of an idea or a situation. Their prodigious mental energy requires them to feed it interesting life puzzles to solve, and they will do a lot to avoid feeling bored.

Virgo is the Mutable Earth sign, so they understand better than anyone that even their practical, skill-driven abilities are no guarantee that things will go according to plan. Their ability to see, understand, and analyze the component parts of anything they are involved with can devolve into self-defeating worry when they are either attached to or in fear of a particular outcome.

Sagittarius is the Mutable Fire sign, so their passionate pursuit of truth is flexible enough to allow for the investigation and acceptance of truths different from their own, acknowledging the uniqueness and validity of differences of culture, philosophy, geography, and everything else that makes the world's peoples seem so differentiated despite our common human traits.

Pisces is the Mutable Water sign, so theirs is the most diffuse and waterlike sign emotionally of the three Water signs, with Cancer and Scorpio being the other two. The sign's symbol, the Fishes, with one fish swimming one way and the other swimming the opposite way, perfectly captures the sign's definition of empathetic connection, often to the point of losing the sense of self and individual identity. This is why Pisces-influenced people need to be the most careful with anything that negates the self, addictions of all kinds, and especially dependence on alcohol and drugs (even prescribed medications).

I realize that I have just given you a lot of information, but there is no need to commit the Three Qualities (Cardinal, Fixed, and Mutable) to memory. I will include them with the twelve Rising Signs in the hope that you will see the logic in each sign having associated with it one of the Four Elements (Fire, Earth, Air, or Water) and one of the Three Qualities (Cardinal, Fixed, or Mutable).

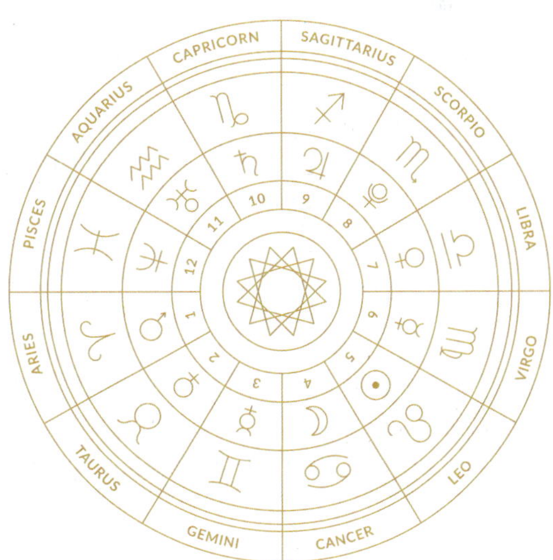

THE TWELVE RISING SIGNS

Aries Rising ♈

ELEMENT: *Fire (impetuous)*
QUALITY: *Cardinal (goal oriented)*

It's easy for others to think Aries Risings are self-confident and/or arguing with them. If they feel weak, no one knows. They need to dial down their fiery passion when they want to appear nice.

FAVORABLE PERSONALITY TRAITS: Energy, enthusiasm, skill at promoting ideas. An inherent force and willingness that can help reach the top. Ambitious, proud, high-spirited, independent, and chivalrous.

ADVERSE PERSONALITY TRAITS: Domineering, conceited, impractical. Not good at sustained effort. Loses interest quickly, branching off into something else. Can engage in conflict with imaginary enemies or pursue futile goals.

People will usually see an Aries Rising as honest, independent, and a go-getter who knows the best way to start a project, though once things get going, they may feel that the Aries Rising appears eager to move on to other projects before the initial goal is accomplished.

It is important for Aries Rising natives to remember that people are inclined to interpret their words and their actions as forceful, passionate, and focused mostly on their need to be the boss in the situation at hand, even when this is not the case, and they are not trying to give this impression. Those who have a negative view of people who present themselves and their ideas strongly may be put off by Aries Risings' manner.

Also, those who have problems seeing themselves as confident and powerful may project and react to an Aries Rising the way they dialogue with their inner self, getting overwrought and even outright angry with them for no apparent reason.

If an Aries Rising senses this reaction in someone they care about—be it someone they love or someone who is important to their plans—the Aries Rising must dial down their natural tendency to bravely say what is on their mind and the energetic way they want to say it. Aries Risings need to know that it is not cowardice to modulate their tone and choose their words with care. As Shakespeare said, "Discretion is the better part of valor."

It is fine for them to appear brave, strong, and aggressive when the situation warrants it. They need to keep in mind, however, that not everyone is able to feel comfortable with someone who is apparently so sure of themselves and their beliefs that they appear to have little or no regard for the beliefs of others.

More than almost any other Rising Sign, Aries Risings need to use their innate ability to be old-school "pioneers" and their considerable behind-enemy-lines skills to move into the uncharted world of individual interpersonal interactions with the same care an explorer would use in an unknown land. Even when they and those they interact with speak the same language, they must learn the nuances of that language and the customs of those they encounter if a successful and enjoyable journey is what they desire.

Taurus Rising ♉

ELEMENT: *Earth (determined)*
QUALITY: *Fixed (stubborn)*

It's easy for others to see a Taurus Rising person as slow and deliberate but dependable, desirous of the finer things in life. They can use their expressionless poker face when they are not sure what to do or say.

FAVORABLE PERSONALITY TRAITS: Faithful, practical, responsible, steadfast. Fond of home, adores children, usually agreeable and genial. Likes family life, good community standing, meticulous about paying bills.

ADVERSE PERSONALITY TRAITS: Stubborn, obstinate, likely to keep on to the bitter end, even if on the wrong track. Undemonstrative and takes affection lavished on them for granted. Sometimes coarse or neglectful of courtesy. Bad-tempered when aroused, sees red like a bull.

People will usually see a Taurus Rising as patient and kind. Their appreciation of and knowledge about the good things in life and what is truly valuable to themselves and to others will be admired.

It is important for Taurus Risings to remember, however, that when they are trying to work their will on the world, people will be inclined to interpret their words and their actions as being based on their desire to avoid change, discomfort, and personal loss. That loss can be of prestige, finances, or anything the Taurus Rising considers to be valuable. As is the nature of the Rising Sign concept in general, they are likely to be perceived in this way even when this is not the case and they are not trying to give this impression.

Taurus Rising people should be aware that some people like to think way outside of the sturdy, beautiful, self-protective bullpen, or box, that Taurus Risings strive to create and maintain. People who themselves have a negative view of those who are resistant to change or who push back on alterations to an existing plan may be put off by a Taurus Rising's bull-headed ways. Even in the rare occurrences when a Taurus Rising is championing a potentially disruptive or revolutionary concept, it will take skill on their part to present it in a way that does not seem to be done for selfish motives.

Also, those who have problems seeing themselves as dependable, persevering, and able to cope with difficult circumstances may project and react to a Taurus Rising the way they dialogue with their inner self, stubbornly refusing to cooperate and even acting like a bull who sees a red cape.

If a Taurus Rising senses this reaction in someone they care about—be it someone they love or someone who is important to their plans—they must dial down their natural tendency to start seething and dig in their heels at the first perceived sign of someone trying to get them to do something that they do not want to do, especially when it involves giving up on something or someone. Taurus Risings need to take comfort in the fact that they will not be seen as weak or easily discouraged even if they judge themselves to be so.

More than almost any other Rising Sign, Taurus Rising needs to use their innate ability to confront and overcome obstacles to inspire others or, if the opposite outcome is desired, to show an adversary that they are going to persevere, and further resistance is futile.

Gemini Rising ♊

ELEMENT: *Air (quick thinking)*
QUALITY: *Mutable (adaptable)*

It's easy for others to see a Gemini Rising as smart, versatile, and changeable. Those who have strong opinions see them as uncertain and vacillating. They need to speak more clearly and slowly than they think they should.

FAVORABLE PERSONALITY TRAITS: Brilliant, versatile, flexible, charming, stimulating, scintillating, and fascinating. Good at multitasking, repartee, entertaining, and amusing. A flair for writing fiction and telling stories.

ADVERSE PERSONALITY TRAITS: Irritable and quarrelsome. Expresses a point of view only to change it the next minute. Can be untruthful if feeling pinned down to one opinion. Often suffers from nervousness.

Gemini Risings are usually seen as smart, shrewd, and fast learners. Their appreciation for and knowledge about the latest developments in virtually all aspects of modern life will always be appreciated.

It is important for Gemini Risings to remember that when they are trying to work their will on the world, people will be inclined to interpret their words and their actions as if they are inconsistent in their beliefs about the subject at hand. Gemini Risings can be perceived on a spectrum from appearing merely unconvinced all the way up to seeming to have a split personality disorder, as if there were two or more people inside them and other people cannot be sure which one they are going to get.

Gemini Risings need to remember that some people are firmly anchored to their unquestionable beliefs and many people simply need to arrive at a definitive conclusion before they can feel secure. Those who have a negative view of people who are prone to thinking out loud or otherwise giving the impression that they seek to see all sides of an issue may be put off by the Gemini Rising way of interacting with the world. Even if the Gemini Rising native is simply seeking to learn as much as they can prior to deciding, interpersonal problems can arise because Gemini Risings rarely appear to have arrived at a definitive view, a final decision, or even a reason to cease deliberating.

Also, those who have problems seeing themselves as open-minded, undecided, or able to see all sides of an argument by listening to another's point of view may project and react to a Gemini Rising the way they dialogue with their inner self, getting nervous and tongue-tied, sputtering words of resistance for no apparent reason.

If a Gemini Rising senses this reaction in someone they care about, they must dial down their natural tendency to get nervous and start saying and doing things to forcefully counter attempts to pin them down. A Gemini Rising will not be seen to be slow to catch on, a poor communicator, or boring even if they judge themselves to be so.

More than almost any other Rising Sign, a Gemini Rising needs to use their innate ability to keep ideas and communication flowing, despite all obstacles, to either inspire others or, if the opposite outcome is desired, to use their quick mind and command of language to show that their ideas are the best way to go forward at this time, even if that means deciding not to decide just yet.

Cancer Rising ♋

ELEMENT: *Water (caring)*
QUALITY: *Cardinal (nurturing)*

It's easy for others to see a Cancer Rising as sensitive, shy, caring, and s/mothering (the *s* being added or not depending on how strongly they insist on being obeyed).

FAVORABLE PERSONALITY TRAITS: Domestic, sympathetic, understanding, peaceful, soothing, nurturing, and cheery. With strong protective instincts, a good partner and parent. Respect for tradition. Self-sacrificing.

ADVERSE PERSONALITY TRAITS: Too yielding, sensitive, impressionable. Suffers from hurts and slights, real and imagined. Has a fear of being made to look ridiculous.

Cancer Risings will usually be seen as caring and interested, someone people can rely on. Their ability to help a person, project, or business grow through thoughtful and down-to-Earth means will be appreciated.

It is important for Cancer Rising natives to remember that when they are trying to work their will on the world, people will be inclined to interpret their words and their actions as if they are shy about expressing their true beliefs even when they have a real emotional connection to the subject at hand. Cancer Risings can be perceived as anywhere from hiding and not appearing at all, like the Crab that is their symbol, doing what they can to avoid interacting with harsh or overbearing people and situations, all the way up to being a mother bear for some person or cause.

Cancer Risings need to remember that some people mistake kindness for weakness and will do anything they can to avoid showing how they feel, the way Cancer Risings do. People who have a negative view of those who are considerate of others—usually because they themselves are not considerate and feel judged—may be put off by the Cancer Rising way of interacting with the world, and others may ignore or be inconsiderate of these natives for the same reason. Even if a Cancer Rising is seeking to be a neutral party or to gently nudge people in a particular direction for their own good, problems can arise because Cancer Risings give others the feeling that they can be themselves, including those who act out because they are emotionally damaged or sick.

People who have problems seeing themselves as shy, passive, or considering their own or others' feelings may project and react to a Cancer Rising the way they dialogue with their inner self, getting overly sensitive and emotional with the Cancer Rising for no apparent reason.

If a Cancer Rising senses this reaction in someone they care about—be it someone they love or someone important to their plans—they must dial down their natural tendency to withdraw completely from the situation. Cancer Risings need to remind themselves that they deserve and have a right to live their life as they see fit and to have their needs met and themselves respected because that is how they treat others. A Cancer Rising will not be seen as brash, egotistical, or uncaring even if they judge themselves to be so.

More than almost any other Rising Sign, Cancer Risings need to use their innate ability to help themselves and others feel safe enough to be their authentic self and grow into the person they say they want to become despite all obstacles.

Leo Rising ♌

ELEMENT: *Fire (demonstrative)*
QUALITY: *Fixed (self-confident)*

It's easy for others to see a Leo Rising as a leader, dramatic and ego-driven with no shyness at all. They usually seem to be doing great and so no one ever feels sorry for them. They must guard against being too familiar.

FAVORABLE PERSONALITY TRAITS: Loyal, generous, magnanimous, industrious. Executive ability and personal magnetism. Born to rule. Sense of noblesse oblige, fond of children, fun, and entertaining.

ADVERSE PERSONALITY TRAITS: Bossy. Adores adulation, susceptible to flattery. Must have the center of the stage. Exhibitionist complex. Boastful.

Leo Risings will usually be seen as having a magnetic personality, interesting, and fun to be around. Their ability to offer advice about how to creatively solve a problem will be appreciated.

It is important for Leo Risings to remember that when they are trying to work their will on the world, people will be inclined to interpret their words and actions as if they expect others to know them well and praise them and acknowledge them as their leader; merely saying "Good idea" will not appear to be enough. Leo Risings can be perceived on a spectrum from generously helping others but appearing to make it plain that they want them to show their appreciation to being quite demonstrative about how they want things to be done to giving the impression that they are a megalomaniacal, my-way-or-the-highway aspiring dictator.

Leo Risings need to remember that some people mistake self-confidence for self-importance and an overly inflated ego. Those who have a negative view of people who are proud of themselves, their achievements, and the way they are living life—usually because they are doubtful about their own abilities and whether they are living life to the fullest—may be put off by the Leo Rising way of interacting with the world. Others may push back or be inconsiderate of a Leo Rising for the same reason. Even if they are seeking to help someone succeed, come into their full power, or avoid making mistakes, problems can arise because Leo Rising people give others the impression that they are acting out of their own personal needs, especially their need for aggrandizement.

Also, those who have problems seeing themselves as the center of attention, judged by their achievements and attributes, or being the person everyone wants to know and spend time with, may project and react to a Leo Rising the way they dialogue with their inner self, getting overly dramatic and acting out for no apparent reason.

If a Leo Rising senses this reaction in someone they care about—be it someone they love or someone who is important to their plans—they must dial down their natural tendency to act as if everything is a big deal and very important to them. Leo Risings have a right to live their life as they see fit, to be respected and have their needs met, but they have to be careful to not appear phony. A Leo Rising will not be seen as shy, unsure of themselves, or unimportant even if they judge themselves to be so.

More than almost any other Rising Sign, Leo Risings need to use their innate ability to organize, motivate, and act in service to others. As *The Book of Tao* says, "One who would lead must follow all." Or, if a Leo Rising sees that others will not listen to reason, their acting ability can come into play. No one is more capable of acting as if something were true than a Leo Rising.

Virgo Rising ♍

ELEMENT: *Earth (skilled)*
QUALITY: *Mutable (analytical)*

It's easy for others to see Virgo Rising as skilled, fidgety, or worried, no matter how they are feeling. Some may see them as innocent, unjaded, and childlike in a good way.

FAVORABLE PERSONALITY TRAITS: Analytical, excellent conversationalist. Systematic, orderly, and conscientious. Usually on the side of peace and stability. Industrious and practical.

ADVERSE PERSONALITY TRAITS: Critical and complaining. Elitist. Nagging. Too thrifty, becoming cheap. Unwilling to admit making mistakes.

Virgo Risings will usually be seen as logical, discerning, and expert analysts. Their appreciation for the little things in life and their interest in and knowledge about the details and mechanics of everything will be appreciated.

It is important for Virgo Risings to remember that when they are trying to accomplish a task, people will be inclined to view them as overly concerned with what others may consider petty or superfluous details, not able to see or be interested in the big picture. Virgo Risings can be perceived on a spectrum from appearing merely bored or going through the motions to make the best of a bad situation to appearing to be overthinking the matter at hand to being so worried and fearful about the outcome of something and their ability to influence it as to drive themselves to distraction, thereby undermining their own efforts more than anything or anyone could ever do.

Virgo Risings need to also remember that some people are not detail oriented and prefer to think in broad terms and see things from a bird's-eye view. Those who have a negative view of people who are prone to be critical thinkers or otherwise give the impression that they are focused on looking for flaws in a system, a product, or a partner may be put off by the Virgo Rising way of interacting with the world. Even if a Virgo Rising is seeking to help by analyzing something so that they can improve it, problems can arise because they rarely appear to have arrived at the end of their attempt to diagnose a situation or even appear to want to reach a definitive conclusion.

Also, those who have problems seeing themselves as overly fussy or fault-finding or doubt their ability to correctly analyze a problem and create (and stick to!) a plan that details a logical and practical method for dealing with it may project and react to a Virgo Rising the

way they dialogue with their inner self, overly critical and sarcastic for no apparent reason.

If a Virgo Rising senses this reaction in someone they care about, they must dial down their natural tendency to be anxious and fretful about their ability to do things the "right way" and calmly remember that their best is all that they or anyone can ever do. A Virgo Rising will not be seen as unskilled, full of themselves, or ignorant even if they judge themselves to be so.

More than almost any other Rising Sign, Virgo Rising needs to use their innate ability to prove the expression "God/dess is in the details" and confine themselves to working at what they are best at, staying in their comfort zone, and showing the rest of us what happens when skill, determination, and hard work are combined. No other Rising Sign can be as helpful to those who have bitten off more than they can chew and need guidance on how to salvage a difficult situation.

Libra Rising ♎

ELEMENT: *Air (measured)*
QUALITY: *Cardinal (thoughtful)*

It's easy for others to see Libra Rising as refined, unflappable, and seeking harmony. They can get away with being a bit nasty sometimes because others will not see that is what they are doing.

FAVORABLE PERSONALITY TRAITS: Sociable, good-natured, talented, and artistic. Always ready to grant a favor. Excels as fashion or beauty experts. Somewhat easygoing—dislikes discord—but can take a firm stand.

ADVERSE PERSONALITY TRAITS: Tendency to become a yes person. Can appear to lack backbone. Evasive and occasionally too subtle. May seem naive or indifferent because of not wanting to seem to feel emotions too strongly.

Libra Risings will usually be seen as attractive, refined, and skilled intermediaries or negotiators. Their appreciation for the beauty in life and their obvious interest in bringing peace, love, and balance to the world will be highly regarded.

It is important for Libra Risings to remember that when they are trying to accomplish a task, people will be inclined to view them as overly concerned with seeking a consensus or compromise. Libra Risings can be perceived on a spectrum from deciding not to decide to agreeing with things they do not really agree with to avoid disharmony or harshness to appearing to be completely undecided regarding the matter at hand to being willing to do whatever it takes to achieve their goal, including acting aggressively. Aggression is not something usually associated with Libra, but many Libra Risings are willing to fight for peace and justice. Libra is comfortable being in the middle of a situation weighing the various components, like the balance scale that is its symbol, with a goal of a fair resolution.

Libra Risings also need to remember that not everyone is interested in elegant beauty or improving the way things look. This can apply to not only people's surroundings but also their physical appearance, reputation, or public-facing images. Some individuals' default method is to do whatever it takes to get the job done, even if it is not pretty or leaves a bad taste in people's mouths. No Libra Rising would ever appear to

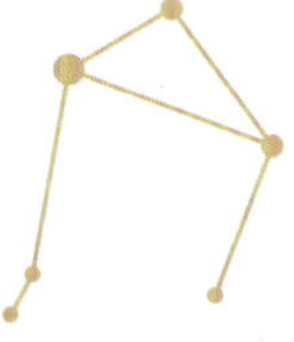

want to make things more disharmonious, even if that were their aim.

Those who have a negative view of people who appear to be desirous of rising above the harshness of life, are continually concerned with appearances, or otherwise give the impression that they believe they are somehow better than other people may be put off by Libra Rising's way of interacting with the world. Even if they are simply trying to be one of the blessed peacemakers this world so desperately needs, problems can arise because Libra Rising people have to work extra hard to appear to be decisive enough to work well with those who have opinions set in stone and who have a strong distrust of others.

If a Libra Rising senses this reaction in someone they care about, they must dial down their natural tendency to show that they see the justice in both sides of the matter at hand and make a special effort to communicate that they know how this person feels and that they are only trying to be fair and treat others as equals. A Libra Rising will not be seen as harsh, cruel, or overly opinionated even if they judge themselves to be so.

More than almost any other Rising Sign, Libra Rising needs to use their innate ability to help other people arrive at a decision that is beyond questioning. No other Rising Sign can be as helpful and respected a counselor to those who have lost their sense of perspective about life and how to live it successfully as Libra Rising.

Scorpio Rising ♏

ELEMENT: *Water (deep)*
QUALITY: *Fixed (penetrating)*

It's easy for others to see Scorpio Rising as sexy, mysterious, and judgmental. Since they are so passionate and direct, it's easy for Scorpio Rising to be misunderstood by those who are not that way.

FAVORABLE PERSONALITY TRAITS: Strong willpower. Can break through obstacles. Ambitious and faithful to friends. Intense, deep, and courageous, and can put up a fight for a cause.

ADVERSE PERSONALITY TRAITS: Jealous, dominating, and unscrupulous. Can justify using any means to gain an end. Ruthless. Quick to anger, hot for revenge. Greedy.

Scorpio Risings will usually be seen as intense, powerful, and not to be trifled with. Their ability to see to the heart of any matter, to keep secrets and detect the secrets of others, and to uncover lies, plots, and cover-ups of all kinds will be appreciated.

It is important for Scorpio Risings to remember that people who are not being their authentic selves or who are uncomfortable in their own skin will be inclined to view a Scorpio Rising as seeing right through them and judging them harshly, as they themselves, consciously or unconsciously, do. Scorpio Risings can be perceived on a spectrum from getting to the heart of a matter quickly to saying the right words at the right time to almost magically make a person aware of what they are actually saying and doing to being seen as so judgmental that they appear to condemn other people's words and actions in preparation for cutting them out of their life.

Remember, however, that some people are not always as self-assured and confident as they appear and are therefore unable to handle the powerful gaze and apparent judgment of a Scorpio Rising. The sensuous quality of a Scorpio Rising adds the element of sexual attraction to every encounter and can further throw a person off balance and unable to accurately determine what a Scorpio Rising is trying to say or do. Someone suffering from past traumas or in a confused state could easily misinterpret a Scorpio Rising's self-contained and powerful presentation to the world as disrespectful.

Those who have a negative view of people who appear to be secretive, who are comfortable with their sexuality, or who do not engage in small talk but only speak when they have something they consider to be important to say may be put off by a Scorpio Rising's way of interacting with the world. Even if a Scorpio Rising is simply thinking about their own situation or daily life's mundane challenges, problems can arise because Scorpio Rising people have to work extra hard to appear to be kind, friendly, and interested in others who present themselves in a confused, inauthentic, or superficial manner.

If a Scorpio Rising senses this reaction in someone they care about, they must become aware of their natural tendency to stay silent and just observe, experiencing life on the deepest, most profound, beyond-words level, and instead make a special effort to show that they are or can be totally committed to being there for others and to using their seemingly magical Scorpio Rising powers for their benefit. A Scorpio Rising will not be seen as unattractive, indecisive, or ineffectual even if they judge themselves to be so.

More than almost any other Rising Sign, Scorpio Rising needs to use their innate ability to penetrate all illusions and get to the heart of every matter. No other Rising Sign can be as helpful and respected a detective in revealing truths that need revealing.

Sagittarius Rising ♐

ELEMENT: *Fire (seeker)*

QUALITY: *Mutable (broadcaster)*

It's easy for others to see Sagittarius Rising as wise, honest, and blunt, sometimes blurting out what they should keep secret. Sagittarius Rising can often feel like they are a stranger in a strange land, even if they never leave their hometown.

FAVORABLE PERSONALITY TRAITS: Frank, honest, loyal, and unselfish. A lucky idealist. Engenders faith and inspiration wherever needed. A great sense of humor.

ADVERSE PERSONALITY TRAITS: Too blunt for their own good. Restless and difficulty committing. Rash and oversensitive. Irresponsible. More interested in the hunt than in the capture.

Sagittarius Risings will usually be seen as seekers of truth, broad-minded, and knowledgeable about the various cultures around the world even if they do not agree with significant aspects of their way of life. Their desire to learn from the best practices and biggest mistakes of the world's many nations and peoples and to share or adapt these concepts will be appreciated.

Sagittarius Risings can be perceived on a spectrum from giving the impression that they are not totally comfortable with the cultural mores they grew up with to learning another language or experimenting with different ways of living to being seen as having a lack of tolerance and respect for those who have demonstrated their own lack of tolerance and respect for people with different backgrounds and their customs.

The Sagittarius Rising gives the appearance of being committed to speaking the truth even when such honesty is detrimental to others, to themselves, and to their stated purpose for speaking out. To further complicate matters, Sagittarius Risings are legendary for revealing secrets, usually at the worst possible time. Some people cannot handle the truth spoken at any time. The old saying "The truth hurts" is all too true for most people, even some Sagittarius Risings.

Those who have a negative view of people who appear to be overly philosophical, long-winded, and unsure of what they believe, or who are tolerant or actively supportive of foreign views and beliefs, or who seem to worship the flora and fauna of nature and need to commune with it as much as possible will not be comfortable watching a Sagittarius Rising's uniquely fiery enthusiasm for life and may project and react to a Sagittarius Rising the way they dialogue with their inner self, acting tactless for no apparent reason and saying words they will regret.

If a Sagittarius Rising senses this reaction in someone they care about, they must become aware of their natural tendency to let the world in on their inner dialogue and make a special effort to show that they are as interested in another person's journey as they are in their own and that their appearing to be committed to conflicting beliefs is part of their effort to arrive at the truth, a goal they assume is shared by all. A Sagittarius Rising will not be seen to be unjust, closed-minded, or prejudiced even if they judge themselves to be so.

More than almost any other Rising Sign, Sagittarius Rising needs to use their innate ability to seek, communicate, and establish truth, justice, and fairness in service to others. No other Rising Sign can be as powerful an example of what being true to oneself can accomplish.

Capricorn Rising ♑

ELEMENT: *Earth (authoritarian)*
QUALITY: *Cardinal (career minded)*

It's easy for others to see Capricorn Rising as serious, extremely competent, and like a stern parent who disapproves of their actions. Capricorn Rising seems to become younger as they get older.

FAVORABLE PERSONALITY TRAITS: Reliable, capable, ambitious, and patient. Gains wisdom through experience. Thrifty. Successful organizer. Respects tradition and those in prominent positions.

ADVERSE PERSONALITY TRAITS: Melancholy. Pessimistic, brooding, influenced by head instead of heart. Stingy. Tendency to toady to the top, overbearing with the underdog. Yearns for power.

Capricorn Risings will usually be seen as no-nonsense, capable people deserving of respect, knowledgeable and respectful of the laws, rules, and traditions of whatever they concern themselves with, even if they do not agree with significant parts of these things. Their ability to do what is necessary to achieve recognition and success as they define it will usually be appreciated.

It is important for Capricorn Risings to remember that people who are not happy with the way things are and especially not happy with those in authority will be inclined to interpret Capricorn Rising as trying to put undue pressure on them to stop "complaining." They can be perceived on a spectrum from being successful examples of what happens when you do what you have to do and not just what you want to do to appearing to want to emulate people they respect or who are in authority and can help them on their path to becoming an authority to being seen as so rigid, negative, or taciturn as to make others sad and worried that they are in danger of being clinically depressed.

Capricorn Risings need to remember that some people cannot handle their discipline and seriousness. They can give the appearance of being disapproving, though this usually takes the form of sarcasm or dark humor. Capricorn Risings are often perceived as "raining on other people's parades."

Those who have a negative view of people who appear to be saturnine, overly concerned with their career, or more comfortable with conserving traditions and going with tried-and-true methods will not give a Capricorn Rising the level of respect they desire. Also, those who have problems delegating or who overburden themselves and others with more work and responsibilities than they should be expected to accomplish, and especially those who were given too much responsibility as children, may project and react to a Capricorn Rising the way they dialogue with their inner self, acting like they are the teacher or superior to them in some way for no apparent reason.

If a Capricorn Rising senses this reaction in someone they care about, they must become aware of their natural tendency to not let others see that they too are burdened by tedium and overwork and make a special effort to show that they consider themselves a part of the group. They need to make it clear that they are not haughty and aloof, just tired and overworked. A Capricorn Rising will not be seen as lazy, unambitious, or frivolous even if they judge themselves to be so.

More than almost any other Rising Sign, Capricorn Risings need to build relationships using their innate ability to plan, execute, and establish something that can survive the test of time. No other Rising Sign understands the harsh realities of life and how important the satisfaction of deep emotional needs is. Remember that the sign's symbol is a Goat with a fish's tail, and in astrology, fish and water have to do with emotion.

Aquarius Rising ♒

ELEMENT: *Air (forward thinking)*
QUALITY: *Fixed (unsympathetic)*

It's easy for others to see Aquarius Rising as inventive, cold, eccentric, or weird. Taking the best from the past to make the future better is their thing. Aquarius Risings are friendly but oddly reluctant to let people get too close to them.

FAVORABLE PERSONALITY TRAITS: Understanding and humane. Often far ahead of their time. Kindhearted and helpful. Happy to oblige when asked for a favor. Communicative.

ADVERSE PERSONALITY TRAITS: Temperamental, unreasonable, and contrary. Often out of step with associates. Loves to stir up trouble; delights in stubbornness and rebellion.

Aquarius Risings will usually be seen as unemotional, calm, and unique in some way. Their honesty about their desire to do what is necessary to achieve a better future for those they care about will usually be appreciated.

It is important for Aquarius Risings to remember that people who are not happy with things changing too much or too quickly will be inclined to interpret their words and actions as trying to put undue pressure on them to radically alter their lives. Aquarius Risings can be perceived on a spectrum from giving the impression that they are pleasantly eccentric to appearing to be committed to being the change they want to see or the model citizen for the new age they are trying to bring forward to being seen as seriously unbalanced and out of touch with the norms of daily life.

Aquarius Risings also need to remember that some people cannot handle the apparent disinterest of the Aquarius Rising in the disruptive consequences that would obviously manifest if their plans for change actually were implemented. Aquarius Risings often give the appearance of being unemotional to the point of being perceived as a bit inhuman and more than a little robotic. To further complicate matters, Aquarius Risings are often perceived as the amplification of the oddest aspects of their particular Sun and Moon signs, adding an element of "What are they going to say or do now?" to their interactions with others.

Those who have a negative view of unusual people or those who appear to be uncaringly rebellious, too concerned with the past and the future but not concerned enough with the present, or overly detached and distracted will not feel comfortable in Aquarius Rising's presence. They have to work extra hard to appear like they have an emotional connection with other people. Also, those who have problems with people who seem to be going out of their way to show the world how unusual, unconventional, and unashamedly uncaring of what other people think about them and their way of living may project and react to an Aquarius Rising the way they dialogue with their inner self, acting cold and distant with them for no apparent reason.

If an Aquarius Rising senses this reaction in someone they care about, they need to make a special effort to show that they do, in fact, care about other people but sometimes get lost in their head and their desire to envision a future where their problems are solvable. An Aquarius Rising will not be seen to be ordinary, predictable, or overly emotional even if they judge themselves to be so.

More than almost any other Rising Sign, Aquarius Risings need to use their innate ability to innovate and think outside of the box. Most people do not get a chance to actually change the world, and so for an Aquarius Rising, changing their world has to be enough.

Like their symbol, the old man pouring out water for all who are thirsty to drink, Aquarius Rising people need to be satisfied with just getting their ideas out there for those thirsty for their version of the future.

Pisces Rising ♓

ELEMENT: *Water (otherworldly)*
QUALITY: *Mutable (uncertain)*

It's easy for others to see Pisces Rising as listening to a disembodied psychic voice or as if there is something wrong. All their passing moods and intuitions show on their face and in their body language.

FAVORABLE PERSONALITY TRAITS: Charitable. Charming, sympathetic, and agreeable. Loves beauty and delights in art. Champion of the underdog. Capable of inspirational achievement.

ADVERSE PERSONALITY TRAITS: Timid, weak, and supersensitive. Enjoys the role of the martyr. Too talkative. Inferiority complex. Escapist behavior.

Pisces Risings will usually be seen as sensitive, compassionate, and caring people. Their obvious desire to do what they can to help individuals in need will usually be appreciated.

It is important for Pisces Risings to remember that people who are not comfortable with those who appear to be overly selfless and willing to give others the shirt off their backs will be inclined to interpret Pisces Rising as trying to put undue pressure on them to be more understanding, forgiving, and charitable to those they may not want to help.

It is also important for Pisces Risings to remember that some people cannot handle the moody behavior typical of their sign. Pisces Risings often appear lost in thought or psychic connection, seemingly inspired or hearing voices from somewhere that others do not hear. This can make other people think that something is wrong, that Pisces Rising is upset or unhappy, either with them or because of some unknown cause. Pisces Risings are actually stronger than most people because their faith and connection with the unseen world gives them true metaphysical fitness.

Those who hold negative views of people who are ready to sacrifice their own interests or otherwise disrupt their daily routine for the good of another will not give Pisces Rising the level of respect they need and deserve. Even if they are simply trying to stay true to their religious or other core beliefs, problems can arise because Pisces Risings have to work extra hard to appear that they are not trying to make others look less spiritual, humane, and devoted to their religious obligations. This is further complicated by the fact that Pisces Risings always have that "I'm listening to you but also to my inner voice" look.

Also, individuals who have problems with caring, spiritual people who ask a lot of personal questions in their desire to understand how best they can be of service may project and react to a Pisces Rising the way they dialogue with their inner self, acting hurt and demoralized for no apparent reason.

If a Pisces Rising senses this reaction in someone they care about, they must stifle their natural tendency to see someone who needs help as having somehow asked them for help and instead wait for them to request assistance before going into helper mode. A Pisces Rising will not be seen to be uncaring, miserly, or selfish even if they judge themselves to be so.

More than almost any other Rising Sign, Pisces Risings need to use their innate ability to truly connect with people to feel fully alive. No other Rising Sign understands loneliness, the fragility of life, and the tenuous connections shared by all beings as they do. Remember that Pisces's symbol is the Fishes, each swimming in opposite directions, so they sometimes seem to be in blissful exaltation and sometimes in seeming anguish. Only a Pisces Rising can allow both energies to exist in themselves at the same time, a rare feat, which is apt because in my experience, Pisces is the rarest of the Rising Signs.

REVIEW: THE SIGNS' ELEMENTS, QUALITIES, AND CHARACTERISTICS

RECAP: *The power in knowing your Rising Sign is that by knowing how what you're trying to say/do is being perceived, you can modulate it accordingly. I hope you can see how adding the element and quality to a sign helps you better understand someone who has it as a Sun, Moon, or Rising Sign and any planets in that sign.*

Here is a list of the signs with their element and quality added and a brief description of primary characteristics.

- Aries is Cardinal Fire, goal oriented and pushing ahead to the frontier without forethought.
- Taurus is Fixed Earth, stubborn and desirous of holding their ground or overcoming obstacles.
- Gemini is Mutable Air, possessing a million ideas and multiple opinions about everything.
- Cancer is Cardinal Water, committed to nurturing their families and establishing a secure base.
- Leo is Fixed Fire, burning with passion like the other Fire signs but very content with who and where they are.
- Virgo is Mutable Earth, practical but flexible and not as sure of themselves as Taurus or Capricorn.
- Libra is Cardinal Air, committed to achieving the idea of balance, fairness, and harmony.
- Scorpio is Fixed Water, intimately connected with the highest and lowest in all things.
- Sagittarius is Mutable Fire, burning with the light of truth, which can change depending on cultural mores.

- Capricorn is Cardinal Earth, goal oriented to achieving authority and respect from those they respect.
- Aquarius is Fixed Air, always trying to bring their ideas into reality to make lasting change.
- Pisces is Mutable Water, truly compassionate but susceptible to being overwhelmed by emotion.

YOUR CELESTIAL TRILOGY

To help you understand the concept of what Amy and I call your Celestial Trilogy—how your Sun, Moon, and Rising Sign are functioning for you—I'm going to share with you my proprietary and nifty way of understanding your Rising Sign/Ascendant. It uses an old-school movie projector as a metaphor, requiring that you know how they looked and worked.

A movie projector is basically composed of three components:

- A light source (the Sun in an astrology chart)
- A curved mirror to concentrate the light onto the film (the Moon in an astrology chart)
- A lens to focus the image from the film onto the projection screen (the Rising Sign)

The Sun in your astrology chart is the light source; it's how you look out on the world. It's your ego. It radiates heat and a light that is colored by the sign it is in.

For example, my Sun, my ego, my purpose, my identity is colored by the zodiac sign Aquarius; Amy's, by Aries.

You have that light from your Sun sign, and it gets concentrated by and reflected off your Moon, which in Earth's sky reflects the Sun's light and in astrology symbolizes your reflective mirror.

So in my case, my emotionally cool light from my Sun in Aquarius's light, one of the three Air (idea) signs, gets reflected and concentrated by my Moon, which is in the very emotional and compassionate sign of Pisces, one of the three Water (emotional) signs.

Like cooking, reading your cosmic blueprint requires blending and mixing. In my case, my scientific, emotionally detached Aquarian desire to aid humanity by taking the best of the past (astrology) and inventing ways to use it and the newest technology to make a better future gets blended with my Pisces Moon's unique ability to empathize with the feelings and situation of another person, one-on-one, like you, dear reader. This allows me to set my mind free to solve problems by theorizing, but with the ability to add much more compassion for the effect my possible solutions may have on individuals as well as on humanity—hey, we Aquarians think like this!

My Celestial Trilogy is in full operation when my Aquarian Sun's light bounces off of my Pisces Moon mirror and gets concentrated and reflected out through the lens of my Rising Sign, Leo. When you see Leo, think "lion," because Leos definitely want to be the leader of their pride. (That term is, incidentally, a word for a group of lions and one of the keywords for the sign.) When you see Leo, you should also think, "Showtime!" Leo Risings have a different definition of "stage fright": We get scared when we're *not* on stage!

In my case, my Leo Rising enables me to *display* the results of my quest to create a *new and futuristic* world (Aquarius) with Pisces Moon–style compassion *to help humanity* (Aquarius again) using the very ancient and yet futuristic practice of astrology and to show others how to have a good time doing so (Leo). The Leo Rising pride and Aquarian detachment also help me deal with my human sensitivity (Pisces) to the inevitable rejections and thoughtless words that are bound to get directed at anyone who is trying *to change the world* (Aquarius) even in some small way.

Amy and I have already added our unique contributions to empowering individuals to make better decisions using our published oracular creations, or, as we call them, our spiritual power tools. We also see our influence in the current strong interest in astrology, tarot, and oracle cards and the proliferation of people who are creating their own oracles. Here's an Aquarian prediction: Our work and other metaphysical books will one day be taught in public schools to help children learn who they are. I am hopeful that this book will be one of the first over the wall of ignorance keeping children from being empowered fully.

RECAP: *Always remember that all signs, planets, and houses have a spectrum of meanings, and we are challenged to use our free will to manifest the best parts of these spectrums for our highest good and greatest joy. Your Sun, your ego, and/or your purpose gets reflected off your Moon, your emotions, your habits, and your attitude to both of them. In addition, your personal and unique light mixture gets projected through the lens of your Rising Sign. What people see is the light through the lens, your surface appearance, your persona, your mask, and not the real you (unless you're born at sunrise and are therefore a double sign).*

So, once again, if someone is just meeting you or knows you but has not had a chance to really get to know you, they will most likely respond to you as they would to someone whose Sun sign is the same sign as your Rising Sign. This is crucial to keep in mind because, as you can imagine, some Sun signs are more sympatico with certain Rising Signs, and so the potential for judgments and misjudgments is real and ever present.

For example, a Scorpio Sun is usually not loud or showy, but someone who can be described as quiet, taking everything in before deciding whether or not they will gain or lose power by saying or doing anything. Most Scorpios do not suffer fools gladly and, being quite judgmental, prefer to keep quiet rather than risk the consequences of volunteering information. A Scorpio Rising appears to have these qualities.

Some Scorpio Risings, Suns, or Moons are downright secretive. So if they encounter a very inquisitive Rising Sign, like Gemini, or its opposite sign, Sagittarius, two zodiac signs strongly associated with communications of all kinds, and the Scorpio-influenced person then becomes on the receiving end of a barrage of questions about a whole host of things, this is almost certainly going to be very off-putting to these quiet, reserved, and often-secretive Scorpio-influenced natives.

I hope you can see the logic of this previous example and that you are starting to enjoy thinking about how the signs of the zodiac interact. Thinking about sign interactions in this manner is one of the best exercises for any astrologer, beginning or experienced. As we all know about exercise, it needs to be done often, and the ones that are done with regularity are usually the ones you enjoy the most.

Here is another interaction for your consideration: Surprisingly, a secretive Scorpio Sun or Moon might be equally put off by a Scorpio Rising! Why? Because Scorpios are the detectives of the zodiac. The powerful, judgmental gaze and sly inquisitiveness of a Scorpio Rising, coupled with the fact that Scorpio Risings are so direct and passionate that they are often misunderstood by those who would never show themselves to be so direct and passionate, might manifest as subtle probing. This might not be as off-putting as the direct questions of the Gemini or Sagittarius Sun, Moon, or Rising Sign, but the secretive Scorpio Sun or Moon would think they were seeing through the Scorpio Rising's stealthy ways.

The trouble would be that Scorpio Risings, the Rising Sign so pure and intense looking that the rest of us often misunderstand them, can be standing there trying to remember whether they left the water running when they left the house, but those who dare to meet their gaze would think by their intense look that the Scorpio Rising was looking right through them and seeing their flaws and secrets. I am exaggerating, of course, but not by much. If you have Scorpio prominent in your chart or the chart of someone you care about, you know what I am talking about. Scorpios invented the saying "Revenge is a dish best served cold."

I know that may have been a lot to process, but I have just given you a peek at how we astrologers get to have fun thinking deeply about the way the signs interact. As your reward for staying with me as I explored my Celestial Trilogy and revealed some secrets of the secretive sign of Scorpio, here is our guide for putting together your cosmic blueprint's Celestial Trilogy.

IF YOUR SUN, MOON, AND RISING SIGNS ARE ALL THE SAME SIGN OF THE ZODIAC

You are what is known as a triple Aries, Taurus, or whatever sign you have been blessed to call yours. You are just about the purest example of your sign possible, and with you, what you see is what you get to a level not known by the rest of us. You need to concern yourself not with blending two or more signs harmoniously but only with blending the various aspects of your sign's meanings. You will, however, have to contend with a world in which almost everyone else has a more complex, complicated, and often-conflicted way of thinking, feeling, and doing what they do.

IF YOUR SUN, MOON, AND RISING SIGNS ARE ALL THE SAME QUALITY, EITHER CARDINAL, FIXED, OR MUTABLE

You too are a pure blend but of a different way of living. If you are all Cardinal signs, you are goal oriented to a degree most other people will find difficult to understand. If you are all Fixed signs, you are stubborn and will not want to change anything in your life, especially your beliefs, unless you finally conclude that you are wrong and there is something better that is attainable for you. If you are all Mutable signs, you are flexible and changeable to the point where it may be difficult for others or even you to know what your core beliefs are. As it is with having one's Sun, Moon, and Rising Signs all in the same sign of the zodiac, you too will have to contend with a world in which almost everyone does not so totally subscribe to either a goal-oriented, stubborn, or changeable way of life as do you.

IF YOUR SUN, MOON, AND RISING SIGNS ARE ALL IN THE SAME ELEMENT, EITHER FIRE, AIR, WATER, OR EARTH

You too are a unique and pure blend of ways to approach daily existence. If your Celestial Trilogy is in Fire, you are a person to whom action, having faith, and always being truthful come naturally. If your Celestial Trilogy is in Air, you dwell in the realm of ideas, theories, and concepts of how things are and how they could be. If your Celestial Trilogy is in Water, your world is one dominated by feelings, emotions, and intuitions that are usually beyond words and beyond the realm of logical thought. Finally, if your Celestial Trilogy is in Earth, you live in the real world and understand its beauty, bounty, and limits more than others could ever know.

IF YOU HAVE TWO PIECES OF YOUR CELESTIAL TRILOGY IN THE SAME SIGN, QUALITY, OR ELEMENT

You should pay particular attention to those two pieces—Sun and Moon, Sun and Rising Sign, or Moon and Rising Sign—and the meanings associated with the sign, quality, or element they share. Compare those meanings with the meanings associated with the sign, quality, or element of that third piece of your Celestial Trilogy and you will see whether there is a harmonious synergy in the three pieces or whether the meanings conflict or cancel each other out. If there is conflict, you can use your favorite strengths from each piece to help you counteract or compensate for the aspects of your personality with which you are not comfortable.

IF YOUR CELESTIAL TRILOGY IS ANY COMBINATION OF FIRE, AIR, WATER

You have been gifted with the ability to take action to bring the ideas you have into reality through your ability to have an emotional connection with those you care about—either those you cherish or those who are important to the attainment of your goals. Be aware that you must try extra hard to apply your harmonized logical mind and emotional intelligence to a plan of action you are considering before you actually embark on it. The goal of this prior consideration is to make sure that what you are about to do with your precious time on Earth is practical to attain and useful to enough people if it is attained.

IF YOUR CELESTIAL TRILOGY IS ANY COMBINATION OF FIRE, AIR, EARTH

You have been gifted with the ability to take action to bring into reality any ideas you have for improving your reality and that of other people. You do not have to plan when it comes to the practicality and usefulness of what you are about to do. You do, however, have to make a special effort to understand how your actions and the implementation of your ideas are going to affect other people on an emotional level. Be aware that other people's feelings about what you do can assist or inhibit the realization of your goals as much as available resources and the purely practical considerations involved with executing your plans.

IF YOUR CELESTIAL TRILOGY IS ANY COMBINATION OF FIRE, WATER, EARTH

You have been gifted with the ability to take action to bring into reality the things you believe you need to have the life you feel that you want to be living. Your actions will be guided by your intuitive understanding and emotional connection to anyone involved in your efforts. You do, however, have to make a special effort to make sure that the actions you take are being guided by your own ideas about how things should be and are not allowing the ideas of others to override your own. Be aware that other people's ideas may have more to do with their own needs and wants and not enough to do with yours.

IF YOUR CELESTIAL TRILOGY IS ANY COMBINATION OF AIR, WATER, EARTH

You have been gifted with the ability to experience, examine, and connect to the real world and the rest of humanity on a deep and profound level. You have a balanced understanding of what it means to be a human being who is inextricably tied to the natural world and of how to best take care of its resources for this and future generations. You do, however, have to make a special effort to turn your ideas, intuitions, and plans into actions that bring them to fruition. Be aware that other people may not need, as you do, regular periods of rest and recharge—and that includes the recharging of your faith in yourself and the rightness of your cause.

Human beings are the ultimate puzzle, and trying to see the intricacies of individual ways of being and their interactions with the world is a lifelong education. I have been doing this for a long time, and yet each time I read a person's cosmic blueprint or write a book and give examples of astrological mixing and blending, I learn something new. I would have loved to describe every specific interaction, but that would require this book to be way too long. I am hopeful that if

I teach you to do it, you will be able to examine the many intricate interactions yourself.

The best way—in fact, the only way—for you to understand this unique blend, your personal Celestial Trinity, is to first become aware of it, which you now are, and then to see how the information stacks up against who you know yourself to be. Amy and I know full well that no one knows you like you know yourself. What we have written is the essence of what we have learned after our decades of astrological practice, presented in a form that you can take into your inner dialogue and see how it resonates with who you know yourself to be. If we have done our jobs correctly, your cosmic blueprint—and *Your Cosmic Blueprint*—can be your guides to self-understanding and self-empowerment throughout the rest of your life.

Now that you know how to derive important information about a person from their Celestial Trilogy, it is time to graduate to the next level of your astrological education: understanding the meaning and the function of the houses of your cosmic blueprint—also known as the twelve slices of your astrological pizza, with each one representing a slice of life.

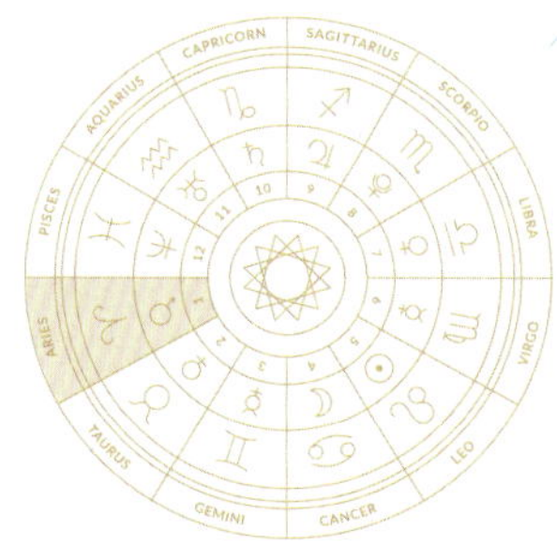

THE FIRST HOUSE

The First House of any astrology chart is the slice of pizza that hangs off and below the horizontal line at the left (east) side of your chart. It is the degree of the zodiac that is on that horizontal line, the symbol of the horizon at the moment you were born, that defines your Rising Sign.

Your Rising Sign degree and the line that defines it also define the cusp (line of demarcation) of the First House of any astrology chart. The Rising Sign is closely linked to the meaning of the First House of an astrological chart, but it is not unusual for your first house to contain the remaining degrees of your Ascendant's sign, part or all of the next zodiac sign, and maybe even a part of the sign after that next zodiac sign.

The First House is similar to your Rising Sign but goes beyond how you appear to the world. The First House of your cosmic blueprint is all about you, including your appearance, but it is the slice of life that also includes how you think about yourself and how you choose to project yourself in relationships, especially with people whose closeness to you almost guarantees that they are going to get to see you as you really are, without filters, by which I mean the things we all have and use to armor ourselves in our dealings with the world. These close people are the ones we allow to see us without our carefully chosen clothes, hairstyles, and makeup, when we drop our outside voices and personality traits and quirks as we kick back and relax into being our private selves.

The First House is where you are the star of your own show. Your personality, how you think about your appearance, and your heart-of-hearts attitude about yourself determine how you will experience your life. If everyone loves you and you don't love yourself, you are not going to experience their love the way you could.

RECAP: *The cusp of the First House of your cosmic blueprint is also known as your Rising Sign and your Ascendant. It is determined by the exact time of your birth and is the degree of the 360 degrees of the zodiac that was exactly on the horizon as you took your first breath.*

If you were born at sunrise, you are a double of your Sun sign and a true representation of your zodiac sign. If, however, your Rising Sign is very different from your Sun sign, then your true nature and your intentions will not be apparent to other people, especially those who do not know you very well or are unwilling to see you for who you really are.

If you have a planet in the First House, you are a planetary agent for that planet! You have that planet's characteristics in your appearance, the way you present yourself, and the way others see you. This also works if you have a planet in your Twelfth House, within 10 degrees of your Rising Sign. If you have one or more planets in the First House, you and your relationship with yourself are much more complex than that of most people.

A BRIEF LOOK AT PLANETS IN THE FIRST HOUSE

The Sun ☉

You are tasked by astrology's tenets to be working on yourself. Therefore, those who don't know you well can wrongly think you're too self-involved, especially when you are stressed. You have a sunny disposition and like to shine at whatever you do.

The Moon ☽

Everyone thinks you're similar to them in some way. The Moon is all about reflection. It makes you a great salesperson. You are sensitive to others even if you try not to show it. If you're angry, people get very anxious because you're usually so considerate.

Mercury ☿

You are skillful at whatever you put your mind to, especially communication. You are quick to learn but prefer to apply what you know and not get bogged down in philosophical arguments about what you have learned. You may have a wirier build than a person might expect.

Venus ♀

You are seen as a lovely person. You are probably more attractive than you think you are and may even work in a field related to beauty, fashion, the arts, or making the world a more beautiful place. You are a peacemaker, a lover, and not a fighter if you can help it.

Mars (Ruler) ♂

You are a fighter, and you do not back down easily once you engage. You show everyone how a person gets the job done by strength of will. Even when you think you are not pushing hard, you are often perceived as being more aggressive than most would be in the same situation.

Jupiter ♃

You are seen as jovial, fortunate, positive, optimistic, and always trying to grow and make good use of anything you get involved with. Be aware that you may expand your waist because of your expensive tastes and appetites. People love having you around them.

Saturn ♄

You are a natural-born teacher. You are disciplined and hardworking. You are realistic but can seem depressed. Those who want to be foolish or lazy consider you a drag when you remind them of the consequences of their actions, even when you are trying to help them.

Uranus ♅

You are inclined to eccentricity, inventiveness, and technical proficiency. You are here to help shake up the status quo and keep life interesting. You have to work extra hard if you need to appear dependable because you can easily seem to be a natural disruptor and rocker of boats.

Neptune ♆

You are inclined to be an inspiration or to appear confused or confusing, depending on whether you want to benefit only yourself or benefit humanity. Choose the latter, and you will succeed and inspire many others. Egocentric or deceitful behavior will backfire on you in the end.

Pluto ♇

You can be perceived as being judgmental. You are surprisingly resourceful. You have a magnetic, attractive, seductive quality and must use it carefully and with kindness because you are an extremist. Make friends with your shadow side—it is an important part of you.

IF YOU DO NOT HAVE A PLANET IN THE FIRST HOUSE OR ANY PARTICULAR HOUSE

Not having a planet in the First House does not mean that you are deficient in any way. This is true for not having a planet in any particular house of the twelve houses of an astrology chart. Wondering about the absence of a planet in a particular house is a logical question that people for whom I read always ask of me. I can almost guarantee that, should you decide to read for other people, anyone whose cosmic blueprint you read will ask you about it.

Having a planet in a house means you are going to be strongly inclined to have to deal with the pleasures and pitfalls of having that planet in that house. It cannot be overstated that every planetary position—sign, house, and aspects (angles between the planets)—has a spectrum of meanings. Our free will allows us to explore this spectrum and decide where we want to be tuned in on this spectrum's dial.

While it is true that some planets are more at home in some signs and houses than others, there is no planetary position that is so "good" that it cannot create problems if its energies are misunderstood and mishandled, and there is no planetary position that is so "bad" that its energies cannot be used in some beneficial way. It may not necessarily be a way you would want to use them if given a choice, but that is the point of living and the reason to use astrology. Life is about problem-solving and choices.

Always remember that everyone and everything has its limits. Interpreting cosmic blueprints is a practice, like medicine and law. We astrologers must dedicate ourselves to doing our best, always, again remembering the words of the great ancient astrologer Ptolemy, who said, "The stars incline, they do not compel." Our free will is very powerful.

An astrology chart is a map that can lead us to many places we might otherwise not go, but we have the choice of what to do with what we learn on the journey. The most obvious choice is to decide whether you or your client want to use what you learn as an excuse for your behavior or as a guide to making your life a success. Astrology has been an essential part of my personal growth. That is why this book is so important to me and, I hope, to you.

The zodiacal degree of your Rising Sign is also the degree of the cusp of your First House. While the Rising Sign is always transmitting how you appear to other people, whether you want to appear that way or not, the First House of an astrological chart is more under your control. It is all about you, your self-concept, what you want to project to the world. The First House is about everything you want people to know about you.

NOTE: *If you are born around sunrise and your Sun is technically in your Twelfth House, above the horizon but within 5 degrees or so of your Rising Sign's degree, you can read it as being in your First House even though it appears to be above your chart's horizon line. This is true for the Sun or Moon near any of the cusps of a chart. Of course, it is in actuality only in one house, but there are interesting nuances to a planet positioned near a cusp, and they can be revealed when an experienced astrologer reads it as if it is in both houses. For now, just read the planet as if it's in your First House.*

A TEST USING YOUR UNDERSTANDING OF THE SUN AND THE RISING SIGN

To test your understanding of the Sun and the Rising Sign, read the following until it makes sense to you: Those born when the Sun was rising near but not on the horizon at the moment they were born and whose Sun is positioned on the first or last few degrees of a sign can find that they are not double Sun/Rising Signs and that their Sun and Rising Sign are as different as those of most of us. If you understand why this is so, you are well on your way to being an astrologer.

Having your Sun, your ego, your purpose, your vitality, the light that you radiate to the world in the First House means that you must be yourself and that finding out who you are is a major part of your life's purpose. The spectrum of meanings ranges from dealing with problems and limitations to being yourself imposed by circumstances beyond your control or by others, or even self-imposed limitations, to showing the world what it means to be a person with a healthy ego who is actualizing their life's purpose and all the way to the extreme of pathological narcissism, believing oneself to be the only person who really exists or matters.

A TEST USING YOUR UNDERSTANDING OF THE RISING MOON

Learning about the Moon in the First House gives you another chance to test your ability to visualize the astrological clockwork of the planets of an astrology chart. I've told you about how having the Sun exactly on the horizon at the moment of your birth makes you a double of your Sun sign. Having your Moon exactly on the horizon at the moment of your birth also makes you a double of that sign.

While having the Sun and the Rising Sign in the same sign aligns your purpose and/or ego with how you have chosen to project yourself into your interactions with other people and the world via all means you choose to explore, having the Moon and your Rising Sign in the same sign aligns the style of emotional intelligence associated with that sign with the same intention. The double Sun/Rising Sign will usually be more self-aware and self-concerned than the double Moon/Rising Sign, which will usually seek to establish an emotional connection as a habitual part of personal interactions.

And if you were born during a new Moon, when the Moon is very close to the Sun, there is a chance that you are a triple of your zodiac sign. Triple Celestial Trilogies are rare, but they do exist. I like to think that these people have a special need to know everything there is to know about that sign and share it in some way with the rest of us.

The rule about your Moon being in the first or last few degrees of a sign applies here as it does to the Sun, so your Moon can be close to your Rising Sign degree but in a different zodiac sign. If this is not confusing you, congratulations! You are an astrologer! It took me a while to understand the nuances of double and triple signs, but it helped me understand the mechanics of what exactly a Rising Sign is.

Triple signs are more than the unique ambassadors of that particular sign. As with a double sign, what you see is what you get. Triple signs, however, are the very definition of their sign. If you meet one, see what you can learn from them. You may be surprised at how eager they are to speak with you about their unique take on the world. They have lived their lives without most people understanding how unique they are, and when you tell them you do understand that, they may confide in you.

We are all unique expressions of our cosmic blueprints, but double and triple signs are . . . well, different. You know what I mean if you are one or know one, and if you do not know one now, you will eventually if you decide to read for other people. I have designed this book to prepare you to read not only your own cosmic blueprint but those of others as well. Many of my students have followed taking my classes by becoming professional astrologers. However, you do not need to do this, and if you do read for others, you do not have to do it professionally. My goal is that either way, you will be prepared to give useful advice to people they would be willing to pay for. By the time you have finished this book, you will have the powerful ability to read people's cosmic blueprints for both fun and profit, giving them useful information that empowers them to change their lives for the better.

It bears repeating that having the Moon in the First House of your astrology chart, especially when it is near your Rising Sign, gives you a rare ability to reflect back at others the emotional connection having the Moon in the First House enables you to make. This connection reflection can make people feel that you are one of them, part of the family, familiar in a good way. It gives you the ability to do very well selling things for a living because others like being with you, feel like you are on their side and understand their needs, and are therefore more inclined to trust you than they trust other people, especially other salespeople.

Remember, the First House is everything you want people to know about you. This is why people with the Moon in their First House are emotional explorers and are challenged to function in the world while feeling everything more deeply than most people, or, at the very least, having to deal with the issue of sharing their emotions, feelings, and reflections about everything with others.

The spectrum of meanings of the Moon in the First House could range from having to deal with problems and limitations caused by one's emotions as a result of circumstances beyond our control to being fine examples of emotional intelligence and appropriate levels of caring, nurturing, and compassionate to being so emotionally tuned in to themselves and others that they are perceived as being extraordinarily empathetic, intuitive, or psychic or to the other extreme of being so controlled by their emotions that they have a hard time living in the "real" world.

The Moon is a powerful planet in astrology, the equal of the Sun in its powerful effect on us all. As I mentioned previously, I have a strong suspicion that the Moon is actually more powerful than the Sun in the chart of someone who identifies as a woman. It may very well be that the interplay of one's Celestial Trilogy is connected to the exploration of gender identity and expression.

I took a chance on you being ready to explore some brief meanings of the other planets of your chart in the First House before I explained in depth the meanings of the various planets themselves. Next, I will introduce you to the planets as I introduce you to the house and sign(s) they rule—another way of saying that meanings and associations of a planet, sign, and house go together perfectly. I believe this is the best way for you to understand your cosmic blueprint. Allow me to introduce you to the ruling planet of the First House, Mars.

MARS, RULING PLANET OF THE FIRST HOUSE

The First House is all about you, and so I would understand if you would logically expect the Sun, the planet that represents one's ego and purpose, to be the ruler of the First House. But astrology, like life, seems to have many contradictions, and it is necessary to be comfortable with that fact and to look beneath the contradictions to find the way the pieces fit together. You need to be able to do this to be a good cosmic-blueprint reader.

As I said when we first began our journey, the meaning of each planet can be found in its symbolic glyph. We spoke about the glyph for the Sun, the single dot, symbolizing our individual self, in the center of the circle, which, taken together, symbolizes our experience of being the center of our personal solar system. The circle is the universal symbol for completeness and in astrology represents All-There-Is, the Great Mystery, the Spirit, or whatever name you prefer to describe the indescribable vastness from which we have miraculously emerged as individuals.

The Moon's waxing crescent glyph can be seen to be the circle cut in two halves, symbolizing each individual's soul cut from the Great Spirit and joined to represent the emotional, nurturing half of the individualized soul. The other semicircle is the logical half of the soul, and we will see it being used in several of the other planetary glyphs.

Though in practice the glyph for Mars is the same symbol as that for male, the glyph for the planet Mars is the cross of matter, the same cross that is the basic structure of the astrological houses, placed over the circle of Spirit. The glyph for Mars uses the cross folded back to resemble an arrow, a strong indication of the active, goal-directed, and aggressive meaning of the ruling planet of the First House. The arrow coming off the side of the circle symbolizes that material goals will be emphasized over spiritual ones, but we are always spiritual beings having a human experience.

Mars is the planet of individual action, the lone pioneer blazing a new trail through the wilderness. In a cosmic blueprint, the sign and the house position of Mars can offer valuable insight into the potential energy available to the native and into the actions that a person may take to get for themselves what their Sun and Moon and, to a lesser extent, their Rising Sign want to have and hold. It can also describe the things the native is comfortable with, how they are inclined to act when they decide to act, or what the native believes they need to do to work their will and make their mark on the world.

Mars is the planet that represents our ability to actualize what our Sun wants to see accomplished. It is related to our strength, our will and willpower, and our ability to go out into the unknown to get what we want. It represents what astrologers of yore used to call "the male principle," the old-school Dark Ages idea of the idealized warrior single-handedly holding back the besieging enemy, taking action to make things the way he wants them to be, and being willing to fight against and overcome all odds and, if that is not possible, to die fighting—a hero's death.

When the energies of Mars in an astrology chart are blocked, stressed, or opposed by other planets (which we will cover later), or if one uses their Mars energy in an overly thoughtless way and they become misdirected, they often burst through in the form of impatience, hostility, accidents, and sometimes violence. Everyone has Mars in their charts, and when your Mars energy is not flowing properly, you can attract situations that will help you realign this energy. This is not always pleasant to experience.

Mars was the god of war in Roman times when war was considered an almost ideal way to develop an individual's strength of mind, body, and character, as well as the strength of the whole nation. At least, that is what their leaders wanted men to think.

Today, the war we are called on to fight is no less challenging. The information overload, chaos, and frenzied pace of everyday life demands that we use our Mars energies to defend ourselves and those we care about and successfully navigate the twists and turns of making a living in the twenty-first century as we work our will on the world. That takes strength of character and the focused willpower of our cosmic blueprint's Mars placement. Knowing which house and sign Mars is in for you is vital to understanding how you approach these issues and how to make Mars work to your benefit.

Mars was called Ares by the Greeks, and so it is easy to see why Mars rules Aries. They are very similar in their energetic and aggressive role in a person's astrological chart. The First House is all about you and what you want, and Mars is the planet that gets it done. The First House is ruled—another way of saying, "is most comfortable in"—by Mars. The archetypal astrology chart has Mars and Aries associated with the First House.

Mars in a person's First House inclines them to be focused on dealing with the energies available to them to actualize themselves as best they can. As I delineate Mars through the signs, you can see how closely that planet's energy is associated with everything associated with the First House and even the Rising Sign (i.e., things that help us interact with the world in such a way that we are participating in it, adding our unique energy in the form of activating our personal will to the mix of energies in which we find ourselves).

The spectrum of meanings for having Mars in the First House can be seen to range from someone who is challenged to deal with the problems and limitations surrounding the issue of personal power and especially how to go about using it to a person who uses appropriate levels of energy—or force, as it is known in physics—to get what they think they want and need all the way to the extreme end of the spectrum: someone overly aggressive to the point where they can do damage and create pushback from their victims, their enemies, and other forces, some of whom may be more powerful than themselves.

Mars in the First House is like having a fast vehicle, a powerful tool, or a weapon—each of these symbols being associated with Mars and Aries. Failure to use them wisely and carefully usually leads to regretful outcomes.

As it is with the Sun, the Moon, and all the planets, what sign Mars was in when a person with Mars in the First House was born strongly colors how they project themselves into reality. Mars is always about aggression in some way—using your energy to change the world or your world. Mars in a chart, and especially in the First House, is the energy that overcomes inertia, gets things moving, and drives us onward no matter what stands in our way.

NOTE: *Though there is a strong connection between the "me first" feeling of the First House of an astrology chart and Mars, and though Mars is the traditional* *ruler of the First House of the archetypal astrology chart, the following delineation of Mars through the signs of the zodiac is not limited to Mars being in the First House of an astrology chart.*

The meanings ahead are what Mars in a particular sign basically means no matter what house of an astrology chart Mars is in. If you want to know what that means in the First House, just imagine Mars in that sign as someone who will be inclined or challenged to deal with being or becoming a warrior, a pioneer, or a unique individual in some way that is aligned with that Mars/sign meaning. Someone with Mars in the First House is very aware of an energy inside them that wants to make an impact—usually, in a lot more than one way.

NOTE: *Refresher on using keywords: At this point in your learning process, I want to remind you about what I consider the most important part of my technique for reading an astrology chart—the linking of keywords as a jumping-off point for you to think about a particular astrological lineup of planet, sign, and house. To familiarize you with the process, I will include an example of this method for each sign position of Mars using one of that planet's most important keywords: driven, as in the case of someone strongly motivated and focused on doing what it takes to accomplish a goal, and a keyword for the sign in which I am delineating the meaning of Mars. As this book progresses, I intend to teach you to synthesize the keywords for planet, sign, and house so you have the skill set that enables you to read a chart without having to look up their various meanings. It may sound impossible now, but that is my challenge, and my personal cosmic blueprint loves a challenge!*

MARS THROUGH THE SIGNS

Mars in Aries (Ruler): Valor ♂ ♈

Driven to be brave

People with Mars in its rulership sign of Aries have an independent nature, a vital mentality, and such self-confidence that they never want to let anyone down—especially themselves. They are brave and others think them fearless, though they are the epitome of the phrase "The only thing we have to fear is fear itself." They are so courageous that fear almost never enters their consciousness, but when it does, it can set off a spiraling feedback loop of fear that can manifest as a panic attack.

Their tendency is to invent, originate, and create. In all things, having the placement of Mars in Aries strongly inclines the person to be the leader rather than the led. They must be careful to control their temper, for once they let it get the upper hand, it can lead them into unpleasantness or worse. Their keen intelligence and ability to size up a situation at once can usually prevent displays of aggression, but only if they believe in their heart that nondefensive violence is the last resort of the incompetent.

Routine or repetition is boring to those with Mars in Aries, and any job that hinders or does not need their initiative or creative ability stifles them and their ambition to finish the job. Aries is a Cardinal Fire sign. They are goal oriented and want action and speed, even if it means plenty of hard work. Expending great effort stimulates in them the production of even more energy. Their courage is equal to any situation. This endows them with a temperament that

thrives on excitement and finds golden opportunity in difficulties that stump other people. They will rarely back down or retreat.

Mars in Taurus: Fortitude ♂ ♉

Driven to persevere

People with Mars in Taurus will be challenged to explore what is truly worthwhile in life. They will often spend a lot of their time building or acquiring things that are tangible and valuable and will vigorously defend against any threat to what they hold dear.

They have a surprising desire and capacity for learning. For them, education is not a mere formality or part of their childhood but a valuable commodity, an enduring process that is constantly illuminating their mind and broadening their outlook in tangible, beneficial ways. Because of this, they have a surprisingly independent mode of thinking that revolts against dictatorial rules that require them to think and act conventionally. Taurus is the Fixed Earth sign, and the placement of Mars therein makes a person practical, realistic, and determined to the point of stubbornly not giving up even if they should. Only when they believe that their efforts have caused or will cause them to lose something valuable will they consider changing course.

There is in their makeup a commitment to taking things slow but steady that causes them to weigh situations and problems before they delve into their solutions. This is particularly true in anything connected to money and the other material things in life. If they could, they would like to have everything be on a cash basis so as to avoid problems with borrowing, lending, and credit. Their association with other people is based on highly ethical ideas, and they want to be known as a reliable person. Disorder and carelessness annoy them because in their heart of hearts, they are systematic, deliberate, and conservative.

Mars in Gemini: Influence ♂ ♊

Driven to communicate

People with Mars in Gemini, the Mutable Air sign, are often unusually versatile, intelligent, and quick to assimilate information. Their minds are always switched on. They have a genius for imparting information. There seem to be endless wells of knowledge and skills within them, which they can call on when occasion requires. This is just how they are, and in the ordinary course of events, they are hardly aware of how different they are from other people. Their scintillating wit and clever repartee give them an audience of admiring friends. Gemini is a Mutable Air sign, and the placement of Mars therein gives a person an ever-changing list of interests, ideas, and even visions about the future.

Mars in Gemini people need to always be using their energies to have influence on at least two projects. Those who work with them have to know that this is a case not of divided loyalty but of having so many skills that two projects are necessary to use them all. That being said, they should be careful not to scatter or overly dissipate the talents with which they have been endowed by this placement, even if their quick mind and often irrational fear of boredom tempts them to do so. Rather, they should do their best to employ their brilliance toward a worthy purpose or two, and then they can achieve their ambitions.

The arts—visual arts, literature, film, drama, and music—appeal to them, and if they can stay focused and not give up on their dreams, they can be successful in these endeavors. Mars generates dynamic power, and when it is in Gemini, those who have this placement often fight for the opportunity to use this power to influence and communicate, but the effort must be sustained over time to realize all the gains that are possible.

Mars in Cancer: Naturalness ♂ ♋

Driven to nurture

People with Mars in Cancer are mentally sensitive to the effect their actions might have on those they care about. This does not slow them down, however. Cancer is a goal-oriented Cardinal Water sign, and so their caring produces rapidity of thought and action guided by the sixth sense we all have: intuition, long considered to be a property of all three Water signs—Cancer, Scorpio, and Pisces. This blend of logical and intuitive mental processes of those with Mars in Cancer are of such swiftness as to sometimes startle even themselves.

This ability extends to other areas. Whereas others pause and ponder the queries of life, they respond immediately to the queries by simply living it. They form the same quick response to the vibrations of color and should be careful about the colors with which they surround themselves, including the colors they wear. Labor-saving devices and gadgets have an appeal to them, and they are always seeking to improve their home life with them.

Outside interference and pressure irritate rather than stimulate them. They like to work around the house and prefer to work out of their home, which they will defend against any threats, real or imagined. A vivid imagination makes it possible for them to enjoy the world outside their world of home and family through tech-enabled vicarious experience when they are not available in reality. However, they should not dwell too much in the realms of fantasy. As harsh as it can be sometimes, they must not neglect their work in the world.

Mars in Leo: Direction ♂ ♌

Driven to show the way

People with Mars in Leo instinctively understand the pageantry of daily life. They can see the extraordinary in the ordinary. They are usually not content to be a mere spectator but need to be seen as an actor and maybe even a director on this stage, putting on a play for everyone else, whether that is their audience or their constituency. A fine sense of discernment enables them to choose their audience in social situations so they are appreciated and not disrespected, wounded pride being one of the few things that can make them lose their cool.

They are courageous, and for the sake of obtaining justice and defending the honor of those they care about, they will do what they have to do. Mars in Leo likes to have fun, and when things are dull, their acting ability and charm are brought into play to enliven them.

Their friends surround them in admiration for their ability to speak in public when they have to. Their innate leadership skills and intellectual scope inspire them. A finely tuned diplomatic ability can allow them to get their own way without appearing to dominate the scene too much, though this is a skill that has to be watched and managed throughout their lives lest they become rigid and controlling. Their aspirations are high, and their fertile mind and vivid imagination are there to help them attain their goals with lasting results, as befits Leo, the Fixed Fire sign. Details are irksome to them, but they must not avoid taking care of the important minutiae because they stubbornly want to just relax and enjoy life.

Mars in Virgo: Capacity ♂ ♍

Driven to do it correctly

People with Mars in Virgo have a tremendous capacity for work requiring great concentration, especially on the small details that can make something that is good enough truly great. Their ability to shut out distractions makes others marvel at what seems to be a veritable dynamo generating power within them.

They are resourceful, inventive, and competent. These traits enable them to overcome mountains of obstacles and successfully attend to a plethora of details. Since they are decisive, alert, practical, and factual, their sense of timing and timeliness leads to the economic expenditure of effort and a highly impressive efficiency. They are experts at critical-path analysis and the mapping out of the order in which a complex project's component parts must be organized.

They are aware of the responsibility of power and position, and for this reason they are usually considerate of those who work with and for them as well as those they serve. Restraint and modesty qualify all they do. People are drawn to them because of these valuable assets and to their prodigious skill set. However, they must not allow their fastidious taste to impose itself too much on their actions. Mars in Virgo, the Mutable Earth sign, is driven to analyze, to digest, and to criticize in a constructive fashion. If criticism is used as a defensive shield or a weapon, if analyzing what is and what might be becomes attached to a particular outcome and becomes endless worry, or if their dexterous use of their skills brings them anxiety because it is not perfect, the gift of having Mars in Virgo will be squandered.

Mars in Libra: Generosity ♂ ♎

Driven to form relationships

People with Mars in Libra love love and romance. They are inclined to seek fairness, justice, and harmony in partnerships, business dealings, or civic life. Libra is the opposite sign of Aries, and there's more than a bit of the Arian ability to stand up for oneself in those with this placement. They are willing to fight for peace and the defense of the weak, being comfortable and proud to be exemplifying this seemingly counterintuitive pairing of planet and sign.

They are surprisingly sensitive and can easily put themselves in another's shoes to the point where they have to guard against becoming overly involved with other people's situations. They try hard to get their own way but value honor and integrity to the point where they use their goal-oriented Cardinal Air nature to avoid underhanded means, always staying true to being the embodiment of the idea of what used to be called righteousness.

They are fiercely independent and know how to take care of themselves and their partners. They usually have a balanced approach to life and a keen sense of judgment, though the balance scales of Libra can swing extremely if they feel misunderstood or disrespected. They are driven to acquire all things that delight the senses because they not only have a developed appreciation of the many forms of art and beauty but also need it to feel at peace. They know what is genuine and are comfortable in the role of critic or teacher. Discord, hate, and focusing too much on the ugly side of being a mortal, fallible, and often inelegant and messy human being can harm their nervous system. They need a harmonious home life and therefore need to be very careful with whom they choose to associate.

Mars in Scorpio: Efficiency ♂ ♏

Driven to extremes

People with Mars in Scorpio are quietly intense. Mars was the ruler of Scorpio prior to the rediscovery of Pluto in 1930. (Sumerian astrologers five thousand years ago knew about the celestial body they called Gaga.)

Mars in Scorpio are naturally suspicious and cautious because they are willing to go all the way in a fight, like the out-of-control raging bull that can be manifested by their opposite sign, Taurus. However, Mars in Scorpio people are smart enough to know how and when to hold themselves back and that violence is the last resort of the incompetent, and they are quite competent. No one can beat them in their ability to pierce the veil of lies and illusion, see clearly through the cloud of details, and hide their intentions from the ignorant, especially when they stop being defensive and settle down to focus on and solve a problem. Their aim in all things is to get at the truth of any matter, and they usually succeed in doing so. Superficiality bores them, but the study of the occult and the profound fascinates them because it can increase their ability to work their will and defend themselves from the will of other people.

Mars generates power, and in Scorpio, this force is expressed in the form of determination that in its extreme form can become the will to dominate. These are people who have to be aware of their desire for revenge as something to be managed, not encouraged. As the Fixed Water sign, once they have aligned their energies with their emotional intelligence and developed a passion for something, nothing will deter them from achieving their aims. There is usually something very sexy and alluring about these natives. Some may also give the impression that they are beyond caring, but this is only the protective covering they assume to win the struggle for existence.

Mars in Sagittarius: Gallantry ♂ ♐

Driven to learn

People with Mars in the Mutable Fire sign Sagittarius, known as the Sign of the Archer, always strive to have the highest of ideals and aspirations. The tawdry and seamy sides of life are almost physically repulsive to them, and they will do almost anything to avoid having to demean themselves. They much prefer to use their powers to raise everything and everyone with whom they come into contact to the high plane on which their thoughts exist. The noble spirit of equity qualifies their every action, so they do their best to be good losers and avoid being arrogant when they win, which is often.

Like their fellow Fire sign, Leo, those with Mars in Sagittarius have a highly developed sense of the dramatic. A keen mentality enables them to hold the spotlight when it is focused on them, enabling them to excel at social media and influencing others.

The driving force of Mars combined with the Sagittarian desire to seek to know and blurt out the truth even if it works against their own best interest is a fact of life that must always be well managed if those with this Mars placement are to attain their goals with the least number of problems. They must also avoid giving in to the temptation to exaggerate, whether it be brilliant experiences or worrisome details. People surround them with affection and admiration because they are adventurous, generous, and ingenious enough. No embellishment is needed.

Mars in Capricorn: Reason ♂ ♑

Driven to achieve

People with Mars in Capricorn have at their disposal an endless energy for achieving any ambition to which they set their intention. While everyone's Mars position propels them toward a goal, Mars in the Cardinal Earth sign of Capricorn excels at being able to energize both the actions and the planning of a long-term project to achieve a level of success that would be considered miraculous had it occurred naturally.

Mars in Capricorn people are willing to defend what they consider the basis for their authority. For this reason, they may find themselves defending people and organizations that do not merit their loyalty but from which the native derives power and income. They can be an able administrator, an efficient executive, or an intellectual leader, but once they are established, it takes work for them to keep up the drive to continue moving onward and upward and risk in any way what they have already achieved. Patience and loyalty prevent them from shirking responsibilities, and tenacity enables them to turn failure into success—unless that success rocks the boat too much.

External appearances can neither fool them nor discourage them. They understand life too well and know how to play the game. They are energetic and willing to work hard for the things they want. They must be aware of their tendency to burn the candle at both ends in order to achieve their ambitions. They need to remember that occasional vacations or other preferred relaxations will renew the forces that they so willingly expend.

Mars in Aquarius: Skill ♂ ♒

Driven to innovate

People with Mars in the Fixed Air sign of Aquarius are usually ultramodern in their outlook and may be said to be ahead of their time. Once an enthusiasm grips them, they expend a mountain of strength in the cause to which they have pledged their allegiance. They usually have a large number of friends, and they come from every walk of life. They can attain recognition for their achievements because they are not shy about stating the often-radical changes they want to make. Therefore, many people know about their quest and eventually are forced to recognize and bestow honor and glory on the Mars in Aquarius native as a way of making up for the stiff resistance they initially put up to their long-term efforts to actualize these profound changes.

Where others must struggle and study for years to attain the skills people with Mars in Aquarius possess, they learn by ear, and acquire knowledge, information, and skills from reverse-engineering whatever they turn their attention to, whether that is how to build or fix something or how to learn an instrument or an app. Following directions is not their strong suit, though they can give directions that are easy to understand. Form, custom, and crystallized convention do not jibe with their spirit of independence. Their slogan is "Let freedom ring," even if it disrupts the status quo.

They must be careful about being taken in by clever schemes or specious trickery, because their dislike for details may lead them into a trap. Like those with Mars in fellow Air sign Libra, those with Mars in Aquarius are protectors of the weak and needy, although they will champion any just cause.

Mars in Pisces: Aptitude ♂ ♓

Driven to connect

People with Mars in the Mutable Water sign of Pisces are motivated to change the world one person at a time by establishing some kind of connection with them, usually on the emotional level. This genuine caring can be done in person or remotely, through volunteer work or philanthropy, through the usual channels for communications or through metaphysical connections like ESP or psychic mediumship.

Pisces, the sign of compassion and the utopian ideal, is obviously a difficult placement for Mars, named after the god of war, and the planet that supplies the energy for us to get what our Sun, our ego, and our purpose want us to have. Mars in Pisces, however, like fellow Water sign Cancer, cares about others, but where Mars in Cancer is family oriented, Mars in Pisces is oriented to what used to be called "the family of man" (an outmoded, sexist way of referring to humanity).

Mars in Pisces can have their already sensitively tuned energy diverted by the needs of a person who is upset or down on their luck. The vicissitudes of life can overwhelm this Mars placement and cause them to manifest escapist tendencies and even addiction as means for fighting against overwhelm. Fortunately, their sincerity and honesty make them want only the best things in life for everyone, but they have to remember to take care of themselves too. Though Pisces is a Mutable Water sign, when Mars is there in a mature person, others find that no argument sways this person's beliefs, because they have an instinctive ability to reach conclusions beyond the realm of reason. They allow experience to teach them many heartfelt lessons, and they apply these.

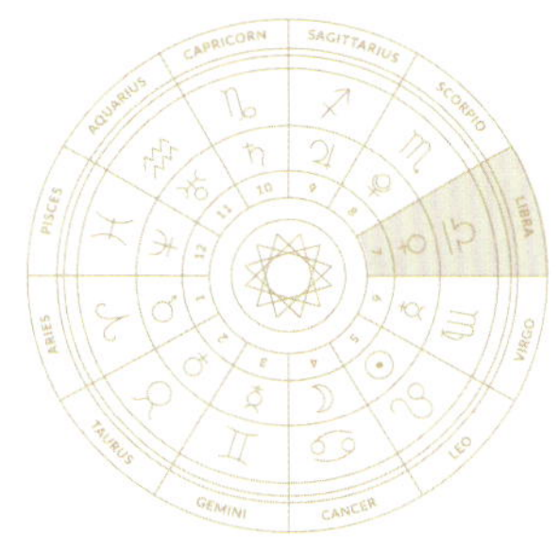

THE SEVENTH HOUSE

RECAP: *Before we move on to the meaning of the Seventh House, I will recap several crucial pieces of information because if you do not understand these things, you will not understand the Seventh House.*

The center point of your cosmic blueprint represents the place where you were being born.

- The horizontal line cutting your cosmic blueprint into upper (the sky) and lower (the Earth) halves represents the surface of the Earth and the horizon.
- The furthest point on the horizonal line's left side represents the direction east, where the Sun and the other planets rise from below the Earth into the sky.
- The degree of the zodiac sign that is rising at the moment you are born is the degree of your Rising Sign, also known as your Ascendant, the sign of the zodiac that indicates how you appear to others, whether you want to appear that way or not.
- The First House of an astrology chart is the slice below your Rising Sign's degree, the horizon's east point at the moment of your birth, and is all about *you* and what you want to project into the world.

If you are comfortable with all that information, I am doing my job—and so are you. It is now my pleasure to introduce you to the Seventh House of an astrology chart. You can see that it is exactly opposite to the First House, and so it is the slice of the pizza that is *above* the horizonal line of an astrology chart on the right side of the chart: the western side, the place where the planets set.

Logically—or should I say astro-logically—since the First House is all about *you*, the house that is opposite the First House is about *others*, especially *your partners*. One of the most important meanings of the Seventh House is *committed partners*, as in contracts, business partnerships, and marriages—legal or otherwise. If you move in together, welcome to the Seventh House.

The Seventh House is also the house of business agreements and partnerships that are contracted or based on mutual trust, including verbal agreements and handshake deals. It is the house to look at for all areas of life where you come before the public in some kind of organized fashion, such as social media, publicity, marketing, and public relations. Your social media friends and followers have committed to you enough to satisfy that Seventh House requirement.

The Seventh House rules committed relationships of a romantic and business nature—not necessarily marriage, but definitely not one- night stands, casual relationships, or fleeting romances. The Seventh House is the house of divinely blessed soulmates or, at the very least, relationships that last a long time. These relationships often involve oral and written contractually binding agreements between people that obligate them to perform specific duties on specific dates and times.

As anyone who has ever had anything to do with the court system will understand, the Seventh House is the house of crafted rules and laws. Court cases, lawsuits, and negotiations are all Seventh House matters. Contracts and business partnerships are often made public, and a marriage is a public declaration of love and lifelong partnership. For this reason, the Seventh House rules coming before the public and publicity. Parties and all social engagements of a formal nature that you attend are ruled by this house.

The symbolism of the First House, the astrological house for *you*—opposite the house symbolizing *others*—is not to teach us that it is us against the world. Rather, it reminds us that interacting with others and the world in a balanced way helps us make our cosmic blueprint and, more importantly, our life work to our benefit. We do not benefit if we lose ourselves in a partnership. Conversely, we cannot be good partners if we are overly concerned with ourselves and our own interests.

Not everyone is ready, willing, or able to live their life in a way that benefits anyone other than themselves. These people can usually be revealed by their cosmic blueprints so you can help them work on themselves, if they want to be good partners, or to accept themselves as they are if they prefer not to be in partnership.

We astrologers need to have the skills to identify and deal with these self-involved people. Understanding our Seventh House helps us understand how we relate to others. In this way, astrology justifies and reinforces our natural caution and self-protective mechanisms of thought and action.

A BRIEF LOOK AT PLANETS IN THE SEVENTH HOUSE

The Sun ☉

You are very partnership oriented. You may have had few periods in your life where you did not have a very close friend or partner. You may have always needed a person close to you to help you accomplish your goals and to become aware of who you really are. You may fear loneliness.

The Moon ☽

Your desire and ability to become aware of and consider the feelings of those you have as partners is going to strongly influence your whole life. You get feelings about people and go by them. You may have a lifelong friend or marry someone described by your Moon sign.

Mercury ☿

You are attracted to people who are intelligent, communicative, quick-witted, and able to keep you informed on just about everything. Your mind is stimulated by working, conversing, or even arguing with others. You prefer broad-minded, young, or young-at-heart people.

Venus (Ruler) ♀

You are in love with love and lovely people, and tend to fall in love easily, so it is important that you learn all you can about potential partners before committing. You may work in a field related to beauty, fashion, or making the world a more beautiful place. You are a peacemaker, a lover, and not a fighter.

Mars ♂

You're a fighter and need to learn how to compromise. If you do not get in touch with and actualize your ability to stand up for yourself, you will either always find yourself at odds with other people or attract a partner who is a no-compromise type of person.

Jupiter ♃

You will be drawn to close partnerships with positive, jovial people or those who benefit you in some way, materially supporting you or otherwise helping you grow into the person you want to be. These people are usually older or more established and successful. Your partners must be very open-minded.

Saturn ♄

Your attitude toward the responsibilities of partnership weighs heavily on you. Fear of not being able to measure up may make you avoid them as much as possible. You may delay close relationships until you are older or partner up with an older person who can teach you about life or any skill or subject that interests you.

Uranus ♅

You want to be free at all times. Any partnership must be with those willing to put up with that. Marriage might impinge too much on your freedom. You and your partner might thrive living in separate houses or in some other unique arrangement. You are probably attracted to unusual people, eccentrics, or geniuses.

Neptune ♆

The ideal of partnership inspires you. Unless you meet a truly spiritual partner, you may find what you thought you saw in someone turns out to have been you deceiving yourself or being deceived. Do not expect to save anyone or anyone to save you. You cannot change anyone. Be aware of escapist or addictive behavior in your partner.

Pluto ♇

You will continually encounter intense relationships with strong-willed and powerful people who may try to transform you or otherwise engage in power struggles with you, maybe because you want them to change. Your partnerships will define your life in some way. You may have the gift of helping others change.

IF YOU DO NOT HAVE A PLANET IN THE SEVENTH HOUSE OR ANY PARTICULAR HOUSE

Once again, it is my duty as your teacher and friend to remind you that not having a planet in a house of an astrology chart does not mean that you will not experience issues related to that house's meanings. As you can imagine, people without a planet in their Seventh House ask this question more than those without a planet in any other house. They often fear that without a planet there, they will not find the partner they are looking for. You must understand that this is not the case.

There is no absolute correlation between having or not having planets in the Seventh House and having a great relationship. For example, neither Amy nor I have a planet in the Seventh House, and those who have known us have given us the great gift of calling our relationship one of the legendary marriages and productive partnerships of their time. We have been together since 1975 and are more in love every day, wanting only for our blessed life together to continue for as long as possible. As astrologers, we know more about life than most people and especially that everything changes and nothing lasts forever, though that doesn't stop us from wanting our love to go on forever. See? No planets in the Seventh House, but lots of love!

The purpose of this book is to prepare you to read both your cosmic blueprint and that of other people. If you choose to read for others, you will soon find that the main reason people go to an astrologer is because of relationship issues. Therefore, as both your astrology teacher and the coauthor with my wife, Amy Zerner, of *The Soulmate Path*, I will briefly share with you the best advice I can give you on relationships, which you can also pass on to clients:

- Be yourself. You're good enough the way you are.
- You can't change anyone. It's hard enough to change yourself.

- Do not waste time with people who do not appreciate you the way you want them to. Also, do not waste time longing for people who were obviously not right for you and are no longer in your life. (You would be amazed at how many people come to a reader wanting to know whether someone who has left them will return.)
- The secret of having a great relationship is for both people to be committed to growing both as individuals and as a couple, because if you do not grow together, you grow apart.
- Put your relationship first, ahead of your family, friends, and even children. Children know instinctively that having caregivers who are an indivisible team provide the kind of secure home on which they can depend.

People with a planet or planets in their Seventh House are inclined to experience the energies of those planets through partnership. They need to know what their partner or trusted adviser thinks about something before coming to know what they themselves believe to be true about that matter. They need to bounce ideas off of their partner.

Not only do people with one or more planets in the Seventh House often need to bounce ideas and concepts associated with those planets off of a partner in order to get in touch with those planetary energies, but they are also drawn to partners who exemplify in some way the astrological meanings and association of the planets found there.

For example, someone with Neptune in the Seventh House would be very idealistic about partnership in general and would be drawn to a person who manifests one or more of the main characteristics of Neptune, the ruling planet of Pisces. Keeping my concept of the spectrum of meanings in mind, a person with Neptune in the Seventh House (in any zodiac sign) could be drawn to a kind, charitable, or otherwise inspirational person, a religious figure or a motivational speaker, a very sympathetic if occasionally overly idealistic or even slightly naive or confused person who often avoids the harsh realities of life, or, all the way on the other end of the spectrum, a person who escapes reality through lies or by succumbing to an addiction of some kind, whether that may be drugs, alcohol, sex, or anything that keeps them distracted from the harshness and disappointment that often accompanies our human experience.

NOTE: *You need to counsel anyone with one or more planets in their Seventh House, especially yourself, with the goal of making sure they know what having that planet(s) there means in terms of who they are attracted to and the quality of a relationship they can expect to encounter with someone who exemplifies the various traits associated with that planet(s) in that particular sign. This is one of the most important parts of being an astrologer, and my keyword technique will help you sort it out.*

VENUS, RULING PLANET OF THE SEVENTH HOUSE

In the archetypal chart used to teach astrology, just as Mars and the zodiac sign Aries rule the First House, Venus and Libra rule the Seventh House.

The symbol for Libra is the Scales, the only zodiac sign that is not a human, animal, or mythological human/animal hybrid (Sagittarius's Centaur). While animate beings have a defined life span and are capable of motion, the inhuman balance scale's purpose is to forever search for and sometimes reach equilibrium—balance—and indicate it by becoming motionless.

For this reason, Libra, the seventh sign of the zodiac and the Seventh House cusp that demarcates the western horizon and the place where Earth and sky meet, is associated with balance, harmony, midpoints, and all points of intersection. Think of how hard it is to identify the point where a sin wave crosses the horizontal line or where two or more lines cross on a graph. Yes, you can identify the point of intersection to a degree that is enough for most purposes, but you can also keep zeroing into the intersecting lines, refining the place of intersection again and again, never reaching a definitive single point. For this reason, Libra also has to do with attempts at conceptualizing infinity.

In ancient times, very large balance scales were used to weigh the harvested produce brought to market in the time of Libra (in the northern hemisphere). The harvest was weighed in satisfaction of the aptly named futures contracts made earlier in the year and done so in public to make sure it was weighed honestly and contracts were honored. These concepts have endured with Libra and the Seventh House through each of them being closely associated with understanding a person's connection to the business practices related to futures and contracts, especially the marriage contract, a public declaration of partnership.

The public aspect of the Seventh House and its association with others is why that house is also the house of public relations, publicity, marketing, and all things associated with the public.

Venus rules Libra and the Seventh House of an astrology chart. (You may have noticed that Venus also has a rulership relationship with the Second House and Taurus, which I will explain when we get to the Second House, the next house we will explore.)

The glyph for the planet Venus is commonly used as the symbol for female. It shows the circle of spirit on top of the cross of matter, symbolizing that with Venus spiritual values, truth, and beauty are more important than material concerns and practical considerations.

I will now delineate Venus through the twelve signs of the zodiac. It is more important that you know the general meanings of Venus through the signs at this point than to know what Venus in each house means. Once you know how to apply my keyword technique to the meanings of the planets in the signs and know the meanings and keywords from the twelve houses of an astrology chart, the basic meaning of the various planets in each of the twelve houses will become apparent to you. Your understanding will increase as I interpret and explain the meanings of each of the planets through the signs and the houses.

Let's now take my keyword technique to a new level, keyword manipulation, showing you how you too can playfully assemble the keywords associated with a planet in a sign—in this case, Venus. The keywords can be in any order that makes sense to you. The purpose of this technique is to trigger in you possible meanings you can adjust to your experience and that of your client, friend, or family member. At this point, if you have not done so already, you may want to get the birth chart of someone you care about and see whether you are able to deduce any information from it using your present understanding of astrology. Going back and rereading what we have already covered as you examine a chart is not only allowed but also strongly encouraged.

VENUS THROUGH THE SIGNS

Venus in Aries: Ardent ♀♈

You are impetuous and always in search of new romantic experiences. Love is only one area of life where you need a constant supply of new thrills. Anyone who wants to be your committed partner has to excite you, never show fear or hesitation, and reinvent themselves in ways either big or small to hold your interest. Though you are sincere as long as your ardor lasts, your enthusiasm often peters out when the battle is won and conquest is attained or the novelty of the romantic interlude wears off. You might be far more attractive to more people if you add a bit of mystery to your conduct instead of simply going full steam ahead, which is attractive to some but certainly not most people. You do well on your own, so anyone interested in you has to be either very attractive or very persistent. Your love of honesty means that anyone who lies, especially to you, is out. You do not give second chances.

KEYWORD MANIPULATION FOR VENUS IN ARIES: Add some of Venus's keywords, like *love, attract, enjoy, beautify, tame, money, improve,* and *"can ignore harsh reality,"* to Aries's keywords: *initiation, challenge, willpower, childlike, adventure, exploration, daring, courage, honesty, competition, innocence, action, aggression, energy, spontaneity, discovery, creativity, "quick to anger"*

SAMPLE PHRASING OF KEYWORD STORIES FOR VENUS IN ARIES: "taming of aggression," "enjoyment of willpower," "spontaneous attraction," "love of courage and honesty," "courageous love," "beautiful energy," "the aggressive energy necessary to make money and make things better," "ignoring a harsh reality provokes anger and aggression"

Venus in Taurus (Ruler): Faithful ♀♉

You are a natural at anything involving beauty, the arts, or matters related to one's money or value system. You are loyal and faithful until death. You may forgive transgressions by your partner others would never put up with. However, though very generous in your own way, you can sometimes seem so focused on plowing through with the matters at hand that you appear to take your loved ones for granted, as if they are set in the place where you want them to be and you do not have to be overly concerned about pleasing them other than by fulfilling the plan. Extending your generosity through material gifts, compliments, or tender words perfects your relationships. Think of the way Venus is portrayed in mythology. Your somewhat chaste and precise behavior leaves the ardor of other signs a bit unrequited. Vary your actions and vocabulary a bit to liven up the formal attitude endowed by Venus, Taurus's ruler.

KEYWORD MANIPULATION FOR VENUS IN TAURUS: Add some of Venus's keywords, like *love, attract, enjoy, beautify, tame, money, harmony, improve,* and *"can ignore harsh reality,"* to Taurus's keywords: *strong, unstoppable, faithful, "slow but steady," values, money, "sticks to the plan," control, security, tenacity, music, beauty, supplies, kindness, calmness, sensuality, organization, nature, construction, luxury, leisure*

SAMPLE PHRASING OF KEYWORD STORIES FOR VENUS IN TAURUS: "faithful love," "loves doing things slowly but steadily," "ignores harsh reality in favor of the beautiful," "loves the finer things in life," "may love money," "loves luxury and leisure," "feels beautiful and in harmony when in control and sticking to the plan"

Venus in Gemini: Gracious ♀ ♊

To you, love is a puzzle or a game in which the elements of uncertainty keep you coming back for more. You long to capture the prize that eludes your grasp, but focusing on one prize or one person does not come naturally to you. You are gracious but somewhat unreliable. You could waste your time focusing on trivialities. When you treat serious things lightly, and do not hold up your end of a partnership, you can be jolted out of your complacency and failure to do what requires hard work. Do not forget that you are mortal, or you may not become aware of a potential love destiny until too late. Inconstancy and a tendency to flirt may cause you to lose face with one you seriously desire. Use your rational mind to overcome your tendency toward dual love affairs. Once you have decided to be faithful to someone you love, admire, and respect, you can not only be happy but also be yourself fully.

KEYWORD MANIPULATION FOR VENUS IN GEMINI: Add some of Venus's keywords, like *love, attract, enjoy, beautify, tame, money, harmony, improve,* and *"can ignore harsh reality,"* to Gemini's keywords: *versatile, flexible, communicative, superficial, gossip, knowledgeable, noncommittal, changeable*

SAMPLE PHRASING OF KEYWORD STORIES FOR VENUS IN GEMINI: "noncommittal about love," "versatile attraction (can use numerous techniques to make one's self attractive)," "communicative about improvements," "superficial to ignore harsh realities"

Venus in Cancer: Peaceful ♀ ♋

Your love plans are almost exclusively bound up with who and what you define as your family. The gathering of the clan is your idea of a good time, and a picnic involving children, elders, cousins, nieces, and nephews is a gala occasion.

Though normally of a peaceful disposition, you will fight fiercely to protect those you care about. You may have secret attractions to others who have no idea of your feelings toward them. Your period of wild oat sowing will be quite a memory in your old age. You have an innate desire to raise a family, but that family does not necessarily have to be the traditional kind. It's family as you define it. If you want children, you have to make sure you do not waste your time with someone who does not share that desire or whose attitude to rearing children opposes yours or, especially, a person who is not going to be able to live up to your high standards of parenting.

KEYWORD MANIPULATION FOR VENUS IN CANCER: Add some of Venus's keywords, like *love, attract, enjoy, beautify, tame, money, harmony, improve*, and *"can ignore harsh reality,"* to Cancer's keywords: *nurture, mother, smother, sensitive, caring, intuitive, "family oriented," "the past," ancestors, shy, reclusive*

SAMPLE PHRASING OF KEYWORD STORIES FOR VENUS IN CANCER: "nurture love," "sensitive regarding the past or harsh reality," "cares about mother and motherhood," "loves sensitivity in a partner," homebody, "shy about money"

Venus in Leo: Dramatic ♀ ♌

You like to show others how things need to be done. Unless you make constructive use of your talent, you develop a tendency to show off. You cannot help putting on an act of some kind but are genuinely affectionate when love comes to you. You are in love with love. A date without some drama, be it last-minute timing, discussions about dress codes and how to act, or the perfect location, would be as inspiring as a salad without dressing. You will do most anything for your beloved as long as your ardent feelings and affection are reciprocated. When your partner's admiration for you wanes, you lose interest. You may be overlooking a chance to build up a real love affair. Volunteer, join an organization, get around more, perform. Romance is an essential part of your life, and you will always go out of your way to attract it. You and anyone wanting to be your partner must learn how difficult faithfulness is for you.

KEYWORD MANIPULATION FOR VENUS IN LEO: Add some of Venus's keywords, like *love, attract, enjoy, beautify, tame, money, harmony, improve*, and *"can ignore harsh reality,"* to Leo's keywords: *dramatic, "show business," showy, demonstrative, lead, pride, self-confident, self-important, affection*

SAMPLE PHRASING OF KEYWORD STORIES FOR VENUS IN LEO: "dramatic love and affection," "enjoys taking the lead," "prideful about money," "can ignore harsh reality by acting self-important"

Venus in Virgo: Discrimination ♀ ♍

You are a perfectionist, and picky about partners because of your skill at analyzing to the point of criticizing just about anyone and anything. You seldom fall head over heels in love, but when you do find someone to love, you go all in, though your romance must progress according to the rules you define. You are attracted to intellectuals whose knowledge, wisdom, and ability to express themselves can stir your admiration. You keep your affections on a mental level, and you analyze them as explicitly as you would an item in a report or term paper. Your nature needs a partner who can stand the strain of theoretical research into the realm of romance. Your oversensitivity to delays and disappointments can keep you from settling down in your love life. Be careful that your keen insight may be considered to be a destructive element by someone who gets tired of being examined. Let your quiet nature and real sympathy, not criticism, speak for you.

KEYWORD MANIPULATION FOR VENUS IN VIRGO: Add some of Venus's keywords, like *love, attract, enjoy, beautify, tame, money, harmony, improve,* and *"can ignore harsh reality,"* to Virgo's keywords: *analytical, worry, skilled, "detail oriented," picky, discriminating, shy, self-effacing*

SAMPLE PHRASING OF KEYWORD STORIES FOR VENUS IN VIRGO: "loves to analyze or worry or be critical, etc.," "skilled with money," "focuses on details to avoid harsh reality," "picky about the partner" (Ruler)

Venus in Libra (Ruler): Appreciation ♀ ♎

You might prefer to be wedded to your art or your work rather than fully commit to a mate because your brand of perfectionism, your love of harmony and beauty, makes you seek companions who can always remain good-natured and attractive, unmarred by the realities of life and especially of the lives you both have chosen. It is this attitude that can cause you to sometimes seem so casual, borderline unemotional, or surprisingly offhand toward your partner. Such apparent lack of enthusiasm could eventually be taken for a lack of affection and cause you to be rejected. You do love fiercely in your way, so be aware of this tendency in yourself and work to prevent it. Remember that the Scales of Libra are very rarely in balance. It is in the act of seeking harmony and love that both are created. In relationships, it is often a better strategy to tactfully seek a compromise and not blind justice handed down from on high by you.

KEYWORD MANIPULATION FOR VENUS IN LIBRA: Add some of Venus's keywords, like *love, attract, enjoy, beautify, tame, money, harmony, improve,* and *"can ignore harsh reality,"* to Libra's keywords: *"seeking beauty," balance, harmony, partnership, public, "rules and laws," infinity, inhuman*

SAMPLE PHRASING OF KEYWORD STORIES FOR VENUS IN LIBRA: "attracts or makes a beautiful partner," "loves to balance and beautify," "public displays of affection," "uses rules and laws to ignore harsh reality ('It pains me to have to do/say this, but it's the rules . . .')"

Venus in Scorpio: Passion ♀ ♏

You center your devotion on one person at a time and stick to this romance through good times and bad as long as you can remain dominant. At times, you are a moody tornado of temperament, so much so that it is difficult for both of you to avoid selfishness and the tendency to be tyrannical. When you can treat your partner as an equal rather than as a lovely necessary object, you are assured the most profound affections and loyalty. Your inner rage and suspicion, however, can cause you to exaggerate minor faults. Let your heart overrule your suspicions and temper; the easiest way to do this is by being generous. Since you love the lavish and luxurious, you can glamorize your love relationship by sharing this sensuous way to live. If you are as ardent in your display of affection as you can be in your love of sex, secrets, and the occasional emotional outburst, you may achieve balance leading to true happiness.

KEYWORD MANIPULATION FOR VENUS IN SCORPIO: Add some of Venus's keywords, like *love, attract, enjoy, beautify, tame, money, harmony, improve,* and *"can ignore harsh reality,"* to Scorpio's keywords: *passionate, intense, secretive, extreme, controlling, sexual, "black or white—no gray," "beyond words," power, mystical*

SAMPLE PHRASING OF KEYWORD STORIES FOR VENUS IN SCORPIO: "loves intense sex," "can tame a controlling partner," "extremely attractive or attracted to mystical people," "extreme passions," "does not seek harmony"

Venus in Sagittarius: Zeal ♀ ♐

Your tastes in romance are dictated by your fervor for spiritual matters, or your devotion to sports, nature, and animals. Nevertheless, you are a good partner, though you can often be fickle in bestowing your affection. Though you are quite ardent, and you mean every word you say in your declaration of love at the time you say it, you do often find it almost impossible not to change your mind when you find someone more alluring. At heart, you are a hunter who enjoys the thrill of pursuit. Though your intentions are loyal and generous because you prefer not to be unjust, you cannot help being attracted to wise, interesting, and attractive people—and not only saying so but also acting on your new truth. Only a very versatile, exceptional, and tolerant person could make a permanent partner for you, for the various facets of that person's being would satisfy the infinite variety you crave.

KEYWORD MANIPULATION FOR VENUS IN SAGITTARIUS: Add some of Venus's keywords, like *love, attract, enjoy, beautify, tame, money, harmony, improve,* and *"can ignore harsh reality,"* to Sagittarius's keywords: *"truth teller," philosopher, blunt, "foreign travel," "the best the world has to offer," "nature lover"*

SAMPLE PHRASING OF KEYWORD STORIES FOR VENUS IN SAGITTARIUS: "love of travel, foreign things, and possibly a person who is foreign to them in some way," "enjoys being a blunt truth teller," "attracts by being a philosopher"

Venus in Capricorn: Usefulness ♀ ♑

You consider marriage important on many levels and are conscientious in your duties to your family. Be aware of a tendency to expect marriage to be a springboard to material success, using it mainly as an incentive to strive for wealth and a high position in your community. You contribute as much to romance as you get from it, but as a rule, you do not become excited emotionally. A comfortable home and steady income are of more significance in your estimate of love than a happy yet impoverished marriage. If poverty befell you and your partner, love might become impossible. Nevertheless, you are so economical that you are quite capable of holding on to money as well as love. Your saving grace is your high sense of honor. Although ambition is strong in you, you would strongly resist furthering it by any unethical act. To attain your heart's desire, you choose diplomacy. Do not ignore your serious need for emotional closeness and sexual release.

KEYWORD MANIPULATION FOR VENUS IN CAPRICORN: Add some of Venus's keywords, like *love, attract, enjoy, beautify, tame, money, harmony, improve,* and *"can ignore harsh reality,"* to Capricorn's keywords: serious, *"success oriented," traditional, conserve, ethical, traditional, humorous, businesslike*

SAMPLE PHRASING OF KEYWORD STORIES FOR VENUS IN CAPRICORN: "serious about love," "attracted to success," "loves a good sense of humor," "enjoys being businesslike and conserving what is worthwhile"

Venus in Aquarius: Faith ♀ ♒

Although you are an altruist and give more than is expected, you resent and usually overreact to the slightest perceived curtailment of your freedom. You assume that your partner is aware of the depth of your emotions without embellishing the relationship with pretty speeches. Friendship is an important part of your love relationship. That person has to be a brilliant, eccentric, rebellious, or, at the very least, a reliably exciting or interesting companion. The absence of what is thought to be the usual and customary aura of passionate or even sexual romance doesn't matter to you. You are faithful and earnest in your associations, and these qualities make you appreciated. The advantage of having fixed desires that, once attained, constantly satisfy gives stability to a sign known for instability and may lead to a surprisingly contented life—the kind of domestic life that, if widely adopted as the way to build a loving partnership, would result in a universal improvement felt by all.

KEYWORD MANIPULATION FOR VENUS IN AQUARIUS: Add some of Venus's keywords, like *love, attract, enjoy, beautify, tame, money, harmony, improve,* and *"can ignore harsh reality,"* to Aquarius's keywords: *unemotional, unusual, eccentric, disruptive, technological, futuristic, cerebral, scientific*

SAMPLE PHRASING OF KEYWORD STORIES FOR VENUS IN AQUARIUS: "love of the unusual," "unusual love," "enjoys eccentricity," "can ignore harsh reality by being unemotional," "tames the disruptive or enjoys it"

Venus in Pisces: Ecstasy ♀ ♓

Because you are a dreamer and self-effacing, you give all for love and expect little in return. Sometimes you are more impractically romantic than any other Venus placement. This leads to disappointment when someone you idealized fails to live up to your ideals or fantasy. An intrigue, secret alliance, or sensuous self-indulgence could tempt you from your path. When you are sustained by the right kind of marriage, every bit of nobility in your character rises to the surface for your success and inspiration. Your innate intuition and sympathy can usually prevent any serious rupture of a committed relationship. The fickle side of your nature might lead you into temptation to escape, but your compassionate nature and sense of truth and beauty, which have guided you for a lifetime, would not tolerate such playing around for long. Be guided by your inspirational love for the finest in life, and you will never descend in your tastes. Avoid intoxication in any form. You are high enough naturally.

KEYWORD MANIPULATION FOR VENUS IN PISCES: Add some of Venus's keywords, like *love, attract, enjoy, beautify, tame, money, harmony, improve,* and *"can ignore harsh reality,"* to Pisces's keywords: *compassionate, inspire, idealize, caring, self-sacrifice, philanthropical, utopian, intuitive, escape, overwhelm, intoxication*

SAMPLE PHRASING OF KEYWORD STORIES FOR VENUS IN PISCES: "escape into idealized love," "attracted to inspiring people," "enjoys philanthropy," "intoxication or self-sacrifice helps in ignoring harsh reality," "loves to escape"

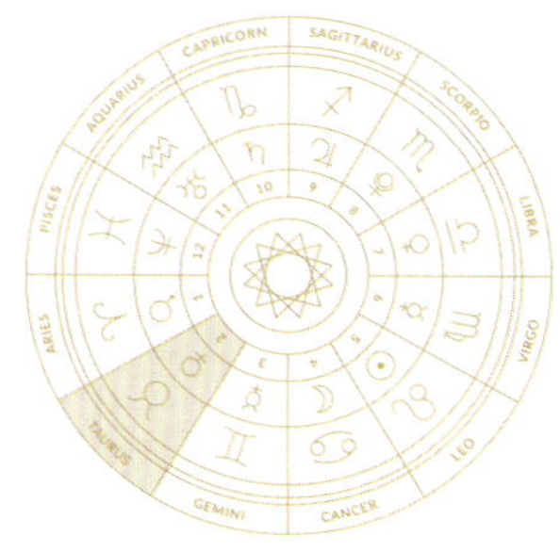

THE SECOND HOUSE

The Second House of an astrology chart is the slice directly below the First House (which is, itself, directly below the horizontal horizon line leading to the degree of your Rising Sign). The Second House derives its meaning from that of the First House.

While the First House is all about you and your vision of how you want to project yourself into physical reality, the Second House is all about your values—what you think is valuable in your life and in life in general. That can include your morals, what you believe that you need in order to do the best job projecting yourself into physical reality for your greatest good and highest joy, and the physical resources that you either have available to you or that you believe you need to have to do so. That makes the Second House the house of valuable, movable possessions of all kinds, and money too. (It is not about real estate, which is the Fourth House, but we will cover that soon.)

The Second House is related to your resources—everything available to you to help live your life the way you want to. As with all the houses, its meaning can be interpreted on the material, the mental, and the spiritual levels. This is why the Second House is about money and material possessions, but it is also about your mental attitude about your available resources and your ultimate value system—your spiritual interface with the reality of belonging to the world of matter as well as spirit.

What you consider valuable and precious will determine what you want, need, and pursue, and what you keep out of your life. Many people trying to walk a spiritual path think they have to avoid money and material possessions. However, it is greed—the *love* of money and the seduction of the material world—and the belief that what we own, including status, rank, titles, diplomas, and other human-created credentials, determines our value, that must be avoided.

Saying that the Second House is about these many things is my attempt to convey to you that everything and anything you can think of related to those Second House keywords are Second House matters. Having one or more planets in your Second House can give you insights into your value system, why you feel the way you do about possessions and money, and even how you go about getting and keeping things, along with concepts and suggestions that might help you improve your life in those areas.

They say money makes the world go around, but it is actually how we feel about money that can either enable us to acquire and use it or have problems in that area. We can either harness our personal power and value system to help magnetize us in such a way that we attract resources and helpful people and situations to us, or abuse or not even use our personal power and value system, a practice that will usually repel valuable people, situations, and material objects. Our strength of will is one of our most valuable resources.

I say the previous as someone who was homeless and broke in my teenage years. I know I am very fortunate that I was able to overcome the natural depression caused by being trapped in my situation, have someone willing to hire me, and literally work my way out of it. I also know that many people are unable to do so, either because of physical or mental limitations, illness, addictions, or a lack of people willing to give them a chance, all too often caused by the atrocity of racism and other prejudices that afflict humankind like some plague from the Dark Ages we are only now coming out of.

The people whose cosmic blueprints you read will most likely not be homeless and broke, though as I write that, I realize that volunteering to read for people who are down on their luck would be a great way to exercise my Pisces Moon. If I did so, I would see people with difficult astrological indications in their charts, and I would expect the majority of them would be Second House related. That being said, I am equally sure that the same difficult astrological indications could also be found in the chart of people who are materially successful. The stars incline, they do not compel.

This brings us to another seemingly odd aspect of reading a cosmic blueprint. The ruling planet of the Second House is Venus, which, as we saw in the previous chapter, is also the ruling planet of the Seventh House of committed partnerships and coming before the public! How can this be? While I never liked it when my parents said, "Because that's the way it is," when it comes to Venus ruling both the Second House and the Seventh House of an astrology chart, that's the way it is because that is the way it has always been. Ugh!

Here's another way I see it: The Seventh House is all about harmony, balance, committed partnerships—including loving partnerships—the beautification of the world, and the peace required for all these things to happen. All those things are easily understandable meanings of Venus.

There are, however, even more aspects of meanings that can apply to Venus. The Second House and Venus in our cosmic blueprint give insight into what we love and find attractive, what we attract, and how we attract it. Attraction is a very powerful force. As gravity, it holds the planets in their orbits around the Sun and it enables us to move on the surface of the Earth and not go flying off into space. Attraction and the keeping of what we attract are very important when we are talking about enjoying life and acquiring resources—especially luxury items and beautiful things.

So, all the meanings of Venus through the signs of the zodiac we delineated on page 150 for the Seventh House can work for the Second House too as long as we remember we are talking about values, beliefs, and physical resources, and not Venus as what and who we attract and how we experience partnerships. Our committed partners are, in a way, our possessions; we say that we give ourselves to our beloved in marriage.

A BRIEF LOOK AT PLANETS IN THE SECOND HOUSE

The Sun ☉

You are focused on having enough resources to be secure and to do what you want when you want to do it. You must beware of having your possessions own you and take you away from living your life. If you can avoid jealousy, you can live up to your highest values.

The Moon ☽

You possess emotions that are strongly influenced by what you have and what you lack. You need to have material things you consider valuable to feel secure and must avoid being too possessive of them and the people you care about. When you feel insecure, you get upset.

Mercury ☿

You think a lot about what you have and want, and that makes you good with money and possessions. You may earn your living in the financial sector through analysis, communications, information technology, writing, or another vocation that lets you explore and share what you find to be truly valuable.

Venus (Ruler) ♀

You love the finer things in life, and you may have a lot of them. It is important that you learn all you can about prospective partners before committing. You may work in a business related to art, beauty, fashion, or making the world more beautiful. You are a peacemaker, not a fighter.

Mars ♂

You're a fighter and need to avoid jealousy and learn the value of occasionally compromising. Get in touch with and actualize your ability to stand up for your values, or you will either always find yourself at odds with other people or attract a partner with issues around compromise.

Jupiter ♃

You may be materially well off or form close partnerships with people who benefit you in some way, teaching, sharing, or giving you the means to help you to grow into the person you want to be. You can be generous when you have enough.

Saturn ♄

The responsibilities of making a living and avoiding poverty and lack weigh heavily on you. Fear of not being good enough may make you work harder than most or not work at all. You may delay close relationships until you are older or partner with an older person who can support you.

Uranus ♅

You value freedom as if it were riches and are inclined to avoid or otherwise reject the responsibilities that possessions require. You are constantly reevaluating your attitude toward finances and often surprise others when you alternately display miserly and spendthrift ways.

Neptune ♆

You can use your intuition and ability to see the big picture in your pursuit of material success. You are charitable and possess compassion for the less fortunate. You must be careful not to be so willing to sacrifice your resources for their benefit that you end up needing charity yourself.

Pluto ♇

You may value having power to change things as if it were riches. You will go to extremes in order to ensure that you have the resources you need when you need them. Sharing does not come naturally to you. You must avoid being overly possessive of people, places, and things.

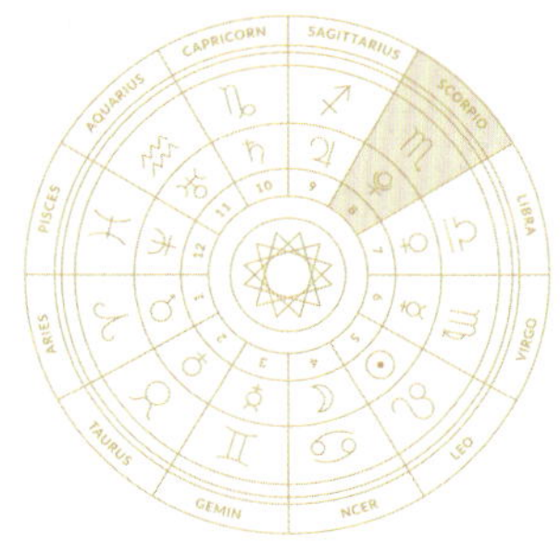

THE EIGHTH HOUSE

It is vitally important to me and my way of teaching you that you see the interconnectedness of astrological houses that are opposite each other. You have seen the star logic of the Seventh House of *others* being opposite to the First House of *you*. You should therefore not be surprised to know that the house opposite the Second House of *your resources* is the Eighth House, the house of *other people's resources*. As the Second House is associated with the resources and values that are totally under the control of the you symbolized by your First House, the Eighth House is associated with *resources and values that are under the control of you and the other(s)*.

If you have read about astrology charts before, you probably read that the Eighth House is the house of legacies and inheritances, and that having your Sun or Moon there inclines you to be able to handle, manage, and protect people's money, investments, and other resources. This can definitely be true but is merely a jumping-off point for us in our understanding of this house. You can inherit a lot more than money, property, and the other things commonly associated with legacies: You can inherit wisdom, ideas, inventions, health, and other genetically transferred traits, as well as guardianships of children, dependent adults, animals, and a host of other things too.

The Eighth House rules both the understanding of and the actual sharing, exchanging, and transmission of resources and other kinds of energy between you and others and between you and the universe. The ability to share, influence, and transform other people's lives through interaction with their resources connects the Eighth House with magic, power, and the mysteries of life, especially sex. It is the house of extremes like good/evil, man/woman, life/death, black/white, and yin/yang, to name a few.

Since no two people feel exactly the same way about virtually any subject, it becomes easy to understand why the Eighth House has come to be associated with the concept of *power*. When two or more people pool their resources, it's usually because they can achieve more with what they have together. But deciding exactly how to use resources that are held jointly immediately poses the question of who has the power to make the decision. Power struggles are not unknown to committees either. But the power gained by people pooling their resources is considerable and, in the long run, usually worth the adjustments or compromises necessary.

The Eighth House, because of its symbolic relationship with power struggles, is connected with the concept of change, and death can be seen as the biggest change possible on this material plane. Whether we succeed or fail in our attempt to use or change the use of other people's resources depends on our ability to use personal power to change a partner's thinking and behavior.

The Eighth House also has to do with extremes of power and transformations—both the good that enables needed change to occur without harm, and the bad, such as crime, obsessions, compulsions, and perversion. Sex, which can be a glorious sharing of love and pleasure between consciously awakened beings or a loveless, meaningless mutual masturbation—such a big part of most people's lives—is an Eighth House matter.

PRO TIP: *Before you judge another person for their unique expression of what sex means to them, it is a good idea to remember that the pioneering psychiatrist Sigmund Freud defined perverse sex as any sexual encounter that is not for the purpose of producing children.*

Sex is also connected with the concepts of the Eighth House for the obvious reason that by joining together as a couple, we can unleash the supreme power of life itself. We thus take part in life's power struggle with death, another Eighth House issue, because our sexual encounters can help ensure the continuation of the species.

The Hindu poets of the ancient tradition of tantric yoga, the spiritual practice of union with the godhead through the practice of specific sexual techniques, even refer to the orgasm as the little death.

Sex and death, two of the greatest mysteries studied by all races of the world, are symbolic of the Eighth House association with the concept of mysteries and investigation in general. Added to this is magic, as in "illusion," as well as magick, which can be described as the attempt to exert power over others for your good or for theirs. Therefore, the sign and planets associated with your Eighth House can provide powerful insights concerning your feelings about all the preceding subjects.

While the Eighth House is the house of other people's money, loans, money that you manage for other people, and inheritances, it also rules resurrection, rebirth, and transformation, including the ultimate transformation: death and the spirit. This association gives the Eighth House, the sign Scorpio, and the planet Pluto, which rules them, a powerful yet frightening or off-putting quality that an astrologer has to realize is an integral part of their meaning and function in our lives.

The meditation on our mortality, on our death, is seen as the highest meditation available to human beings because of its overwhelming power to stop us from focusing on extraneous nonsense and return to our understanding of what is really important for us to be doing with our limited time on Earth. We astrologers have a sacred duty to help ourselves and then others to remember what we are here for: The purpose of life is to be happy.

Admittedly, remembering the reality of our death and the limited existence of all we love is frightening, especially when you first try doing it purposefully. However, doing it as a spiritual practice keeps things in perspective and helps us appreciate the precious, fleeting gift of life in us and those we care about. This practice is especially important for helping those lucky enough to have never lost someone they love to understand those who have suffered a profound loss.

To recap, the Eighth House has to do with legacies and all that is related to it, such as inheritances, transfers, and wills. The sign on the cusp and the planets placed in the Eighth House can often indicate the nature of the native's interest in anything or everything ruled by the Eighth House. The Eighth House is ruled by (closely associated with) Scorpio and Pluto.

PLUTO, RULING PLANET OF THE EIGHTH HOUSE

Pluto is the ruling planet of the Eighth House and Scorpio. It was named for the ancient god of death and rebirth, the lord of the underworld, whose judgment about who went to Hades after they died was absolute.

Pluto's glyph symbol on your computerized astrology chart looks like a combination of Venus and Mercury, only the circle of the Spirit is completely detached from the crescent of the soul and the cross of matter, hovering above both to symbolize the unattainable and ultimate power of the Spirit associated with Pluto.

In our book, Amy's fabric collage tapestry for Pluto has been rendered as a combination of the letters *P* and *L*. PL works for PLuto and is also the initials of astronomer Percival Lowel, who predicted its discovery. It can also be viewed as the cross of matter deconstructed to be a horizontal and a vertical line, symbolizing Pluto's association with breakdown and decay. Completing the PL glyph is the crescent representing both the emotional and intellectual halves of our individualized soul that remains attached to the deconstructed cross, symbolizing the soul's transcendence over death.

You can see why astrologers were aghast when some astronomers tried to deplatform Pluto as a planet. We knew that it would emerge from this life-or-death power struggle as a planet again, like a phoenix rising from the ashes of its old body. Although it is the smallest planet in our solar system, in astrology, Pluto is very powerful. It is the planet of power, transformation, and resurrection.

Pluto symbolizes the part of us that wants to gain and use power of every kind. It is the planet of extremes, and so it rules our personal power to do good. It gives us the ability to never give up and never surrender regarding the house where it is positioned. However, it also rules power struggles, gangsters, dictators, and the terrible things that happen when people try to make themselves powerful at the expense of others. Pluto was rediscovered on February 18, 1930, a time that coincided with the rise of numerous dictators and other gangsters around the world.

Pluto is associated with the mysteries of life, magic, sex, and the ultimate transformation, death. It is also associated with resurrection, whether that may be renovating a home, getting cosmetic surgery, or bringing back into your life something you thought was long gone. It represents the unconscious mind, invisible yet powerful enough to produce compulsions and obsessions seemingly beyond our control. Like Pluto, their purpose is to help us become aware of what needs to be eliminated from our life and to help us do so.

Speaking of eliminations, it is worth noting that Pluto and Scorpio represent our body's ability to eliminate waste materials through the same body parts that can produce life, clear proof of Pluto's extreme nature, just as Scorpios are legendary for taking an extreme view of anything and everything under examination. There is actually another symbolic representation of Scorpio besides the Scorpion: It is the Eagle and the Snake, symbolizing the bird that flies the highest and the reptile that is in constant contact with Earth.

Astrologers have noted that Pluto returns (the time when a planet returns to where it was on the day a person, corporation, or nation was born) usually coincide with an empire's fundamental transformation. Rome's first Pluto return saw it become a republic and its second one saw the emergence of Augustus, the first of the Caesars to rule Rome. As of the writing of this book, the United States is still going through its first Pluto return since its birth in 1776 and seems to be in the unrelenting grip of Pluto's powerful energies for drastic change.

Pluto is usually the planet farthest from the Sun, though its elliptical orbit is elongated in such a way that it occasionally comes within the orbit of Neptune, which is usually the second-farthest planet from the Sun. Pluto takes the longest time of any planet to go completely around the Sun: 248 years.

Because of its long orbital period, Pluto is in the same sign for many years and metaphorically stamps out generations of beings who all have the same planet in the same sign, as does Neptune and Uranus, the other two slow movers, stamping out subsets of these Pluto generations. As I write this book, Pluto has been in only nine zodiac signs since 1900: Gemini, Cancer, Leo, Virgo, Libra, Scorpio, Sagittarius, and Capricorn. Pluto began its journey through Aquarius on March 23, 2023.

NOTE: *Pluto takes on even more power in a chart if it is what is known to astrologers as a personal planet. Every chart has as personal planets those that are closest to the Sun out to Mars—that is, y/our Sun, Moon, Mercury, Venus, and Mars. However, any planet becomes a personal planet, a planet whose power is amplified in your chart, if it is the ruler of your Sun, Moon, or Rising Sign—for example, Pluto in the chart of someone with Scorpio Sun, Moon, or Rising Sign.*

Let's look at Pluto's meaning through the signs that are possible to encounter today, remembering that these dates are approximate and that the chart of anyone born within three years of any date should be checked in an online ephemeris, a book of monthly tables listing the exact positions of the Sun, Moon, and planets, so as to ascertain the exact sign their Pluto was in. You can find an online ephemeris at www.astro.com/swisseph/swepha_e.htm.

PLUTO THROUGH THE SIGNS

Pluto in Gemini ♇ ♊

(1883–1912)

This generation saw the inventions, the rapid implementation of those ideas, and the startling modernization that started a technological revolution that is still ongoing.

Pluto in Cancer ♇ ♋

(1912–1939)

Coincides roughly with the cohort of the US population known as the Silent Generation—those born between 1928 and 1945—who grew up or were young adults during the McCarthy era, when you had to keep your political beliefs quiet. They are also known as the Lucky Few Generation, because they were relatively few and came of age during the prosperous 1950s and 1960s. Pluto in Cancer echoed that sign in that the family was the center that held people together during the dark days of World War I, the Spanish flu epidemic, and the Great Depression.

Pluto in Leo ♇ ♌
(1937–1958)

Coincides roughly with the cohort of the US population known as the baby boomers. This generation rebelled against the Pluto in Cancer's perfect-family trope and ostentatiously echoed the medieval Children's Crusade in a naive wishing-should-make-it-so attempt to have love rule over greed, though they did end the military draft in the US. Their flamboyance upended the old "Children should be seen but not heard" tradition of previous generations. These children were and are all about being seen and heard.

Pluto in Virgo ♇ ♍
(1956–1972)

Coincides roughly with the cohort of the US population known as Generation X, who were reared during the time when women entered the workforce in large numbers and so they were forced to raise themselves while their boomer parents "did their thing." Pluto in Virgo people rebelled against the egotism of the Pluto in Leo generation and worked hard to clean up what they saw as the previous generations' mistakes. Gen Xers seem to have achieved an impressive work/play balance and are solid citizens who do not mind working hard. They worry more than their parents did, and their children have to deal with parents who are very hands-on.

Pluto in Libra ♇ ♎
(1971–1984)

Coincides roughly with the cohort of the US population known as millennials, who are also known as Generation Me, known for wanting to balance their work with play to a degree that, compared to Generation Xers, their lives seem to unrealistically center around playtime, not work time. Their Libran love of harmony, their aversion to open confrontation, and their rejection of the constant criticism, sarcasm, or complaints of the Pluto in Virgo generation have defined them. They are all about fairness and balance to a degree that upsets and imbalances the other generations, who have paid only lip service to "life, liberty, and the pursuit of happiness."

Pluto in Scorpio ♇ ♏
(1983–1995)

Befitting the secretive and power-focused sign of Scorpio, it's hard to put a generalization name on this cohort, though they are sometimes referred to as Generation Z. Rebelling against the Pluto in Libra ideal of everything being beautiful in its own way, they are focused on the dark side of life-and-death issues the previous generation avoided acknowledging, using what was formerly thought of as occult or metaphysical practices in daily life, discovering and exposing secrets, fighting against anyone and anything that restricts their power and sovereignty, and fostering the fundamental transformation of society and of individuals. This is seen in their embrace of gender modification, gender fluidity, and unique take on sexual identification while at the same time completely rejecting anyone's right to push back against the extreme changes they embrace and embody. They can be cynical in the extreme about the possibility of anything they do not agree with.

Pluto in Sagittarius ♇ ♐
(1995–2008)

Coincides roughly with what has been named Generation Alpha, since they are the first people born or becoming conscious completely in the twenty-first century. As of this writing, these people are coming of age, and it seems that they are going the Scorpionic obsession with truth one better. Where the Pluto in Scorpio generation is cynical, the Pluto in Sagittarius generation shares that sign's philosophical optimism, demanding that everything discovered to be underhanded and detrimental to the well-being of the world's population be exposed and eliminated, and insisting that new ways be instituted without regard for national borders. Their philosophy of justice informs their every action.

Pluto in Capricorn ♇ ♑
(2008–2023)

This generation is quite young as of the writing of this book. They started being born during the Great Recession, which started with the collapse of the Lehman Brothers and Bear Stearns firms in the US, and others were born during the global COVID-19 pandemic at the other end of Pluto's transit through Capricorn. The lockdowns and mask wearing have surely contributed to many of them possessing a typically stoic Capricorn sense of the need to endure hard times and to manifest a businesslike demeaner that hides what is going on inside them, since in their formative years, they weredeprived of seeing the full faces of other people and of playing with other children.

Capricorn's focus on authority, combined with Pluto's often-ruthless pursuit of power, may see this generation rebel against efforts to create a one-world government with a digital currency tied to a social credit system. However, my rule of the spectrum of readings is always at work, and so this generation may actually defer to authority and simply get in line and go along to get along. Time will tell. One thing is certain: The Pluto in Capricorn generation will live in a new world order.

Pluto in Aquarius ♇ ♒
(2023–2044)

Pluto entered Aquarius while I was writing this book—on March 23, 2023, to be precise. Since I am an Aquarius and since I am convinced that the Age of Aquarius started on September 11, 2001, I believe that the generation born with Pluto in Aquarius is going to be even more focused on a world where each person is a self-sufficient citizen, or, in the opposite extreme, lives under a one-world government ruled by faceless bureaucrats or, I shudder to think, by artificial intelligence in some fashion.

In the event that planetary alignment does produce a government that will be extremely authoritarian in its use of futuristic technology, this will also presage a generation of those in secret and open rebellion against the curtailment of their freedoms. It is my fervent hope that Pluto in Aquarius will produce the highest expression of Aquarius, a government and a people who exist to make it easier for everyone to be as independent and supported by technology as possible. The children born during this time are going to redefine just about every aspect of daily life.

To a large extent, how this goes will depend on the previous Pluto generational survivors using the constitutions they were born under, many of them (like in the US) having been created the last time Pluto was in Aquarius (1778–1798). Aquarius is all about learning from the past to make sure the future is much better, all about disruptive technologies and policies, and all about being unemotional about getting rid of anything that does not advance humanity.

Pluto is the higher octave of Mars. Whereas Mars represents the energy available to us to go out and work our will on the world, Pluto symbolizes the powerful forces that are beyond our control—death being the most extreme example but one that is universal in its application (the ultimate extreme, the affirmation and the negation of the concept of "This, too, shall pass"). It is a great reminder to me that Pluto, the smallest planet of our solar system, represents overwhelming transpersonal power like that of nature. It is important that every astrologer helps anyone they read for to understand and make friends (sort of!) with their chart's Pluto position.

A BRIEF LOOK AT PLANETS IN THE EIGHTH HOUSE

The Sun ☉

You are focused on having enough power and resources to feel secure and to avoid feeling owned by anyone or anything. Become aware of obsessive behavior. You cannot deny the importance of sex. You are an excellent detective and know how the game of life is played.

The Moon ☽

You possess a powerful intuition. You are sensitive and emotional, strongly influenced by what others have and what you feel you lack. Emotional detachment must be learned. You want to know everything about this life and the next. You may inherit something of value from a woman or caregiver.

Mercury ☿

You think a lot about hidden or unspoken truths. You are good with money and may earn your living in the financial sector through research, analysis, trading, information technology, or a vocation that lets you explore and share what you find to be truly valuable.

Venus ♀

You have a powerfully attractive quality that can benefit you in many ways. Other people will be inclined to share what they have with you. You love investigating the mysteries of life and may become adept at metaphysical practices. Your unique attitude toward life and death is a gift.

Mars ♂

You are intense, passionate, and stubbornly sure of what you believe to be true. Your sex life is a world of its own. You are drawn to strategic financial planning and are willing to do what it takes to make sure you get what you deserve. Compromise is something you bestow rarely, like a gift.

Jupiter ♃

You may materially benefit from your associations with other people, some of whom will also seek your advice about important issues. You know what you want and how to get it and will work hard even when you would rather not if it will help you magically change your life.

Saturn ♄

You have intense, complex emotions but are reluctant to face them or to share them with anyone, because you equate being secretive with being powerful. Limits and boundaries are intimately connected to your sexuality. You need a very understanding partner to feel secure.

Uranus ♅

You have an unconventional attitude toward life, sex, death, and the occult. You are constantly transforming yourself, thereby exerting an almost psychic attraction on those seeking to understand life by experiencing what to most people are extremes. You cannot be manipulated.

Neptune ♆

You exert an almost-mystical effect on all you meet because you seem to understand their secret inner drives and conflicts. You must use your power responsibly and for the good of other people. Your dreams and your idealization of sex, power, and magic can lead to disillusionment.

Pluto (Ruler) ♇

Pluto is at its most potent here. You have enormous personal power and can transform yourself and exert great influence over other people. Your mission in life is to be known for advocating some important aspect of the collective will, shared values, or fervent hopes of your people.

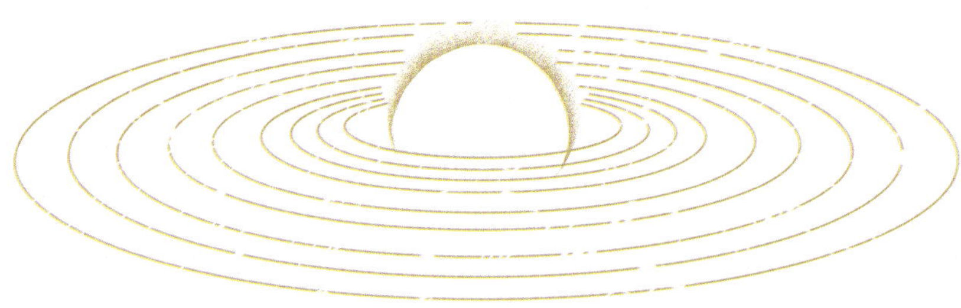

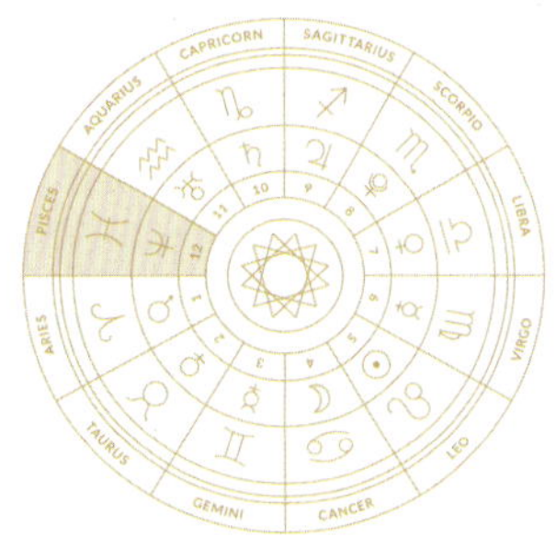

THE TWELFTH HOUSE

Like the Second House, the house that reveals what you consider to be valuable on the spiritual, mental, and physical levels for projecting yourself into reality, the meaning of the Twelfth House, the house directly above the horizon on the left side of a chart, is derived from the First House and the Rising Sign.

Where the First House and the Rising Sign are all about you, how you project yourself into physical reality, and what you want other people to know about you, the Twelfth House negates one's individual identity and ego in some way and represents everything you do not want people to know about you.

If a chart has the Sun in the Twelfth House, it means this birth occurred just after sunrise, the time usually darkest before the dawn, a theme similar to the solitary absence-of-light nature of the Twelfth House. It is a serene time when the birds are starting to sing and we look forward to having another blessed day on our spaceship Earth. We can feel like the only person in the world and still realize how small we are in the scheme of things, a part of a greater whole that is our Earthly family of fellow beings. Knowing and feeling this reality is what most people think of as a very mystical or spiritual way to live.

The Twelfth House is associated with everything that helps you remember that you are a small part of a great whole. The overwhelming beauties of nature, looking at a work of art, or entering a cathedral are perfect examples of this humbling but inspiring feeling. These things can make you feel extremely alone, sad, insignificant, and needing to escape and, at the same time, in awe of the majesty and grandeur of life and its infinite beauty. Both the sorrow and the joy of life can bring us to tears.

The Twelfth House also has a shy, hidden dimension of privacy to it, just like the hour of the first light of dawn. People with one or more planets in their Twelfth House need to be completely alone and undisturbed at least once each day in order to process the information that has resonated with the things in their life ruled by that/those planet(s). If they are not able to be alone for a time each day, they can experience otherwise unexplainable anxiety related to the planet(s) and sign(s) involved.

Just as I mentioned regarding the explanation of a person's Moon sign often being so revealing and important to a person consulting an astrologer as to warrant focusing on it to the exclusion of other information, it is a very gratifying experience to alert a client to this very real Twelfth House need for privacy they may have previously seen as a character flaw.

The Twelfth House rules a person's innermost being, including the subconscious, intuitive, and psychic dimensions of their mind. The old-time astrologers called the Twelfth House the house of self-undoing and related it to secret enemies, as opposed to those who confront you openly and declare their intentions. I believe that not understanding the subtle meanings and blending of planets and signs involving the Twelfth House can, indeed, lead to a lack of self-awareness that could easily cause a person to react and act against their own best interests and cause others, not wanting to be affected by someone who obviously doesn't know what is good for them or anyone else, to act against them.

The Twelfth House is connected to anything that negates one's ego, like being a little cog in a big machine. It rules any large institutions like hospitals, corporations, government, organized religions, the court system, and the armed forces. People with planets in their Twelfth House are usually more comfortable working in the privacy of a studio, not on a stage, the exception being working for a movie, TV, or other kind of infotainment studio where the stage is a controlled and private area.

The Twelfth House has the flavor of the zodiac sign Pisces and is ruled by Pisces's planetary ruler, Neptune. It is related to anything that denotes isolation, seclusion, and both the limitations of personal power encountered by those who go up against large and entrenched institutions and the transcendent power available to those who connect to spiritual realms. The spectrum of possible meanings of planets in the Twelfth House extends from experiencing limitations on being one's self, such as being confined to a hospital or a prison, to feeling a religious connection with All-There-Is and all the way to a divine ecstatic experience of enlightenment.

People with planets here must learn to regard themselves not as a separate being but as a part of the whole, inseparable from it and ever in contact with it, though they may never know what "it" is in its entirety. The Twelfth House involves faith in things unseen, spirituality, organized religion, charity, philanthropy, and the concept of escape, which is best achieved by being alone to process the day's events. Without that release, the person will seek other ways of escaping, which can lead to harmful actions and substance use.

TWELFTH HOUSE KEYWORDS: *spirituality, inspiration, ego-negating, gentle, merge, dream, dreamlike, unclear, union, isolation, escape, hidden, the studio, boundaries, "divine discontent," sacrifice, addiction, self-undoing, "hidden enemies," illusion, subconscious, dissolve, compassion, "large institutions," prison, "cog in a machine," fantasy, "what you do not want others to know about you"*

NEPTUNE, RULING PLANET OF THE TWELFTH HOUSE

The planet that is most closely associated with, and rules, the Twelfth House is Neptune, named after the god of the seas. The glyph for Neptune is obviously Neptune's trident. It can also be seen to be the crescent of the individualized soul impaled on the cross of matter, symbolizing how the material world can make things difficult for a sensitive soul.

Neptune rules our inner fervent prayer for the nobler aspects of human beings to reign supreme and our dream of a better world. Neptune is all about the utopia we could be living in if only—the noble but easily-seen-as-naive carrot dangling from reality's stick that all we human donkeys keep walking toward as we journey forward in life. Briefly put, Neptune is what gives you goose bumps, what inspires you, and, ideally, what enables you to inspire others.

Neptune also rules the human concept of fantasy. Fantasy is an important part of our psyche; idealism is a powerful defense mechanism preventing us from descending into a mindset hardened by the intransigent cynicism that would result if we were only reminded of and exposed to the harshness of life and its many disappointing lessons and our inevitable demise.

Neptune is a difficult planet to clearly define because the planet itself represents the concept of the aspects of our psyche, as well as events and situations we find ourselves in that are difficult if not impossible to clearly define. Neptune has come to be associated with oily, murky, foggy films that make clear sight very difficult. As I showed you when I talked about my analogy describing your Celestial Trilogy, what we now think of as video used to only be seen as the result of the actions of a movie projector, shining bright light through film, creating the illusion that we are watching real things happen.

It is easy to see that Neptune is associated with separating what is real from what is fantasy. On a personal level, this is why Neptune has to do with lying. Whether a lie is told to spare someone's feelings, to avoid having to admit that life is not living up to someone's utopian fantasy, or as a means of luring someone to give up their possession or even their life, a lie is still a lie.

The Neptunian utopian fantasy about lying is that ultimately, the telling of a lie will lead to there being more truth in the world. This could happen because the liar realizes the error of their ways and decides to tell the truth—or at least a

THE THREE GEMS BRINGS SPEEDY RECOVERY FROM ILLNESS WEALTH AND ENDURANCE
THE PINE CONE WORN TO INSURE GOOD HEALTH AND BRING WISDOM AND WEALTH

lot more of the truth and a lot less of the lies—or because the person that is lied to, on discovering the deception, becomes more savvy and less naive and therefore less likely to be duped in the future. Ah, Neptune, you do mean well.

It is imperative, however, that we remember that it is as difficult to impose utopian ideals on the world as it is to stop the tides. If we forget this life lesson, our real-world efforts become undermined like people standing at the ocean shore who either fall or rebalance themselves as the tide removes the sand they are standing on.

Neptune's sign in a cosmic blueprint is an indication of that generation's idealization of the important characteristics of that sign *and* what the people of that generation are willing to lie about and to be lied to about in order to avoid their failure to deal with the murky, messy, imprecise, and unknowable aspects of life so as to preserve their utopian idealization of that sign even in the face of what they know to be true. It is crucial that caregivers help children and young adults understand this concept, or else the Neptune-induced idealization/disappointment/lying energy matrix will negatively impact their lives until it is understood.

Neptune is a most powerful—and, to be honest, a most-dangerous-to-our-ego—planet disguised as an idealistic fantasy lover's planet. It asks us, what is fantasy? Is wanting the world to be a better place a utopian fantasy? Yes, unless we work to make real our dreams. Is psychic phenomena fantasy? Yes, if you do not get over yourself and the Dark Ages ignorance and do the research and the work of developing your intuition and learning about the metaphysical forces that have long been proven to be real by Einstein and the rest of the quantum mechanics physicists, the forces portrayed in the gorgeous sewn-fabric collage tapestries made by my incredible wife, Amy Zerner, that you see in this book.

Neptune takes on even more power in a cosmic blueprint if it is, in that specific chart, what is known to astrologers as a personal planet. Every chart has as personal planets the ones closest to the Sun out to Mars—that is, your Sun, your Moon, Mercury, Venus, and, to a lesser extent, Mars itself.

However, any planet becomes a personal planet (a planet whose power is amplified in your chart) if it is the ruler of your Sun, your Moon, or your Rising Sign—for example, Neptune in the chart of someone with Pisces Sun, Moon, or Rising Sign, or if it is conjunct (on the same degree of the zodiac as) a traditional personal planet.

Neptune in any sign can undermine the fundamental meaning of that sign in that chart by placing an unrealistic expectation that the ideal manifestation of that sign can and will actually occur. An example of that was the disappointment of the Neptune in Libra generation, many of whom became known as hippies, when their peace-and-love dreams failed to materialize as they wanted them to and many of them decided to become focused on making deals (Libra) and spending money to make their lives more beautiful (Libra again) without regard to how and what effect it had on other people or the environment. This is not true for a very large percentage of that cohort, but, like so much of what we are talking about with the outer, transpersonal planets (Pluto, Neptune, Uranus), there are themes that definitely made themselves known to the culture and are therefore worthy of mention and consideration in the reading of a cosmic blueprint.

Neptune takes approximately 146 years to travel around the twelve zodiac signs, spending about 14 years in each sign. Like Pluto, the planet that is usually the slowest and farthest from the Sun, Neptune stamps out generations of people born while it was in a particular sign. Neptune in a sign has a unique effect on everyone born during the 14-year period it spends in a sign.

Let's look at Neptune's meaning through the signs, including the ones that are not possible to encounter in a living person today. I include them in case you want to see what happened in history when Neptune was in a sign or have some idea about the decades to come. While it is true in many instances that the past is prologue, and we can learn a lot from the past about what we are experiencing in the present, I strongly caution against thinking that what we know happened the last time a slow-moving planet (Pluto, Neptune, Uranus) was in a particular sign will be repeated the next time it is moving through that sign. There will be themes that are explored again, but they will be strongly redefined because of the radical difference between our time and then.

Another thing I would caution against is an overemphasis on the keyword *surrender* as an overarching meaning to attach to your other keywords based on the sign and house position of Neptune. While it most certainly can incline a person to surrender or merge with the infinity of the Great Spirit, All-There-Is, or God/dess as you define it, the concept of surrender—in terms of a generation surrendering based on what sign Neptune is in when they were born—does not in my opinion seem to deserve a universal application to that generation. Someone with the Sun conjunct Neptune would be a dreamer and an idealist, possibly a fantasist, but they would not be inclined to surrender their dreams and ideals—quite the contrary.

Always remember that the dates used for the outer, slow-moving planets are approximate, and the chart of anyone born within three years of any date listed here should be checked in an online ephemeris, a book of monthly tables listing the exact positions of the Sun, Moon, and planets, so as to ascertain the exact sign their Neptune was in. And, as with all the outer, transpersonal planets (Pluto, Neptune, Uranus), their meaning in a sign is still more influential in how they impact individual astrology charts, and their meaning in world history should be seen as a mass formed by these individual effects. (Here again is the link to an ephemeris: www.astro.com/swisseph/swepha_e.htm.)

NEPTUNE THROUGH THE SIGNS

Neptune in Aries ♆ ♈
(1861–1875 and 2025–2039)

This book's publication coincides with the early years of Neptune's ingress (entrance) into Aries. I will get to the other sign placements of Neptune in a bit, but first, I will use the Neptune in Aries placement as a teachable moment.

By this point in your astrological education, you should know that the sensitive, intuitive, emotionally fluid, utopian dreamer, often seen as naive and looking to escape the harsh realities of life symbolized by Neptune—which is closely aligned with and rules Pisces, the Mutable Water sign, is not at all like the warriorlike, fiery, impatient, pioneering, one-of-a-kind, go-it-alone energy of Aries, the Cardinal Fire sign. Water can put out a Fire—a useful trait if you want to extinguish a Fire, but not so much if you would rather it kept burning. And Fire can boil Water to sterilize things—including Water—cook food, and otherwise be helpful, unless you needed desperately to drink that Water and now it's way too hot.

Forgive my facetious examples, but the dichotomy between Neptune and Aries is so pronounced that I hope you can see that having Neptune in Aries is a difficult, or at the very least a highly nuanced, placement to have in a young person's chart, especially if they have planets in Aries or their Rising Sign is Aries. If you decide to read the cosmic blueprints of other people, you are undoubtedly going to be reading those of people born with Neptune in Aries.

Using my keyword technique, you should be able to formulate for yourself some basic meanings of Neptune in Aries. These keyword phrases will be suggestive of some of the possible energies that will be encountered during this fourteen-year period.

I will start the ball rolling:

- The idealization (Neptune) of (among many other Aries traits) bravely standing up for oneself in a forceful manner (Aries).
- Aggressive (Aries) utopian idealism (Neptune).
- Idealization, confusion, or a lack of clarity (Neptune) regarding the use of force (Aries).
- The dissolving or diminution (Neptune) of the idealization of the Warrior (Aries).

I'm sure you will have other keyword phrases pop into your mind—at least, I hope you will. Your astrological education is moving right along!

Babies born with Neptune in Aries will probably display, have issues with, or idealize the rugged individualism and feisty attitude of Aries. Each generation produces exemplary role models. This generation will probably attempt to find as a role model one or more people who exemplify their ideals. It may be people who, like themselves, exemplify the various aspects of making real the Neptune in Aries ideals for improving and implementing their utopian ideas in the real world, a spiritual warrior.

When that happens, as it happens with all generations trying to make their mark on the world, they are inevitably going to be met with the resistance-to-change cohort that has existed since time immemorial. They will be criticized by those trying to ignore the truth of what the Neptune/Aries generation is all about for the extreme Neptunian and Arian energies they will use in their efforts. This is a generation that will be radically different from the babies born while Neptune was in Pisces. (See page 187.)

It is worth noting that the last time Neptune was in Aries, the American Civil War took place, a tragedy from a barbaric time whose aftereffects are still reverberating in the United States, a nation that would have become the Untied States if the Confederacy had won the war.

When you think about Neptune in any sign while reading a person's cosmic blueprint, always remember utopian idealization and Neptune's trident, which will help you recall the analogy of the ocean's tide pulling the sand from beneath one's feet, and you will have a good starting point to see how Neptune is affecting them.

Neptune in Taurus ♆ ♉
(1874–1889 and 2038–2052)

While it is outside the scope of this book, using my keyword technique, Neptune in Taurus has to do with *the idealization of material wealth and comforts*. This makes me suspect that this generation's generality would be that, individually, when Neptune becomes a personal planet, they would not want to do anything that would rock the boat and disrupt their good time. During this time, both Karl Marx and his *Communist Manifesto* and John D. Rockefeller's empire attained great power regarding the ownership of wealth.

Neptune in Gemini ♆ ♊
(1889–1902 and 2054–2068)

Another sign position outside the scope of this book. Applying my keyword technique in the hope of getting a starting point for the understanding of this placement, we can focus on the concept of the *idealization of communications, versatility, and learning*, three ideas you should always keep in mind when you see Gemini anywhere in an astrology chart. Back in this time, Germany made what were then revolutionary reforms: the eight-hour workday, no children under fourteen working, working conditions regulated, people allowed to assemble en masse, direct voting by secret ballot, laws taken off the books that put women at a disadvantage legally, public education, and no money supporting a particular religion. These policies increased the literacy rate in Germany and gave it numerous advantages, but Gemini is always connected to duality, and so these wonderful achievements ended up setting the stage for World War I when Neptune's passage through Cancer, ruler of the home and the past, encouraged Germany to expand its homeland through military conquest.

Neptune in Cancer ♆ ♋
(1902–1915)

While the chance of reading the chart of someone born during Neptune's journey through Cancer is probably zero as of this writing, it is crucially important that you be able to blend a planet with a sign, and so what do you get when you blend what you now know about Neptune with what you know about Cancer? Idealization of the mother, land, and the motherland is an accurate response, though an easy one, since I just gave that one to you in my brief paragraph about Neptune in Gemini. This would have been a generation who would have done anything for their idealized vision of what family means. Keep in mind that the spectrum of meanings is always relevant, and so an idealized vision of family is either cherished when said family is nice enough and together enough to warrant it, but that same vision can motivate deception, including self-deception, in someone whose actual experience of family was disappointing or worse. Idealization of the past, of security, of owning land, and of home ownership are all possible meanings. In the US, Rocky Mountain, Glacier, Mesa Verde, Wind Cave, and Crater Lake National Parks were all established while Neptune was in Cancer.

Neptune in Leo ♆ ♌
(1915–1929)

The idealization of the self, the ego, the performer, the person who shows others how things are done, the hero, the celebrity, and the things that supported the emancipation of women, each of whom could be the star of their own show as they dressed and acted like the flappers or the super influential film stars of the 1920s. Neptune rules film, and this period saw the first movie stars of the Golden Age of Hollywood, but this Leo inclination to ostentatious display and performance morphed into the start of not just any depression, but the Great Depression, which caused movies to become even more important and extravagant. The people of this generation, who came to be known as the Greatest Generation, sacrificed, fought, suffered, and died during World War II.

Neptune in Virgo ♆ ♍
(1928–1943)

The keyword combination of "the idealization of perfection" does not really work as a way of helping us in our understanding of Neptune in Virgo. The world of this period was far from perfect, with the Great Depression and World War II strongly affecting this generation because, as children, they had to endure the privations and the constant worry about numerous life-or-death situations, whether that was eat or starve, have a home or be homeless, or have parents who earned a living or ones who struggled to survive—and that became worry about one's father surviving the war effort. It might be the idealization of the service work they all did in order to be able to supply themselves and their family with the basics, like food on the table, a roof over their heads, and of fighting off the real and present dangers that are a threat to daily survival. Perhaps this generation was great because they realized the supreme value of simple things and ordinary days because they had so little of both. However, their difficult childhoods inclined them to be overly critical at times.

Neptune in Libra ♆ ♎
(1942–1956)

The keyword combination of "the idealization of relationships" is the perfect description of the meaning of Neptune in Libra. This is the hippie generation that came of age in the 1960s, idealizing peace, love, and harmony to the point where they overturned traditional social mores but lost their way as drug use, ruled by Neptune, undermined their high ideals. Many of this generation idealized relationships and their partners to the point where they not only expected their partners to lead the way but were also not able to deal with their human frailties and the day-to-day reality of partnership, causing divorce rates to soar. This era also embodies the idealization of the arts, especially visual arts and music, which led to the amazing music scene this generation created and supported.

Neptune in Scorpio ♆ ♏
(1956–1970)

The idealization of power, transformation, and extremes is perfect for this charismatic generation, none of whom want anyone to exert power over them. Their ability in extrasensory perception is naturally more intense than in other generations, and they have to be aware that using their insights into the minds and motivations of other people must be done responsibly and not to control or manipulate others. This generation either loves what was formerly called the occult (the word means "hidden" or "obscured"), such as tarot and other oracle cards, astrology, extrasensory perception, and psychic powers, because it makes them more powerful, or they hate the very same things because they do not want to believe that anyone can have power over them. Scorpio rules emotions and everything else that is beyond words and impossible to explain, and so Neptune in Scorpio in an individual can reduce their ability to communicate the things related to any planet they either conjunct or oppose.

Neptune in Sagittarius ♆ ♐
(1970–1984)

The idealization of truth—especially of telling the truth—and of justice, philosophy, and the best practices known to cultures around the world. This generation may idealize the customs, mores, laws, and even the economic systems of places other than where they were reared. They love the idea of travel and would do so even when the difficulties of doing so would deter people with Neptune in other signs. This generation understands religion and philosophy at a fundamental level, and their experience of both comes to them without traditionally sanctified intermediaries or the need to attend services in traditionally sanctified places unless those religious leaders and places are foreign to their initial experience with organized religion. They want to have a direct experience of the mystical, and since most of them will not have the stick-to-itiveness to devote the huge amount of time and energy invested by true shamanic practitioners, they will be more willing to use psychedelics than any generation in a long time.

Neptune in Capricorn ♆ ♑
(1984–1998)

The idealization of respect, authority, and career drives this generation to approach work and career from an unusual top-down perspective, approaching them both as if they were already successful and respected, expecting the perks that come with achievement that they can easily envision but have yet to attain. Since this sign is generally more comfortable with tradition, people with Neptune in Capricorn are able to present themselves as solid citizens who idealize tradition, and when they then display the aforementioned top-down approach to work and benefits like vacation time and daily personal time, this is often surprising and confusing to members of other generations. If a job does not live up to their expectations or their employer does not respect them in some way, they will leave or do the minimum amount of work that brings in a paycheck until they have found a new job. Capricorn represents the parent or caregiver who helps direct them on their path to work and career success, and so Neptune in Capricorn may cause idealization of that person or of all the caregivers who were admired and respected. The idealization of respect and authority may lead some of this generation to take extreme measures to get power quickly.

Neptune in Aquarius ♆ ♒ *(1998–2012)*

The idealization of the future, technology, and humanity, though, as someone with Aquarius Sun, Venus, and Jupiter, I suspect that there is also going to be in this generation a surprisingly cavalier attitude toward those whose traditions and very lives may be strongly impacted by this generation's tendency to disrupt the status quo in a very drastic manner that undermines the essential well-being of the very humanity they claim to want to help. This generation is going to be very friendly and may actually redefine what *friends* and *friendly* mean. They will have to be very careful not to succumb to Neptune's tendency to make things sound better than they actually are and dedicate themselves to doing the work, not shunning the work that is necessary to achieve the global initiatives that are going to be very important to them. Since technology's ability to save humanity from itself is limited, as is everything in life, this generation may succeed in the goal of making computers more human friendly, which should have a profound impact on robotics and the ethical questions that will arise when machines reach the level of self-aware beings—which may have already happened during this period.

Neptune in Pisces ♆ ♓ *(2011–2026)*

Neptune rules Pisces, and the generation born during Neptune's sojourn through its home sign is going to produce a generation of visionaries, most of whom will idealize just about everything, having what are bound to be unrealistic expectations, which could lead to them being disappointed or not comfortable in our world of limits, lack, and suffering. They may idealize escaping the harsh realities of the less fortunate and the fact that everyone has to work and eat to live—and all the killing and difficulties that the production of our food and other necessities requires, but especially the necessity of protecting ourselves from the damaged people who would do us harm. They might not be willing to take the actions necessary to manage bad people and both isolate and help them, preventing them from hurting themselves and others too.

This generation is going to have to be very careful about ingesting any drug, vaccine, or anything that interferes with their body's natural processes, like alcohol, recreational drugs, or any other pastime that can devolve into addiction as an escape. This will also include escaping into a self-denying frenzy designed to help others, including the less fortunate, but care will have to be taken to avoid giving too much and giving to people things that make them more dependent and less able to care for themselves, an external manifestation of the taking of drugs that make a person's body and immune system weaker and not stronger. This generation will make a lot of progress in restoring the balance in people's mind, body, and spirit that has been severely disrupted by the poorly managed COVID-19 pandemic, which has thrown the world's population into a kind of nebulous, ocean storm–like emotional upheaval and a hard-to-manage and hard-to-predict energy tsunami that are totally Neptune-like in their expressions.

A BRIEF LOOK AT PLANETS IN THE TWELFTH HOUSE

An easy way to remember the difference between planets in the First and Twelfth Houses is that the planet(s) in your First House can represent everything you want people to know about you and the planet(s) in your Twelfth House can represent everything you don't want people to know about you. That is an oversimplification, but it can help you remember the difference in the two houses and act as a good jumping-off point if there are planets in either or both houses.

Traditional astrologers have often called the Twelfth House the house of secret fears, secret enemies, and our self-undoing, and the origin of this description is obvious to me: Any person not aware that we all have an aspect of self-doubt to our personalities and, to make matters worse, any person who dwells too much on their own self-doubts, acts in a weakened, self-defeating manner that creates suspicious enemies along the way. This does not mean that every person with a planet in the Twelfth House acts in such a manner. It does indicate that there is an added, usually hidden, dimension to this person's personality, the exact nature of which is symbolized by the qualities associated with that planet.

PRO TIP: *Since the Twelfth House is the house of a chart just above the horizon line and the Rising Sign's degree of its sign, people with planets there can unconsciously project the energies of those planet(s) in terms of how they appear to other people. This projection of the planet's energies, if not understood and compensated for, can cause problems for the native because it's the Twelfth House, the house of hidden influences, and they are not as aware of how this planetary influence of theirs is perceived by other people the way people with the same planet(s) in their First House would be. For example, I was born with Pluto just over the horizon and into my Twelfth House and in the showy sign of Leo. I do not usually think of myself as having the Plutonic judgment or seemingly Scorpionic appearance and tendencies other people close to me tell me I can sometimes project, especially on the rare occasion when I lose my sense of humor and take offense or otherwise lose my Aquarian Sun's cool. Using keywords, I should know better. Pluto in Leo equals demonstration of power and judgment.*

The Sun ☉

You know that our individual identities are not as important as our oneness with the infinite. Be aware you may downplay the importance of your ego, identity, or life's purpose. You are more comfortable in the studio rather than on the stage. You can do well interacting with large institutions.

The Moon ☽

You can be surprisingly shy. Your emotions connect you to what others call the mystical realms, but to you, it's just daily life as a human. You must be aware of this and not judge and react to others when you think they do not relate well to you. Without daily alone time, you will become moody.

Mercury ☿

Your logical mind is different than most people's. It is naturally attuned to a level of intuitive knowing impossible to describe. You know you are different from most people, and that may cause you to refrain from direct, clear, or honest contact with others. Avoid losing yourself in daydreams.

Venus ♀

You are a lovely, artistic, and spiritual person and may be quite attractive. You love to be alone to both process the events of the day and obtain distance from those judging you on appearances. You embody the transcendent spiritual power of love but should be careful of sacrificing too much for those you care about.

Mars ♂

Be aware of your tendency to use your Mars energies in indirect, hidden, or repressed modes. You can be surprisingly influenced by others but should avoid suppressed resentments that can explode into rage. You can do well with large institutions: corporations, government, courts, the military, and hospitals.

Jupiter ♃

You are a positive person, embodying the tenets of a religion or other codified way of being. You are very considerate of other people—sometimes too much so. You can be fortunate with large institutions. You must learn the difference between escapist fantasy and reality. Avoid excess always and in all ways.

Saturn ♄

Difficulties in early life may cause fears about yourself and your world that cause unnecessary problems for you now. If you want to feel love, stop criticizing yourself. Face, embrace, and understand why you don't feel good enough so you can develop self-discipline and self-confidence that can lead to success as you define it.

Uranus ♅

You are intuitive and have genius-level ideas but can be concerned that they are too naive, different, or disruptive to implement or even share. If you feel misjudged or restricted, you can become rebellious or restless because you feel empowered by those states of mind. Try not to startle people—unless you want to.

Neptune (Ruler) ♆

You are extremely sensitive, intuitive, and compassionate, though you may not want others to know. Your prayers for union with the infinite are often answered, connecting you directly to the energy fields that surround and sustain us. Confront addiction and other escapist tendencies in yourself and others.

Pluto ♇

You are discerning to the point of being judgmental about everything and everyone, especially yourself, and you cannot share the full extent of your inner life with anyone except maybe a loving partner. You must acknowledge and include in some way your shadow side in your self-concept, or you will not feel complete.

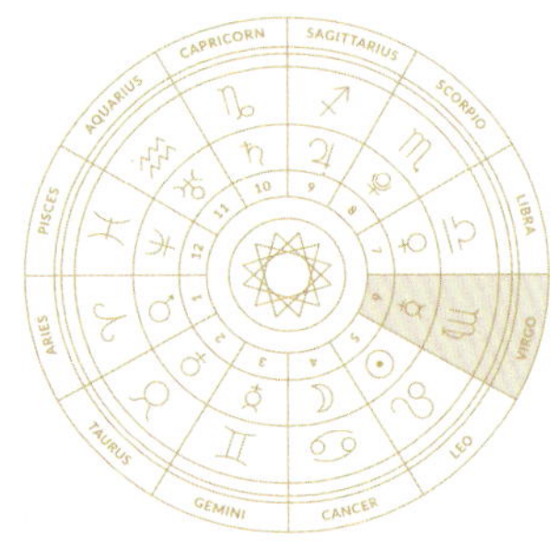

THE SIXTH HOUSE

The meaning of the Sixth House is derived from that of the Seventh House. The Seventh House is all about *partners* who are usually relatively equal to each other, depending on the contractual agreement, and are owners or otherwise have some kind of ownership or equity stake in the partnership. The Sixth House is all about *service work* done for someone else who is employing you. You are not a partner; you are an employee. Someone is paying or otherwise compensating you to work for them.

The Sixth House used to be called the House of Servants, but this is a very limited view from a time when people thought that some people were of a better class than others and that the "lower classes" were meant to be modern-day serfs and do menial work for their "betters." This hideously wrong attitude has slowed, and still retards, the development of nations because it prevents some of their brightest people from being socially mobile and activating their success.

The Sixth House is all about the basics of working for a living, no matter in which occupation or field you are employed. Amy and I both have Venus in the Sixth House and we proudly consider ourselves to be working artists. We write and make books, art, couture clothing, music, poetry, and jewelry, and that work goes into projects and products other people are willing to exchange their hard-earned money for.

The most common expression about working for a living is "putting food on the table." The Sixth House rules food as well as health (without which all other aspects of life and of a cosmic blueprint are redefined and made more challenging). That includes doctors, nurses, psychologists, psychiatrists, bodyworkers, fitness instructors, and healers of all kinds. It rules cooking, chefs, and of course everyone who grows, processes, transports, and serves food in any way. It is the house of workers.

The Sixth House is also about the detail-oriented work that must be done regarding the construction of the table the food is put on and the skills necessary to make everything we need to live. That includes all the building construction, maintenance, and repair trades and everyone connected with supplying them and everything that goes inside those homes and other buildings.

I am doing such a deep dive into the Sixth House because most astrology books do not seem to understand its importance. I suspect that this is because all too many astrologers and astrology books are not doing original thinking but are parroting what their teachers and the old books told them, many of them influenced by the prejudices against service, trade, and even the work of skilled craftspeople, but especially the "rednecks," whose necks got red from working in the sun farming, digging ditches, and doing other physical labor.

I have my Sun, Venus, and Jupiter in the Sixth House, so I know it well and feel privileged to be sharing its meanings with you. I love to exercise and do physical labor no matter the weather. I believe without question that all honest work is noble and valuable. I believe that we would all be better off if everyone, especially those who can afford to have others cook and clean and garden and drive and do whatever they themselves could and should be doing for themselves, would, at least on occasion, fend for themselves, put their hands in the soil while planting something, and get reacquainted with how most of the world lives and works. The world would change overnight.

The Sixth House reminds us of the importance of the little things—the myriad details of our existence as human beings that must be seen to if we are to live a life of quality and meaning. Our health is supremely important, and the purity of our food and water intake is directly connected to our health. Farming and all aspects of food production are Sixth House matters. Hippocrates, the father of modern medicine, who inspired the Hippocratic oath, which in turn inspired the principle of "*Primum non nocere*" ("First, do no harm"), wrote, "Thy food shall be thy medicine."

Although the Twelfth House governs large institutions like hospitals, the military, the government, large corporations, and other major undertakings, the Sixth House, the house opposite the Twelfth, governs "We, the people," the individual beings without whose individual work product these large operations would grind to a halt.

To be clear, hospitals are Twelfth House, but the inclination in a person to become a doctor, nurse, psychologist, or related health and healing worker is Sixth House. The military is Twelfth House; the individual members of the military are Sixth House. A movie studio or a video production company is Twelfth House; the people who do the work are Sixth House. And the work contracts of all the people, crew to management to actors, those agreements are Seventh House matters. I hope you see the differences and that I am not confusing you.

The Sixth House relates to one's job, one's work. In physics, the formula for determining work is "Force multiplied by distance," and the Sixth House rules work that is actually done, that accomplishes something measurable in some way, whether that is digging a ditch or working with digital information.

I hope you do not mind my bringing in something out of sequence, which I'm about to do because I respect you as a fellow astrologer. Try your best to understand the following: If a job's task is asked about and/or worked on in your chart reading, it's a Sixth House matter, but if a *career* is asked about and/or worked on, that is a Tenth House matter, and we will discuss the distinction in depth when we get to the Tenth House. Suffice it for now to say that job equals Sixth House and career equals Tenth House.

An important distinction between the Twelfth House's rulership of working for a large company, institution, or government agency and the Sixth House's work done for someone else is that when you do Sixth House work, you may personally know and often see the actual person or persons for whom you are working. This may be working in a service capacity in or on people's homes or in businesses where the boss is an individual or a group of individuals you may see or you may get the chance to interact with.

When you do Twelfth House work for a large corporation, the military, the government, the court system, a hospital, a university, or any very large enterprise, you most likely do have an immediate superior or three whom you see and you interact with, but your "customer," the being(s) for whom the whole large enterprise is designed to serve (ideally!), is a transpersonal entity, like citizens, voters, patients, consumers, the state, clients, the nation, society, "we, the people," or humanity.

Animals are crucial Sixth House matters. The animals that various cultures and individuals choose to kill and eat give them life. It is hard to imagine how important the horses, mules, donkeys, oxen, elephants, and other animals that work for us were before the advent of machines and their engines, whose output is measured in horsepower to this day. The amazing abilities of dogs are applied in numerous fields as well. In addition, our pets are our sort of servants, though anyone with a beloved pet knows the roles are usually reversed.

It is important to say again that Sixth House work is related to the Seventh House of partnerships and can be seen as helping one or more of the people in the partnership fulfill the terms of their agreements and everything related to being able to perform their function.

Psychological health is also Sixth House. There is stress anticipating and fulfilling the needs of others and dealing with the fact that you are working for someone else and not on an equal footing with them. It is difficult for some with Sixth House planets to be constantly reminded that they're not the boss, and if they cannot work under those conditions, they need to find other employment before they are demoted or fired.

There is a negating of the ego that is a necessary prerequisite for doing this kind of helpful work. Anyone who has done Sixth or Twelfth House work knows this and has probably encountered people ill-suited for this kind of use of their body/services, either because they are entrepreneurial and need to be using their labors to further their own business or because they have difficulty with authority or with being a team player, something also ruled by the Sixth House. Good workers are usually capable of being team players, though a strong Mars or Aries influence in the Sixth or Twelfth House can indicate someone who might be more comfortable working alone or on their own piece of a team effort.

RECAP: *The Sixth House rules how things work—your job, your employees, machines and devices that work for you, and your own body. It has to do with what you put into your body and the state of your health, including the mind/body connection. This house rules food, drink, farming, planting seeds, cooking, tradespeople, physicians, dentists, servants, anyone connected to health and healing, and exercise.*

The Sixth House has to do with the services people perform for each other—everything from manual labor to doing someone a favor. The negative aspect of the Sixth House is work done against your will or against your own best interests, either by you or someone else. (This is why traditional astrology assigned suffering and open enemies to this house.) More pleasant categories ruled by the Sixth House are pets and small animals in general.

The Sixth House is an important house for those whose work is connected with healing, whether that be licensed and credentialed medical professionals, those whose work involves a desire to help others with their healing process, or those who sell the products and services connected with healing in its many forms.

MERCURY, RULING PLANET OF THE SIXTH HOUSE

The Sixth House is associated with Virgo, and the ruling planet of Virgo is Mercury. In mythology, Mercury was known as the Winged Messenger, bringing communications from the gods to we mortals here on Earth. In astrology, Mercury also rules communications of all kinds.

The glyph for Mercury shows the mental half of the crescent of our individual soul resting on the circle of Spirit, which is, in turn, resting on the cross of matter. It is as if the symbol for Venus, with all of its power to love, beautify, desire, and attract, has been crowned with a parabolic reflecting antenna (similar to that of the Moon). Mercury's glyph suggests the ability not only to focus with pinpoint accuracy on the particulars of what is mentally desired, but also to concentrate on and communicate those personal ideas to the universe.

In the pages ahead, we will analyze how your life is affected by the dynamics of Mercury, exploring the meanings of Mercury through the twelve zodiac signs.

MERCURY THROUGH THE SIGNS

Mercury in Aries: Speed ☿ ♈

You think like a pioneer has to think in order to survive blazing a new trail. Your prodigious mental capacity and power of speech means that you can excel in politics or in a profession calling for contact with the public. Your ability to quickly assess any issue enables you to make helpful suggestions in a crisis. You never back down from what you think is right. Your aptitude for logic and debate, combined with versatility, makes you a good counselor. Your confidence is admired by others. Your vibrant force and dynamic personality impress all those you meet. If your creativity can be combined with your vivid imagination and pioneering spirit, you may create objects, situations, circumstances, and talents that cause you to be remembered for generations. If you are involved with people who do not give one hundred percent to their endeavors, you rebel and make your own rules. You are not afraid to be different and will always remain in the vanguard of progress.

Mercury in Taurus: Endurance ☿ ♉

You are the epitome of slow but steady wins the race. You are not rash or careless in your communications. You are measured and deliberate, making certain each word or step in your plan is safe before you take it. You prefer to concentrate on the tasks at hand, strive to complete them and get them out of the way before you move on to other, possibly greater achievements. You are keenly sensitive to financial fluctuations and are aware of impending changes in money standards and anything having to do with the world of finance. You can estimate clearly and without confusion the interrelated economic currents, a skill you can use to make your living. Even though you do not have the reckless tendencies of most people, regardless of your chronological age, you will always hold fast to the spirit of youth and will be comfortable around the young. You have much to teach them and enjoy doing so.

Mercury in Gemini: Enthusiasm ☿ ♊

You are interested in everything and know enough about how to speak carefully, not revealing what you do not know, so you are able to speak intelligently on a variety of subjects. You can be perceived as impersonal because you talk to everyone, and your mind reflects life as you find it. Your pleasing personality is refreshing, especially when things are moving too fast for most people. You are never, ever boring.

Mercury is the ruler of Gemini, the sign of duality and communication, and not only do you put ideas and people together, but you can also see both sides of any situation, which makes you a valuable friend. Touching life at so many points, you stimulate interest in new concepts, ideas, and schemes. You are welcomed by all because you fit in everywhere. Your thinking is dynamic, and you want to remain young in your attitude toward life. Stale notions and obsolete beliefs have no place in your mind. You believe in being hopeful about what tomorrow may bring, and that is infectious to all you share it with.

Mercury in Cancer: Insight ☿ ♋

Your thoughts are shaped by how secure you feel. You are naturally self-protective in the extreme and this focus extends to being protective of those you care about. You are always thinking about your past, home, and family. This feeling extends to your country, to the world, and to humanity at large. You are a champion of the public welfare. History fascinates you because it is a record of a bigger family that is replete with traditions. You are good at taking the pulse of the public and appealing to large groups of people through your innate knowledge of human psychology. You have a high sense of honor, and *patriotism*, for you, is not a dirty word—and you make sure that others know this. Accuracy is one of your highly developed traits. System and order are your ceaselessly unending aims. You are also acquisitive and a natural collector of all manner of things. If you train yourself, you can become an authority on matters antiquarian. But whatever your work, your thinking is strongly influenced by Mercury's unceasing desire to make connections and Cancer's flexibility.

Mercury in Leo: Production ☿ ♌

The secret of your success lies in your ability to organize your thoughts and present them to others as definite, reasonable plans. You have a convincing manner and are masterful when there is a presentation to be made or confusion that has to be overcome. You are usually calm and seldom afraid to face unpleasant facts. What you do not handle well is being ghosted. You can go too far in your performance and give the impression that you are domineering, weakening your ability to lead. When you are cooperative, you usually win a coveted goal of yours—leadership. You are kind, but you dislike sloth or laziness. Everyone knows your word is your bond and you will not break a promise unless it's for the benefit of everyone. For this reason, you want your word to be the law and you will not permit negligence, carelessness, sloppiness, or neglect. You know all too well how being careless about seeming trifles threatens success.

Mercury in Virgo: Analysis ☿ ♍

Your sharp, analytical gift enables you to detect faults in people and things, but unless you feel threatened or insecure, you do not seek errors for the sake of troublemaking. Your usual aim is to better conditions. You never hesitate to call attention to matters you believe need correction. With your avid desire to learn everything about a subject in which you are interested, you sometimes appear unduly persistent in your searches for perfection. You forge ahead. Your mind is versatile, observant, and penetrating. Once you conquer your fear of not doing something perfectly, you meet each situation with hope and confidence because you know how things work and how to fix them when they don't.

Virgo is the sign that rules the critical faculties, and, like Gemini, it is also ruled by Mercury, the planet of the mind. Gemini, an Air sign, is focused on the realm of ideas, but Virgo, an Earth sign, gives you a unique advantage in displaying physical skills of all kinds. Avoid attachment to a particular outcome, and do not allow your thoughts to devolve into worry and destructive criticism.

Mercury in Libra: Dexterity ☿ ♎

Your considerate and deliberate way of thinking can give you a better-than-average chance of success and recognition. You must be careful, however, because although you are ordinarily well-balanced, there is danger that you will take extreme views at times, usually to your own advantage, but you may swing from one extreme to the other as you decide what you believe is the better position. If you can be aware of this tendency, you are better positioned to take advantage of the fact that despite the aforementioned inclination, you have an excellent sense of ethical and material values and could do well in various professions or in commercial work where you can use your natural diplomatic and artistic instincts.

Libra is the midpoint sign of the zodiac, and this may be the reason that, so often, Mercury in Libra is found in the charts of those who possess a wide variety of talents and abilities. You can probably make a living from using any one of these several gifts if it helps you feel calm and balanced.

Mercury in Scorpio: Confidence ☿ ♏

You act on the impulse of the moment and like to lead a life where you feel like you are on an adventure, not just going through the motions of daily life. Adaptability is one of your key traits, so much so that you would rather accept what destiny has to offer than to just attempt to cope with problems you encounter. You are guided by your emotions, arriving at your conclusions through instinct rather than by systematic reasoning. You are inclined to be stubborn, and this can extend to your dedication to obtaining satisfactory payback from those you feel have wronged you in some way.

Mercury in Scorpio makes you determined, penetrating, and versatile in anything related to the areas ruled by Scorpio. You know your own mind, and you desire freedom for yourself and everyone else. You do not like to be restricted in thought or action and will do what it takes to get your way. You are resentful of restraint and independent in your opinion, though you won't waste it on the ignorant.

Mercury in Sagittarius: Intuition ☿ ♐

You are not shy about much, especially about how you despise all that is petty and mean, setting an example that inspires others to match your standards. Admiration and acclaim for your bravery are necessary for you to avoid withdrawing into yourself. You want to be worthy of the limelight; genuine praise warms you and spurs you on to greater effort. To win, you overcome obstacles, dominate every circumstance, take risks. You have an intuitive perception that enables you to gauge instantly the turn of events for better or worse. You don't like drab ideas, dull people, or dreary surroundings. You like everyone and everything to be on their best game, and if you think they are not, you do whatever is necessary to get them back on track. You are always seeing in your mind the extreme high and low of every idea, searching for the truth. Truth is so important to you that you may work against the best interests of both you and those you care about by sharing what you believe despite the consequences.

Mercury in Capricorn: Eagerness ☿ ♑

You direct your mind to achieve a practical thought process whose goal is to attain authority, with the amount of material and financial success and status you acquire used as metrics to prove to yourself what you have accomplished. You may very well attain these things, despite your fears to the contrary. However, you may be hampered by self-imposed limits to your ability to see the whole picture of your situation and what you have to do if you do not place enough importance on the equally valuable and ultimately more meaningful accomplishments you garner that cannot be measured so, such as your spiritual development, ability to teach others, and sense of humor.

You are a hard worker, careful and calculating. The quality of your success depends on your ideals. Powerful friends usually back your efforts to get ahead because you think like they do. Although your popularity may fluctuate, your ability to attain prominence is strong and should carry you forward despite any temporary setbacks.

Mercury in Aquarius: Valiant ☿ ♒

You are open and straightforward in your thinking and communications with everyone about everything because you have the scientist's lack of tolerance for anything that is not measurable, provable, or able to stand a rigorous inquiry. When you find it necessary or desirable to criticize, you do so. Though you may not think of yourself this way, you are an unusual type of extrovert because you do not fear to let people know what you think. You abhor injustices and are motivated to be a part of changes for the better whenever possible, especially against corruption and injustice. Routine and restriction distract you immeasurably. Personal freedom is the breath of life to you. When you are restrained in any way, it undermines your ability to think clearly and is damaging to your spirit. You rebel against injustice, intolerance, and stupidity. Many of the great inventors and writers were born when Mercury was transiting Aquarius. You think outside of the box to a degree that others cannot comprehend.

Mercury in Pisces: Imagination ☿ ♓

Your strong imagination enables you to visualize scenarios that allow you to see the myriad causes of problems and their solutions, but this same ability can incline you to exaggerate or outright lie on occasion if you think that doing so will be helpful in some way. Nevertheless, it serves you well in many ways, especially your ability to connect with and inspire others, a major asset. You must be very careful when ingesting drugs, even those prescribed, because your logical mind is in the sign most associated with addiction and escape from reality. Coming events often are revealed to you through psychic impressions and unbidden hunches. With this knowledge, you can give warning to others, but here your liability ends. You do not interfere with the freedom of action of the individual, even though your assistance in perilous times would make you almost a public resource. Dreams and prophecy are no strangers to you; through them, you shape your course in accordance with the revelations you receive.

MERCURY RETROGRADE

The concept of the Mercury retrograde has worked itself into the modern lexicon. Most people have some superstitious association with Mercury retrograde as a time when communications are much more difficult than they usually are and when you should not start anything or buy anything new, nor should you be signing papers, planning new projects, or traveling. This is definitely not true. Let's take a look at what the word *retrograde* means before we get on to the true meaning of "Mercury retrograde."

Retrograde Planetary Motion Explained

The zodiac is used by both astronomers and astrologers. It is used in plotting the positions of the planets of our solar system, all of which travel through the imaginary but universally agreed-on band of space we call the zodiac. The planets all move through their orbits around the Sun, and their positions can be plotted against the zodiac so we can tell where they are, have been, and will be so that astronomers, astrophysicists, and other scientists can plan trips to visit them.

To understand the retrograde, you have to imagine in three dimensions the planets orbiting the Sun, and you also have to remember that we look at the planets from our vantage point of Earth. The planets are usually scattered around the Sun but still in their orbital paths through the zodiac. They do bunch up sometimes, as measured against the background of the zodiac, which is why some charts have most if not all of the planets in one or just a few houses of an astrology chart.

A planet is said to be retrograde when we on Earth see it as moving backward through the zodiac. (The word is a synonym for *backward.*) We astrologers know that a retrograde planet is not really moving backward, just like we know that it is the Earth that orbits the Sun. It's like when you are on a fast train overtaking a slower-moving train, and it appears to be moving backward.

Remember that a retrograde planet is not really moving backward, but because of the relative positions and speeds of the Earth and the rest of the planets, we on Earth, who are plotting the position of the various planets against the band of the zodiac, can see that planet as going retrograde. Another way of saying this is that a planet is displaying retrograde motion.

NOTE: *The Sun and the Moon are never retrograde.*

There are usually three Mercury retrograde periods each year, though sometimes there are four, with each one lasting approximately three weeks. The vagueness of the number and duration of the Mercury retrograde are clues to its meaning.

If you really want to know how long a specific retrograde is going to last, you cannot depend on your memory or on the period of the last retrograde; each has its own duration. To ascertain the exact dates, you have to slow down, focus, and do a bit of research using an ephemeris, a book listing the positions of the planets for a specific day. That is why I always tell people that with retrogrades in the sky or in your cosmic blueprint, you are challenged to either be aware or beware.

Another key to understanding planets with retrograde motion is in the word *retrograde*. The prefix *re-* means "again." REtrograde periods are good times to do anything that can be described with a word beginning with *re-*, such as *REdo, REvise, REsearch, REnovate, REnew, REalign, REbrand, REthink, REmake, REmember*, and maybe even *REbel*.

One major *re-* word I have not mentioned is *REverse*, and that is at the heart of visualizing the implications of the Mercury REtrograde. Imagine the planets moving through the zodiac as a horserace on a racetrack. When the horses are running in the same direction, all that the jockeys riding the horses have to concentrate on is moving forward as fast as they can and avoiding colliding with the horses around them. However, if one or more of the horses decides to go backward on the track, it becomes a different kind of horserace, a race where being careful is a supremely useful skill and those who are not careful quickly regret their actions.

People born with Mercury or any planet REtrograde are often surprisingly cautious regarding the things ruled by that planet. As a rule, they do not rush into things, and they take more time to consider the consequences of their actions than people whose planets are not REtrograde.

The important thing to remember with Mercury REtrograde and all the other planets when they are REtrograde in a chart or in the sky right now is that we must be careful. The good news (and there is always good news with every planetary lesson) is that a REtrograde is actually a chance to have a do-over, to go back and do your best to understand a lesson you might not have handled as best you could, and maybe even to fix it. REtrogrades are the perfect time to RElearn lessons you have forgotten.

Why this is so is contained in the fundamentals of REtrograde motion itself, which brings us to the special time in each planet going REtrograde: the stationary period. When Mercury or any planet is appearing to slow down in preparation for becoming REtrograde, it reaches a point where it appears to be standing still, known as stationary REtrograde. This apparent standing-still phenomenon also occurs when a retrograde planet appears to slow down in its REtrograde motion as it prepares to go direct again. This standing-still time is known as stationary direct.

People born when Mercury or any planet is stationary REtrograde or stationary direct usually have a special relationship with that particular planet in some way. For example, I was born with Neptune stationary REtrograde, and I have devoted my life to manifesting in myself and later in life to sharing with others the Neptunian inspiration and connection to the unseen energy realms around us. Knowing that I was probably much more affected by my childhood and homeless period than I was aware of, I studied various spiritual theories on the nature of consciousness and personal reality.

There is an old saying, "When the student is ready, the teacher appears," and when I met Amy, she was studying astrology and I was studying Amy, so I learned astrology. In my thirties, I was finally able to help people beyond my ability do individual astrology chart readings through my books about metaphysical subjects. This happened only when I took myself out of the escapist and self-defeating aspect of Neptune that comes when you choose to lead the cliché of the rock musician's life, which I left in 1981. Seven years later, my decision was tested, and I passed when *Karma Cards*, my first book, was published to great success.

Another example is my wife, Amy, who was born on a Uranus station—stationary direct, to be more precise—the planet associated with the humanitarian and revolutionary sign of Aquarius. She displays the fearless dedication to using her artistic genius to benefit humanity with work that disrupts the status quo—in this case, the art world. She does this by bringing through her pioneering, award-winning fabric-collage style and through her art couture garments the awareness of our inseparable connection to the scientifically documented energy fields that underlie all being, including the astrological energies we are studying.

The number of days a planet is stationary depends on how far it is from the Sun. Mercury stations usually last less than a day, while Neptune stations can last more than two weeks, some years even more than Pluto, which is usually the farthest planet from the Sun. This is because Pluto's orbit is so elliptical that it is sometimes squeezed so as to make its station shorter than that of Neptune.

I was born when Mercury, Venus, Saturn, Uranus, Neptune, and Pluto were all retrograde. You may find it hard to believe that someone who has chosen the freelance artist's life over work that produces a steady paycheck and health benefits is cautious, since I have so many planetary horses going backward on my astrology-chart racetrack, yet that is the truth. People with REtrograde planets are adept at using the things related to that planet in a cautious way, thereby gaining a powerful ally in the energies of that planet because those energies are used more deliberately and cautiously.

A lot of astrologers believe that the Mercury REtrograde period does not end when Mercury goes stationary direct, but rather ends only when Mercury returns to the exact degree of the zodiac it was on when it previously went stationary retrograde. Keep this concept of the shadow period in mind as you live life with your newfound astrological take on it, but only if it appeals to you. In my opinion, adding the shadow period to the Mercury REtrograde period results in too many days spent using extra caution, so I count Mercury as going direct from the time it goes stationary direct until the next time Mercury becomes stationary retrograde.

If you think about it, this shadow period is a time when we get to REtrace our steps and finalize decisions *for the third time.* Mercury has moved forward, then retraced its steps during the REtrograde period, and then gone forward again, going over the same degrees of the zodiac for the third time. I think the shadow period gets its reputation from people not realizing this and not concentrating on making the right decisions and taking the right actions. There is a saying, "The third time is the charm," and I hope that would be true. Sometimes, however, people do not realize the gift of the carefully thought-out and practiced do-over a retrograde planetary period offers us.

NOTE: *My take on the existence of the shadow period of Mercury REtrograde is just one area of many in astrology where my opinion is decidedly different from that of other astrologers. Therefore, I remind you of my previous request that you not share my teachings with anyone, especially someone who says they know astrology, until after you have read this book to the end and will be able to understand my conceptualizations of various astrological information. You will then be better able to decide what resonates with you.*

Steps You Can Take to Deal Successfully with the Mercury Retrograde

The Mercury REtrograde has gotten its bad reputation because all too many people are not willing to do the REsearch about what a REtrograde is and how to best REvise their normal way of thinking and acting so as to flow with the astro-weather energy matrix in which we find ourselves each and every day. Those are the times that miscommunications, missed appointments, lost notes, and lots more unfortunate things happen. It's probably the time when the notion of Murphy's law—what can go wrong will go wrong—came to be.

Since Mercury goes REtrograde three to four times a year, for several weeks each time, it is important to remember my maxim: Be aware so you do not have to beware. The first thing to do is to remember that Mercury REtrograde is a great time to finish things you started a while ago: REorganize. REnew. REnovate. REad. This is an excellent time to REflect and otherwise work on your inner life, tie up loose ends, and file things away.

Since you know Mercury rules communication, clear thinking, truth, and travel, be sure not to take things too personally. Because their thinking is clouded, and their communication skills are out of sync, people will often say offensive things they don't mean around this time. Or it could be you who says something that someone else does not want to hear. Forgive if you want to be forgiven.

Backing up your data is always good advice, but never more so than when Mercury is REtrograde. Quite often, Mercury REtrograde does seem to affect the smooth working of computers, phones, and all technology. Of course, life doesn't stop just because of Mercury REtrograde, so if you absolutely have to purchase a costly item such as a computer or phone, recheck your paperwork and make sure you have a good warranty.

Also remember, everyone is a bit confused and stressed during Mercury REtrograde, so someone selling you something may be giving you bad information by accident or on purpose. Or you might be thinking you hear someone—perhaps not simply a salesperson—saying one thing when they mean something different.

If you buy something and then change your mind, do not be angry. That happens a lot. People who buy something during a REtrograde, even those who do their due diligence, are much more inclined to change their mind once Mercury goes direct. It then becomes the issue whether to take action to return something or get out of a contract. Read the small print on any contracts. Ask lots of questions. Double-check any information you're given, especially as it relates to travel. Buy insurance, and check times, delays, baggage allowances, reservations—all arrangements.

If you want to wait until the Mercury REtrograde passes before making major decisions, that is your choice, but there are definitely going to be times when you have to sign something, buy something, or travel during a REtrograde period. To paraphrase the Bible's words about the Sabbath, "Astrology was made for human beings, not human beings for astrology."

A BRIEF LOOK AT PLANETS IN THE SIXTH HOUSE

The Sun ☉

You are a modest, organized, detail-oriented, hardworking person who needs to be proud of their work. You are very body aware, and health, healing, food, exercise, and stress reduction are constant in your daily thoughts. You will do menial work if you feel it's for a greater good.

The Moon ☽

You feel more emotionally content when working for or with someone than on your own. You have a special affinity for animals. Being out of work or not feeling that what you are doing is really helping one or more people is harder for you than it is for most people.

Mercury (Ruler) ☿

You quickly comprehend all aspects of any task you put your mind to. You can see the most efficient order in which tasks must be done to complete jobs on time. You are able to develop a surprisingly varied skill set. Mental stress affects you more than most.

Venus ♀

You either need to love your work or work for someone you love. You may have an easier time than most people finding a good job. Your love of all Sixth House things, including animals, and dedication to them can cause you to have remarkable healing abilities.

Mars ♂

You need work that allows you to make an impact using your energies to the full. Even in a sedentary job, you must feel like your influence helps get the job done correctly in a no-nonsense, almost-military fashion. Once you start a project, you will do what it takes to complete it.

Jupiter ♃

Your positive attitude and ability to see nobility in all work and all workers inclines others to want to help you. What starts as a job may become a successful career. Experiencing the best of everything Sixth House related may benefit your health, but avoid excess.

Saturn ♄

You are very disciplined and hardworking, and this extends to staying as healthy as you can. You must do work you and others respect, or you will not do your best. You are either totally dedicated to service work or you avoid it completely.

Uranus ♅

You are inclined to do work that allows you to feel free from the interference of others, work for yourself even if providing services for others, or be part of the movement to manifest an improved future. Boring work or doing things the old-school way is not good for you.

Neptune ♆

You must do work that inspires you, others, or, ideally, both. You are very sensitive to the energies you experience when working and must avoid toxic work environments. You must be realistic about what you can expect from a job, or face disillusionment.

Pluto ♇

You should do work that enables you to make major transformations in the lives of the people you work for, either through affecting the things they own or the people themselves in some way. Doing work you judge inferior will cause you to work against yourself.

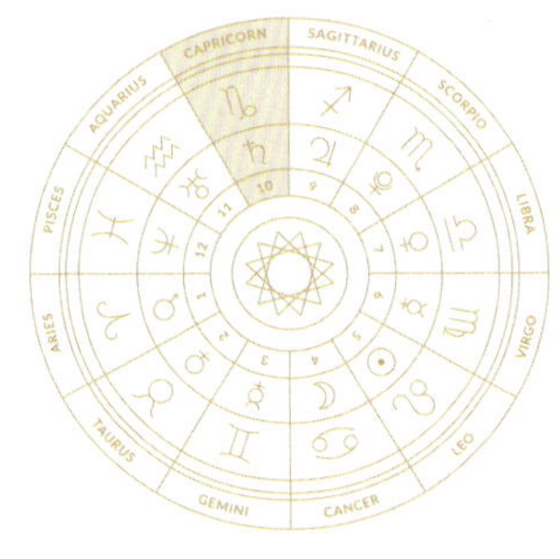

THE TENTH HOUSE

The Tenth House of an astrology chart is demarcated by the uppermost point in a chart, the point at the very top of the cross of matter, the cross formed by the horizontal and vertical lines set at right angles to each other that is the skeleton and foundation of every chart. This point is the cusp, the beginning of the Tenth House, which is the house to the left of the vertical line. The cusp of the Tenth House is also called the Midheaven because it is supposed to represent the point in the sky directly above you at the time of your birth, the point where the Sun would be if you were born exactly at high noon. It is the point in the sky where the planets stop ascending and start their descent.

The astrological meaning of a chart's Tenth House is everything connected to *where you are going, your career plans* (as opposed to your Sixth House job requirements), *what you aspire to*, and especially *becoming a person respected by those whom you respect*. It can also be related to being recognized, attaining awards and honors among your peers, and even fame with a segment of the general public.

The Tenth House can also give you information about how a person experiences authority, dealing with the authority of others, and becoming an authority, and how they handle the responsibilities and power of authority once it has been attained. It also rules how you feel about those who have authority over you both then and now, including how you think they feel about you, and how you feel about standing up and publicly sharing what you believe to be unquestionably true.

The issue of authority extends to how you experience the person or persons who functioned as the caregiver who helped guide you on your path to all Tenth House matters. Traditional old-school astrology assigned this role to the father, and very often it does represent one's father, but it is not accurate to limit its meaning to a person's biological father. We modern astrologers have led the way to a more accurate description of the person or persons who are actively involved caregivers and help someone successfully navigate Tenth House matters.

The Tenth House represents how you experienced the parent(s) or caregiver(s) in your home while you were growing up, those who imposed structure, rules, and discipline. It would also be the place to find out how those who did not have a person or persons who imposed structure, rules, and discipline would be inclined to react to this challenging absence. It could also show the consequences of this lack of structure and discipline on the native, on both their life and their career.

Whether you respect yourself and how you experience, value, and respond to the respect of those you do and do not respect are vitally important Tenth House matters.

The Tenth House also relates to your calling in life, whether you feel you have one, and, if you do feel that way, how you go about answering that call. It is all about the ideas, plans, and actions necessary for you to establish your personal dynasty and create what will live on after you pass away in time.

Achievement and everything that achievement requires and produces, and how your life is affected by achievement or lack of it, are all Tenth House matters. Fame is another issue—your attitude toward fame and famous people, and your capacity for becoming famous and dealing with the perks and problems that arise as a natural consequence of any measure of success. Whether we are rich, poor, or in between, we all have to deal with the limits and problems that are a natural part of life, not just the issues associated with our station in life. That immutable fact brings us to the meaning of the Tenth House's ruling planet, Saturn.

SATURN, RULER OF THE TENTH HOUSE

The ruling planet of the Tenth House is Saturn, the planet of discipline and the cold, harsh facts of reality.

The glyph for Saturn shows the crescent of the individualized soul descending from the bottom of the cross of matter. This symbolizes Saturn's role as showing us how material concerns dominate the purely intellectual and emotional halves of our being human and born into our physical bodies.

The astrological meaning of Saturn harkens back to the model of the traditional stern father, which I have updated for modern times to represent any caregiver who explains to the younger person that making one's way in the world can often be a difficult, lonely, and unforgiving experience and, therefore, one cannot fool around forever with childish things but must grow up, the sooner the better. This person inculcates the understanding that this achievement requires a person to be as

realistic and disciplined as possible and to use one's limited time on Earth doing what must be done, not just what one wants to do, if one is to achieve anything worthwhile and lasting over time.

In mythology, the other name for Saturn is Chronos. (This term is from the Greek word meaning "time.") Our limited time on Earth is the ultimate reality, and Saturn is the ruler of all things connected to time and timing. Saturn is both the authoritative teacher who reminds us of and enforces the rules of time, in the sense that everything living has only so much time to live, and the ruler of everything conceptualized and actualized that is meant to last, to endure the test of time.

Since I believe it is useful for astrologers to view astrology as a psychological language, that prompts the question, "What aspect of our psyche does Saturn correspond to?" It's the part of us that knows that our time is limited and knows what we should do, what is expected of us by others, and, more importantly, what we expect of ourselves.

Our capacity for self-discipline is intimately tied to our Saturn's sign and house placement. As with all the other planets, a balanced approach is key. It is important to balance the usually critical and doleful influence of our Saturn on our inner dialogue with a healthy dose of self-appreciation and self-love; otherwise, Saturn will prevent us from being comfortable enough with ourselves to live our lives with enjoyment and will limit even the simplest of our pleasures in ways small and large.

Saturn is all about limits and endurance. Saturn is the teacher of all things that are real and true but difficult to hear, accept, and act on. Saturn tests one's ability to be dedicated and consistent in the working of a plan of action. Saturn knows that the way to become recognized for something is practice, practice, practice.

Pay close attention to whatever sign or house Saturn is in when you are reading a cosmic blueprint. Never give it anything less than your undivided attention. Saturn's house and sign in an astrology chart can represent either a strengthening or a blockage in the expression of the energies represented by that house and sign.

However, it can also represent that this person takes these matters so seriously that their thoughts and actions regarding these matters can be made in isolation from the rest of the chart. This can explain why people seem to act strangely, impractically, or against their own self-interest, as if they have a blind spot, in the things related to their Saturn's house and sign position. Treat Saturn seriously because Saturn rules everything that is serious in a person's life.

SATURN THROUGH THE SIGNS

Saturn is a very important and necessary energy in our lives. It is the discipline we need to accomplish anything we want to accomplish and make our presence felt on Earth in an impactful way. If you want something to have impact and value, to be remembered, and to have influence for a long time, you must thoroughly understand and use your Saturn energy wisely, with your undivided attention, and with compassion for being a human, with all the limits that entails.

Our Saturn's house and sign position can indicate areas of life where we are trying to be so practical and follow the rules so as to avoid feelings of lack and limits on our abilities to act exactly as we want to act in those areas that we end up thinking in a limited fashion, lacking the inclusion in our thought process of other things we know just as well—maybe better.

Saturnine thinking, planning, and acting is often revealed to be driven by our desire to be overly logical or emotionally intelligent regarding matters ruled by the sign and house Saturn occupies and to display a slavish adherence to the tried-and-true, hardly allowing our own experiences and the other planetary energies to inform the matter. Saturn is all about crystallization, and as anyone who knows crystals can tell you, their molecular structure is strong and beautiful and enables them to conduct powerful energies that make daily life possible. See the work of the brilliant scientist Marcel Vogel if you want to know more about the importance and power of crystals.

What is to be avoided is an effect on the individual that can be likened to calcification, a hardening of energies, opinions, modes of operation, and attitudes that prevents growth as a person and forward movement in the game of life. Saturn's influence on us is beneficial when it enables us to have goals and to create a strong foundation in the skills we will need so we can reach those goals. It can work against us when we are not open to adjusting our strongly held beliefs to the lessons and situations in which we find ourselves as we move along the river of time. There are countless examples of good, smart people who work hard and become authorities on a topic but refuse to be open to other ways of looking at what has become their area of expertise.

Anything connected with time, or the timing involved in a plan, usually a long-term one, is a Saturn matter. Since astrology is a psychological language, Saturn's rulership of time, endurance, discipline, and both learning and teaching show that it is an immensely powerful area of our psyche and one of the most important.

The Sun (ego), Moon (emotions), Mercury (logical mind), Venus (personal magnetism), and Mars (how we work our will) are our personal planets. Saturn takes approximately thirty years to go around the Sun and is in a sign for approximately two and a half years, so it stamps out subsets of the longer-spanned generations stamped out by Pluto (17–31 years because of its very elliptical orbit), Neptune (13–15 years), and Uranus (6–8 years).

However, it is Jupiter (how we grow), which we will learn more about soon, and Saturn (how we learn) that allow us to be part of our peer groups and potentially feel part of a cohort of fellow children and students who were born when Jupiter was in a sign (approximately one year) and Saturn was in a sign (approximately two and a half years). This allows us to feel part of a larger whole and prepares us for adulthood when we are going to be interacting with a lot of people who have their outer planets—Uranus (what renews us), Neptune (what inspires us), and Pluto (what transforms us)—in the same sign as ours and in different signs.

Just like the glyph for Saturn shows the crescent of soul reaching down, our Saturn's house and sign are like an anchor holding us and our personal identity safe and secure in a world that easily can be seen to be threatening to our very existence, with constant change and never-ending uncertainty. When you see Saturn in a sign or a house, visualize its meaning as either a strengthening and a deepening of the meaning of that sign and house or as a limiting blockage of those energies. The truth can be revealed by doing so.

Though Saturn can indicate a vitally important, disciplined application of a sign or house's attributes, for our purposes here at this stage of your education—because I am preparing you to read a cosmic blueprint, and seeing potential problems is half the battle—when you see the word *Saturn* in this book from now on, think of the word *problems.* I will tell you when to stop thinking of Saturn in this way. For now, I want you to think of Saturn in a person's chart as representing the area where they often do not think as accurately or as logically as they believe they are doing. It represents an area of their life they are working on and will be working on all their days.

It is imperative to realize that even when you have identified and started to get a handle on what limiting thoughts and beliefs are afflicting you via Saturn's influence, *you are still not going to think completely accurately about that area of your life*! Yes, it will diminish and get better, but no, it won't go away. Saturn is the teacher, and if you don't fight the lessons to be learned, but rather use the problems and difficulties to build lasting strength and endurance in yourself, you will understand that Saturn is the planet that helps us achieve maturity and wisdom, enabling us to stand strong and maybe even stand out as an authority or a role model in the lives of our contemporaries.

Remembering this and staying in touch with and increasing your understanding of the limiting thoughts, beliefs, and habits associated with your Saturn is like exercising, eating right, or, more specifically, brushing your teeth; you must do it after every meal. Just like every time you see a problem coming, are in the middle of it, or are dealing with the aftermath, you should remember where your Saturn is and what that means. Thinking "I've got that!" and ceasing to do the work required by Saturn when you should be thinking about what Saturn's position wants you to learn is a sign that you have not "got that" yet.

For example, I have Saturn in Virgo. Simple keywords: problems with worry. Do you think knowing that stops me from overthinking or worrying? No. Is it a tragedy, the end of the world? Also no. Being aware of it does help and mitigate it somewhat but only sometimes—not always. Having Saturn in Virgo helps me to be a much more precise and organized person—in this case, a disciplined writer who is willing to take on the many years it took to write this book, all the while having as precise a conversation as I can have with you, dear reader. It also makes me a better teacher.

NOTE: *When I say things like "problems with worry" or "problems with being bossy," that can mean problems with worrying too much or not enough or with being too bossy or not bossy enough. It could also refer to problems you do not have but that you are forced to deal with in another person because of your attitude or reaction to other people being bossy or exemplifying one of the other problems I list.*

ALSO NOTE: *You are more likely to encounter the energy of your Saturn from someone else if you have it in the Seventh House—the spectrum of meanings, remember. In general, it is the extreme ends of the spectrum that are the most problematic. This is true for every keyword mashup of the planets, signs, and houses of astrology.*

Saturn in Aries ♄ ♈

Problems with acting quickly and without forethought, honesty, lies and liars, being a pioneer, being alone, being bossy, being aggressive, being brave.

Saturn in Taurus ♄ ♉

Problems with possessions, money, coping, adapting, sensuality, values, stopping, inertia, laziness, being strong, stubbornness, giving up.

Saturn in Gemini ♄ ♊

Problems with communicating, attention, connections, multitasking, boredom, learning, duality, gossip, understanding your and others' core beliefs.

Saturn in Cancer ♄ ♋

Problems with nurturing, the past, feeling supported, real estate, intuition, security, (over) protection, one's mother or the caregiver(s) who fulfilled that role.

Saturn in Leo ♄ ♌

Problems with pride, status, taking a chance, coming before the public, leadership, ego, organization, embellishment, acting out, romance, creativity.

Saturn in Virgo ♄ ♍

Problems with worry, perfectionism, order, cleanliness, overthinking, analyzing, health, service, not seeing the big picture, thinking too small.

Saturn in Libra ♄ ♎

Problems with balance, agreements, commitment, coming in front of the public, judgment, compromise, partnerships, relationships, being too accommodating.

Saturn in Scorpio ♄ ♏

Problems with power, change, sexual matters, eliminations, waste removal, deception, detecting, magic, secrets, the metaphysical, extremes, death.

Saturn in Sagittarius ♄ ♐

Problems with the truth, honesty, things foreign, laws, philosophy, the uneducated, natural healing, long-distance travel, horses, religious matters.

Saturn in Capricorn (Ruler) ♄ ♑

Problems with authority, limits, structure, time and timing, sensual needs versus business at hand, being responsible, teaching and learning, being serious, career.

Saturn in Aquarius ♄ ♒

Problems with being different, disruption, freedom, revolution, scientific advances, friends, hopes and wishes, overreacting, distraction, being ahead of one's time.

Saturn in Pisces ♄ ♓

Problems with sensitivity, compassion, psychic matters, matters beyond words, overwhelm, balancing the personal with humanity, ego destruction, solitude.

You now can stop thinking about Saturn as only being related to problems. You can now think of it as the Lord of Discipline, time, timing, and all things that reinforce a realistic view of the world so that we can create and anchor our beliefs, our core identity both internally and out in the world, and do and build things that have the potential to last a long time, even past our time on Earth. If you want to build a dynasty, use your Saturn energy creatively.

A BRIEF LOOK AT PLANETS IN THE TENTH HOUSE

NOTE: *The closer a planet is to your Midheaven/Tenth House cusp, the greater will be the chance that the following delineations seem to be amazingly accurate.*

The Sun ☉

You are inclined to either identify with or reject any similarities with your caregiver who explained the harsh realities of life and influenced your career path. You need the respect of those you respect more than most people. You have leadership abilities that may be widely recognized.

The Moon ☽

You feel more emotionally content when you are pursuing your career goals. You have a deep-seated need to use your exceptional level of emotional intelligence to rise in your chosen profession until you become an unquestioned success and authority figure.

Mercury ☿

You are almost always thinking about bettering yourself and the lives of those you care about, always on the alert for opportunities for advancement. You may become recognized for knowing more than most people about all aspects of what you choose for a career.

Venus ♀

You feel favorably toward and identify with the caregiver who played the archetypical Tenth House role in your life. You may be attracted to a career that involves the arts or the beautification of people, places, and things. If you love your career, you will succeed.

Mars ♂

You are driven to succeed. You may not take career advice well, causing friction between you and caregivers and any advisers who try to guide you. This might cause you to have a problem with those in authority, but if you can use this energy positively, you will be one of them.

Jupiter ♃

Your career can appear blessed. You and your positive-role-model caregiver will know how your growing as a person has led to worldly success. If you can avoid excessive optimism and moderate your desire to always keep expanding your goals, you can accomplish a lot.

Saturn (Ruler) ♄

You and your role model(s) have always known that you have an important calling in life and what you must do to achieve success. One or more stern caregivers, or the lack of one, made you who you are or were. You are now dedicated to being an authoritative person of substance.

Uranus ♅

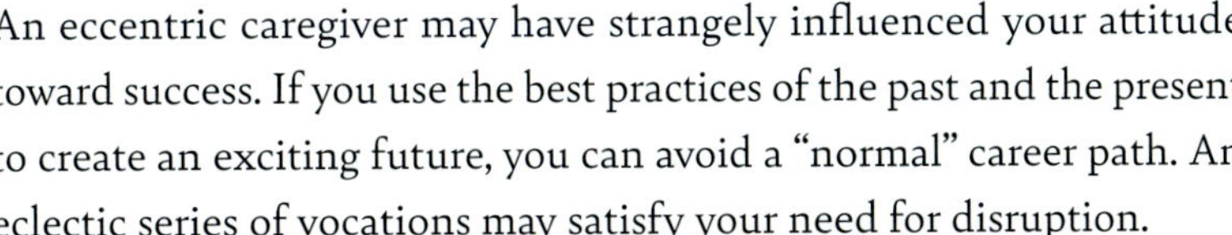

An eccentric caregiver may have strangely influenced your attitude toward success. If you use the best practices of the past and the present to create an exciting future, you can avoid a "normal" career path. An eclectic series of vocations may satisfy your need for disruption.

Neptune ♆

An idealistic caregiver who could have had escapist tendencies may have inspired you to inspire others or caused you to feel a career path was beyond your abilities. If you use your innate intuition to guide your career, you can accomplish more than anyone thought you could.

Pluto ♇

You may have struggled with an often-overbearing caregiver who tried to impose their will on you. You need a career that allows you to either feel important or be important. If you resist the urge to defy or constantly confront those in authority, you can become one of them.

RECAP: *The Tenth House is related to authority of all kinds. It represents how you experienced the parent(s)/caregiver(s) who imposed structure, rules, and discipline while you were growing up. It also rules how you feel about those who have authority over you now, including how you believe they feel about you, and how you feel about becoming an authority and wielding power.*

Saturn rules the Tenth House and is the planet of time, timing, discipline, authority, teaching, the wisdom and problems of age and aging, and the part of our psyche that is so important to us that it both anchors our identity in reality and can cause us to overcorrect our thinking and behavior based on our wanting to be "realistic" to the point that we limit our thinking, either ignoring the metaphysical ("beyond the physical") realities or dwelling on them too much for our own good.

THE FOURTH HOUSE

The cusp of the Fourth House represents the point directly beneath you, behind the Earth when you are born and took your first breath. (I want to say it is the point beneath your feet when you are born, but you are far from standing when that blessed event takes place.)

In astrology, the Fourth House does represent where you stand, your home, what makes you feel secure, your past, and real estate and all resources that cannot be moved. It also represents where you will make your stand, the people, places, core beliefs, and boundaries that you will try to maintain at all costs.

With so many people working from home these days, an important distinction to keep in mind is that while the Fourth House represents one's home, it is the Tenth House that represents business offices, factories, warehouses—whatever we consider our working "home"—and so the Tenth House represents one's home-office area and one's attitude toward working at home.

The Fourth House is the house opposite the Tenth House. While the Tenth House can be associated with the stern-father cliché of old-school astrology—the person(s) who showed you the cold, hard facts of the ways of the world—the Fourth House represents the person or person who "mothered" you, especially the person who gave birth to you.

The Fourth House is related to your experience of the unconditional love, nurturing, and support a child needs to feel secure. This means it relates to whether you had those things, as well as the quality of what you experienced if you had the good fortune to have someone like that in your life. It almost goes without saying that your childhood experiences of this nature will strongly influence your adult experience of home, family, and even workplace and work family, making your understanding of the Fourth House and any planets that occupy it vitally important to the reading of a cosmic blueprint.

Of course, new cultural norms and the scientific miracles of our time have also called on astrologers to expand their minds and be open to new definitions of mothering: caregivers who are relatives of the child, friends of the family who take them in and raise them, paid childcare workers of any kind (governesses, nannies, people paid by governmental, nongovernmental, or religious organizations), and includes surrogates, in vitro fertilization, and families that are composed of two (or more) people who would not traditionally be called mothers. All these things are Fourth House matters.

The Fourth House is ruled by the Moon, which we have delineated through the signs starting on page 69.

A BRIEF LOOK AT PLANETS IN THE FOURTH HOUSE

NOTE: *The closer a planet is to your Fourth House cusp, the greater will be the chance that the following delineations seem to be amazingly accurate.*

The Sun ☉

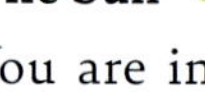

You are inclined to either identify with or reject any similarities with the caregiver who was supposed to nurture and love you unconditionally. If there was no one who fulfilled this role, the sign it's in gives you clues to how you have nurtured yourself or why you do not do so.

The Moon (Ruler) ☽

You feel more emotionally content when you are home with family or engaged in activities that connect you to the past. You nurture others in the way you received nurturing as a child. You have a natural affinity for things connected to home ownership.

Mercury ☿

You are almost always thinking about the past, the way you were reared, and what makes you feel secure. This makes it easy for you to know what is necessary for establishing and maintaining a home or any base of operations that runs smoothly and efficiently.

Venus ♀

You are inclined to always care for the nurturing caregiver(s) in your life. You need to live in a nice place or one that connects you to your past in some way in order to feel secure enough to make it your "nest." You may do well in industries that buy, sell, and improve homes and land.

Mars ♂

You are driven to feel secure. You may have experienced one or more of your caregivers as overly aggressive, and this has shaped how you feel about closeness, kindness, unconditional love, family, or the past. You may always be searching for the perfect place to call home.

Jupiter ♃

Your personal growth is tied to exploring what makes you feel secure and your experience of home, family, the past, and caregivers whose positivity you may emulate. Your home may be large, welcoming, or otherwise impressive. You can be lucky in real estate speculation.

Saturn ♄

It may have been difficult to receive the unconditional love and nurturing you needed, and that feeling of lack, insecurity, and otherwise having a difficult early life may still linger. You have cultivated self-discipline and may, over time, acquire an impressive real estate portfolio.

Uranus ♅

An eccentric caregiver may have strangely influenced your definition of caregiving, home, family, and security. For you to call a place or situation home, it has to allow you to be your authentic self and have freedom to move on. You have an unusual attitude toward owning property.

Neptune ♆

An idealistic caregiver, one you idealize even though they could have had escapist tendencies, may have influenced you to feel secure only when you are helping others. Your home may be seen as a spiritual center. You may have an unclear or idealized picture of your past.

Pluto ♇

You may have struggled with an often-overbearing caregiver who tried to impose their will on you. Your home life and past may have been much more difficult than that of most people. You are willing to do a lot to feel secure. You may be involved in power struggles over property.

RECAP: *The Fourth House is the house on the bottom and to the right of the vertical line that separates the two halves of an astrology chart into right and left. It is opposite the Tenth House. While the Tenth House is all about your career, your office or other work "home," work "family," and the direction you are headed into the future, the Fourth House is all about what home, family, and the past mean to you.*

The Fourth House is where you are coming from, both literally and figuratively. It represents your inner self, who you are when you are home and no one is watching or listening. It is about what makes you feel secure. It usually is related to how you experienced your mother or the parent or parental figure who cared for and nurtured you the most and gave you any unconditional love, if you were lucky enough to receive any while you were growing up. Now that you are older, the Fourth House is related to your past experiences, people and places from your past, and how you feel about them. It is also related to buying, selling, renting, and owning land, buildings, and other fixed forms of wealth.

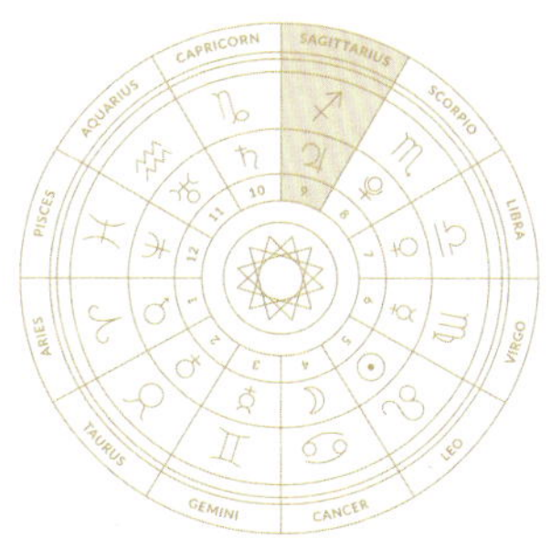

THE NINTH HOUSE

The Ninth House and the Eleventh House of an astrology chart can be understood as being strongly related to the Tenth House. The Tenth House is the house of authority. The Ninth House is all about what enables a person or an entity to become and stay an authority.

The Ninth House is all about the laws, rules, philosophy, higher learning, and the increase of knowledge and of what one knows to be true that is necessary to keep an authoritative entity in power, whether that entity be human, governmental, corporate, or any other form that has influence and power. That increased knowledge, understanding, and wisdom comes from study, travel, and the sharing of all the knowledge and wisdom of all the people of all the nations, cultures, and philosophies out there in the world.

The Ninth House is also associated with everything that takes what you know about the world to those beyond your usual places, neighborhood, friends, and family. This is why the Ninth House rules books, publishing, videos, podcasts, webinars, conferences, broadcasting, and any and all things related to disseminating and expanding the level of information one needs to function as someone who deserves to be a Tenth House authority. The Ninth House can be viewed and remembered by you as the support "staff" of the Tenth House.

The Ninth House rules laws, including the painstaking, word-by-word crafting that takes place to get the intent to be as clear as possible and codified as accepted laws, while the Seventh House rules the debate about the philosophies and laws based on those philosophies, as well as the legal trials based on the interpretation of those laws, and the Twelfth House rules the judicial system as a whole operating and functioning system.

The following is designed to help you understand the distinctions between the houses in the above sentence:

Ninth House? Philosophy, higher learning, the crafting of laws.

Seventh House? Weighing one consideration against the other in debate and in trials designed to apply those Ninth House laws.

Twelfth House? The legal system, the court system, governments, and any large institution where a person is subject to the rules of that particular ecosystem, including the military, corporations, the educational system, and similar entities.

The Ninth House's rulership of philosophy extends to the codified tenets, the ideas, words, and rules of organized religions, and the teaching and study of all subjects one would find both in a religious context and in a university or other enriched learning environment.

The Twelfth House rules organized religious orders as if they were any other large institution where one's individual ego is negated and where you are a cog in a machine dedicated to helping followers of a particular religion—including charitable institutions and all large organizations dedicated to advancing a particular religion or philosophy.

The accumulation of wisdom and knowledge is also a Ninth House matter, and that is the reason that this house is commonly known as the house of foreign travel. There is an old expression, "Travel broadens one," meaning it widens one's perspectives on many subjects, and while this can be, and often is, true, there is a finer distinction between Ninth House travel and, as you will soon see, Third House travel.

If you walk across the room and you receive an "Aha!" moment of insight, that is Ninth House travel just like a trip around the world is. If you are forced by circumstances to routinely visit the same place, even if you have to travel thousands of miles to do so, and do not have any "Aha!" moments or insights from that trip, that is Third House travel.

Ninth House travel is any travel that expands your mind, by which I mean expands your understanding of a particular subject, especially of what it means to be a human being facing mortality, which is the basis for virtually all religions. Planets and the signs they are in if they are in your Ninth House can indicate one's attitude toward the search for and sharing of ultimate truth through organized religions, alternative and more personally evolved spiritualities, higher education, academia, long-distance travel, and the search for and sharing of the best the world has to offer.

The Ninth House's concern with matters that are supposed to be universally beneficial to so many people binds it with its ruling planet, Jupiter, also known as the greater benefic, with Venus being the lesser of these two fortunate planets. Jupiter is all about how we grow as we live and learn.

JUPITER, RULER OF THE NINTH HOUSE

In the psychological language that I consider astrology to be, we have learned that the Sun represents our ego, the Moon our emotional intelligence, Mercury our logical mind, Venus what we love and how we attract it to us, Mars the desire and energy we possess to go out and work our will on the world, and Saturn how we benefit from being realistic and doing the hard work required of us.

Jupiter represents how we grow and expand from being positive and grateful, expecting things to work out, how we benefit from realizing how lucky we are, no matter what our situation (trust me—things can always be worse), and from having an awareness of the riches given to us in the many forms in which they can manifest—often very well disguised, but riches nonetheless.

The glyph for Jupiter shows the half-circle representing the intellectual and emotional halves of the individual soul connected to the cross of matter at its left-hand point, the same place on a cosmic blueprint that determines its Rising Sign. This represents the beneficial aspect Jupiter brings to the individual soul harmoniously interacting with material reality.

The word *jovial* comes from *Jove,* the other name Romans used for Jupiter. While Jupiter does sometimes bring good times and good fortune to things related to the house it is in, it is much more usual for it to indicate to us how we grow, how we increase in knowledge, wisdom, and understanding, or how we grow and expand our business, family, or just about anything else. Jupiter, like all the planets, does have its spectrum of meanings, and the negative extreme of Jupiter is excess, gluttony, overexpansion, or expansion that is ill-timed.

Jupiter is deceptively important in astrology. While Saturn requires detailed explanation and warnings regarding its meaning, sign, and house placements in our cosmic blueprint to help us avoid or mitigate its indications of major challenges to our enjoyment of our precious time on Earth, Jupiter is closely tied to that enjoyment and indicates an area of respite from the challenges posed by Saturn.

It is my firm belief that our cosmic blueprint is one of our strongest tools for helping us fulfill our most important task on Earth: to grow into being ourselves fully. Our Jupiter shows us how we can best do so and thereby enjoy life to the max.

JUPITER THROUGH THE SIGNS

Jupiter gives without being asked. As mentioned above, Jupiter represents how we grow, as well as expansion, good fortune, or just plain simple or amazing luck. Keep in mind as you read the following delineations of Jupiter through the signs that when I say, "Growing by learning about . . ." you can be growing by learning about how it feels to be lacking something as well as by having it. Never forget my advice about the spectrum of meanings. It will keep you balanced, and when you provide astrological readings, you will give useful advice, not just pat answers.

Jupiter in Aries ♃ ♈

Growing by learning about being first, being honest, coping with lies and liars, being a pioneer, being alone, being bossy, being aggressive, and about fighting for what you think is worth fighting for.

Jupiter in Taurus ♃ ♉

Growing by learning about possessions, money, coping, adapting, sensuality, values, starting, stopping, inertia, laziness, being strong, being weak, being stubborn, giving up, anger, desire, wealth, and music.

Jupiter in Gemini ♃ ♊

Growing by learning about learning, communicating, paying attention, making connections, multitasking, boredom, understanding, dealing with duality, sophistry, debating, and ultimate truths.

Jupiter in Cancer ♃ ♋

Growing by learning about nurturing, the past, feeling supported, real estate, home building, intuition, security, protection, one's birth mother or the caregiver(s) who fulfilled that role, and homemaking.

Jupiter in Leo ♃ ♌

Growing by learning about ego, pride, status, risk-taking, gambling, performing, leadership, politics, organization, embellishment, acting out, romance, creativity, the lion's share, and having a great time.

Jupiter in Virgo ♃ ♍

Growing by learning about worry, perfectionism, tidiness, order, cleanliness, overthinking, analyzing, food, animals, health, service, seeing the big picture, thinking small, procrastination, and being a virgin in some way.

Jupiter in Libra ♃ ♎

Growing by learning about balance, harmony, contracts, agreements, commitment, coming before the public, judgment, compromise, partnerships, relationships, compromise, beauty, and peace.

Jupiter in Scorpio ♃ ♏

Growing by learning about power, resurrection, change, sexual matters, eliminations, other people's resources, deception, detecting, mysteries, magic, secrets, extremes, things metaphysical, and death.

Jupiter in Sagittarius (Ruler) ♃ ♐

Growing by learning about truth, honesty, secrets, things foreign, laws, philosophy, higher education, good fortune, natural healing, long-distance travel, large animals, nature, and things religious.

Jupiter in Capricorn ♃ ♑

Growing by learning about authority, discipline, limits, structure, time and timing, sensual needs versus business at hand, responsibility, teaching, learning, being serious, funny, older, and businesslike.

Jupiter in Aquarius ♃ ♒

Growing by learning about being different, disruption, freedom, revolution, scientific advances, the future, being ahead of one's time, overreacting, distraction, emotions, friends, hopes, and wishes.

Jupiter in Pisces ♃ ♓

Growing by learning about compassion, sensitivity, psychic matters, emotions, overwhelm, idealism, personal needs versus humanity's, charity, large institutions, ego negation, solitude, and utopian dreams.

A BRIEF LOOK AT PLANETS IN THE NINTH HOUSE

The Sun ☉

You are inclined to have a philosophy of life you live by. It can be constantly evolving as you search for ultimate truth, but you will continually strive to never violate your personal code. You have an open mind and want to fill it with the best ideas so you can share them.

The Moon ☽

You are always on the move, both physically and emotionally. If you cannot change your residence or travel, you have to always be learning, teaching, and growing as a person. Your philosophy of life is based on what is true for you emotionally.

Mercury ☿

You are almost always thinking about or traveling to faraway places and how what you are experiencing at that time fits in with your ever-evolving philosophy. You are a born communicator and need to be sending out and receiving ideas constantly.

Venus ♀

You love to travel and do anything else that allows you to experience, share, or learn about the best the world and its peoples have to offer. Your philosophy of life is inextricably tied to your ability to attract and bring love to a world that so obviously needs it.

Mars ♂

You are driven to learn about and leave your mark on the world, whether that is through travel, higher education, speaking, writing, and all manner of communications, or the making and implementing of rules and laws. Beware of defending your beliefs too aggressively.

Jupiter (Ruler) ♃

Your personal growth is tied to exploring the best the world has to offer in terms of culture, philosophy, laws, and more. You are a citizen of the world, much more open-minded and understanding of religious and racial differences than other people with similar upbringings.

Saturn ♄

You take the world very seriously and see its flaws, dangers, and the difficult but needed remedies you believe in. You may travel more than most people but, even going first class, it will be difficult for you to enjoy it. You need to see the necessity for joy in your worldview.

Uranus ♅

You are aware of humanity's need to disrupt and shake off the old ways that have outlived their supposed usefulness. You can be part of this movement if you join forces with those not precisely on your page. Your philosophy and style of traveling are quite unusual.

Neptune ♆

You care about the world and are willing to do your part to help, even if that means traveling to places that are dangerous or that have primitive living conditions. Your worldview is both compassionate and inspiring. You can be truly spiritual, highly intuitive, or religious.

Pluto ♇

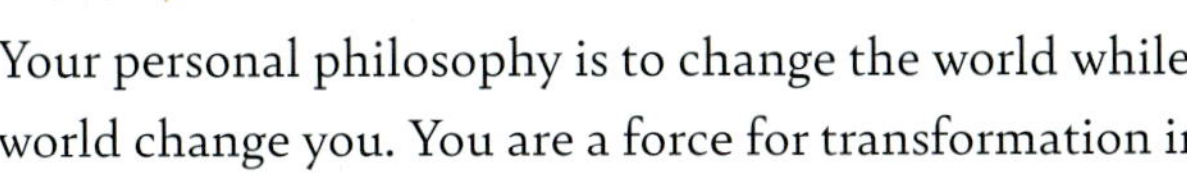

Your personal philosophy is to change the world while not letting the world change you. You are a force for transformation in whatever role you choose, though you may prefer to do so as an unseen force working away quietly in a position where you exert raw power.

RECAP: *The Ninth House has to do with the transmission and exchange of important information between you and the world. One aspect of this is travel and everything that helps you travel—travel that broadens your understanding of the world or that allows you to exchange ideas with many people. Other ways to learn about the customs and beliefs of people who are not in your neighborhood are by reading books, newspapers, magazines, and electronically transmitted information of all kinds through avenues like the internet, television, radio, and other wireless communications devices. The communications ruled by the Ninth House are about sharing college-level thinking, expert advice, historical facts, philosophy, cultural anthropology, cartography, and research of all kinds.*

The Ninth House also has to do with justice, which is not the same thing as the laws of the Seventh House. Justice requires that you apply law with the wisdom that the Ninth House rules. Justice should not be blind. The Ninth House is ruled by Jupiter, the planet that in astrology represents how we grow in wisdom and understanding and very often it represents how we grow when things are going well. Saturn, of course, represents how we grow when things are challenging. Jupiter represents the tools used to aid growth in knowledge and understanding. While Mercury represents attention to the little things, the details, and the piece-by-piece perception of individual facts, Jupiter represents assembling the pieces to make the finished puzzle, the big picture. Jupiter is the "forest" to Mercury's "trees."

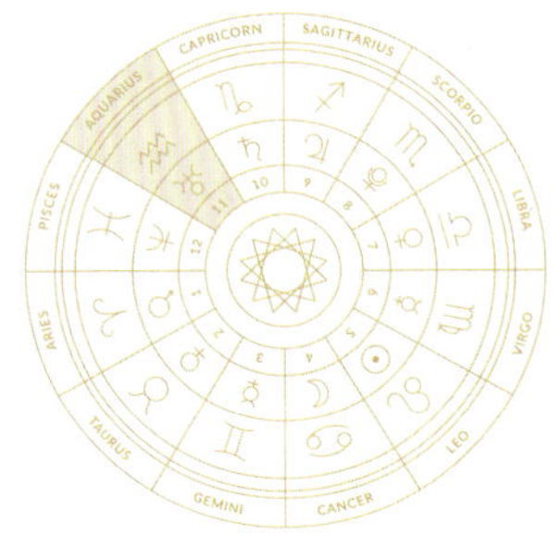

THE ELEVENTH HOUSE

The Eleventh House of an astrology chart, like the Ninth House, can be understood as being strongly related to and its meaning derived from an understanding of the Tenth House. As I hope you remember, the Tenth House, ruled by Saturn, is the house of authority, and the Ninth House, ruled by Jupiter, is all about the laws, rules, philosophy, higher learning, and the equally important increase of knowledge that comes from foreign, mind-expanding, long-distance travel that can teach the open-minded things they could not learn in a book or a classroom.

The Eleventh House is traditionally known as the house of friends, hopes, and wishes, and though that can sometimes be true, I have discovered that the Eleventh House is the house of people who band together for the common goal of using the strength of their numbers and the pooling of their resources to be able to act like an independent, powerful authority, either to support or oppose an existing authority. This can even be a group that has gotten organized to bring disruption and revolution to an existing authority or social order.

At the other end of the spectrum, Eleventh House matters can be organizations composed of experts and/or successful people who, as authorities themselves, band together to determine licensing requirements and advise governments on policymaking, scientific theories and currently accepted definitions, and the imposition of conventions and paradigms of all kinds.

Group meetings of those in a particular industry, career, or lifestyle are often called conventions. At many of these conventions, those who want to effect change gather, network, and further organize—all things that are Eleventh House matters.

The Eleventh House relates to any group of individuals who get together for a common purpose. They may not love or even like each other, but in union there is strength, or at least the appearance of strength. I'm sure that, like Amy and I, you have often been surprised at how many trade groups, fraternal societies, and especially religious groups, associations, and organizations there are, clustered around a particular cause, and how much publicity and other attention they receive. They might not have great numbers behind them, but they are making use of the old ways from the old days, a time when an organization with an impressive name was afforded great respect whether it actually deserved it or not.

In the information age, it is getting harder and harder for a small organization of people devoted to a cause to present themselves as a large one, though it still seems that anthropologist Margaret Meade's famous saying is still true: "Never doubt that a small group of thoughtful, committed citizens can change the world. Indeed, it is the only thing that ever has." Another of her brilliant sayings is one that should be on billboards around the world: "Never depend upon institutions or government to solve any problem. All social movements are founded by, guided by, motivated and seen through by the passion of individuals."

The Eleventh House has to do with people who are passionate about authority, like trade unions, fraternal organizations, fraternities, sororities, trade shows, political parties, rallies, nongovernmental organizations (NGOs), clubs, and all groups of people who come together for a common goal.

It is important to note that the reason organizations of people are respected by those is authority is because people in power know that the hold they have on other people is tenuous and that a large group of people united for a cause can overwhelm the forces of authority if they are dedicated and organized enough and willing to risk their jobs, their reputations, or even their health and safety.

URANUS, RULER OF THE ELEVENTH HOUSE

The Eleventh House is ruled by Uranus, which takes approximately eighty-four years to go around the solar system. Dividing that number by twelve, we see that Uranus stays in a sign approximately seven years, though that can change because of its elliptical orbit and/or retrograde motion and last eight years.

The glyph for the planet Uranus shows both the intellectual and the emotional crescents of the individualized soul pulling on opposite sides of the horizontal axis of the cross of matter, which is, itself, above the circle of Spirit. In this glyph you can see the glyphs of both aggressive Mars, the circle of Spirit with the cross of matter above it (before it becomes folded into an arrow symbol), and the glyph of loving Venus but standing on its head, a clue to Uranus's love for the unusual and extreme.

Planetary Returns: Essential Information for All Astrologers

I would like to point out again that the slower-moving planets mint—stamp out like coins—generations of people born with a particular planet in a particular sign. When a planet has gone around the solar system and returned to the spot it was on when the observing of its motion commenced, we say that planet has a return.

It bears repeating that the most famous planetary return is that of your birthday—the Sun's apparent return to where it was when plotted against the background of the zodiac when you were born. (This is the origin of the expression "Many happy returns.") Take note of the fact that your actual solar return, when the Sun is on the exact degree and minute of the zodiac, can sometimes happen a day before or a day after your traditional birthday.

If you want to be a good astrologer, you have to look at the age of your client and see whether they are at or near the age when one of the following outer-planet returns is happening in their chart. These returns, especially the returns of Saturn and the opposition of Uranus to where it was on the birthday of the person whose chart you are reading, mark significant periods in a person's life and are always worth being examined during the reading.

The Jupiter Return

Jupiter stays in a sign for about a year, taking about 12 years to go around the Sun and return to where it was when a count started. The time of a person's first Jupiter return is the approximate time when a child starts to be treated more like an adult, usually receiving gifts, in true Jupiterian fashion, to commemorate the transition. Jupiter returns are usually pleasant and are accompanied by some form of gift—often that of personal growth, though it can sometimes be a tangible gift that reinforces Jupiter's reputation for being the planet of good fortune.

The Saturn Return

Saturn stays in a sign for about 2½ years, taking about 30 years to go around the Sun. Because of retrograde motion, this can occur anywhere from when a person is 27 all the way to 33 years of age, when young people start worrying about being "old." The Saturn return does mark the transition from youth to adulthood and is invariably a noticeably difficult time in everyone's life. One can no longer do the often-silly things one used to do as a youth without experiencing adult consequences—especially those things people often do even though they know doing so is not good for them.

The Saturn return is one explanation for the infamous 27-year-old curse, which saw Jimi Hendrix, Janis Joplin, Jim Morrison, and many other lesser-known young adults not survive their Saturn return. Had they consulted a skilled astrologer, they would have learned that there has not been a person born who, at the time of their first Saturn return, did not feel depressed and believe that their life was not moving fast enough, that they had not accomplished enough, or that their life was, by some definition, a failure.

The passage through this time and these feelings is a vital step in becoming a mature person in true Saturnine fashion. It happens again around the age of 60, the passage from being an adult into being a sage, a teacher of the wisdom you've accumulated. And if you're lucky to live long enough, it happens again around 90 years of age. I'll let you know what that passage presages when I get there. It may mean a release from discipline.

The Saturn return can be very difficult for people who have shirked their responsibilities, taken shortcuts, or refused to do what they know they have to do and grow up. The Saturn return can sometimes reward a person for not taking shortcuts, doing the work, or putting in the time. The form of this reward, however, is often disguised as more work or responsibility or overshadowed by the problematic events and dour moods the Saturn return often engenders.

The Uranus Return

Uranus stays in a sign for about 7 years, taking about 84 years to go around the Sun. As you have seen, I don't think it is relevant to your astrological studies to learn much beyond their period of return, but Uranus, the planet that rules not only Aquarius but also astrology itself, is different. Uranus rules being different, and it demonstrates just how different one can be by its unique way of orbiting the Sun. Unlike every other planet, Uranus does not spin like a top as it orbits the Sun—with one of its poles pointed at the Sun, it spins like a spinning wheel as it makes it journey.

Uranus is the planet that can tell astrologers that the person whose chart they are looking at is going through their midlife crisis. Since it takes about 84 years to go around the Sun, it is 180 degrees opposite the place it was on when a person or entity was born when that person or entity is around 40 years old. With retrograde motion, this can be anywhere from 38 to 44 years old, so if someone is around those ages, look closely and you will see whether they're having their Uranus opposition, the time when many people quit their job, their marriage, their lifestyle, and opt instead for freedom and unusual experiences. These are people who have not been what psychologists call their authentic self. They have not consciously and deliberately brought newness and excitement into their lives in a natural and gradual way, and so the Uranus opposition "helps" them do so—often at the worst possible time in the worst possible ways.

The Neptune Return

Neptune stays in a sign for about 14 years, taking about 165 years to go around the Sun. Neptune conjunctions, when Neptune is on the same degree as another of the planets, are difficult for the person whose chart you're looking at because, like the sea pulls the sand from beneath your feet as you stand at the shoreline, Neptune weakens and confuses the energy of any planet it touches. The Neptune square happens around the same time as the Uranus opposition, further confusing things at the age of approximately 40 years. The Neptune opposition and the Uranus return happen around the same time, making the time around 80 years of age equally powerful and potentially difficult to navigate. Because astrology has been around for a very long time and these effects have been noted, astrology can help a person prepare for the various contingencies that can be expected to be encountered.

The Pluto Return

Pluto stays in a sign for between 14 and 30 years, because of its very elliptical orbit, which sometimes takes it inside the orbit of Neptune on its 248-year journey around the Sun. As it is with Neptune, no person ever experiences a return of Pluto. The Pluto square happens around 62, plus or minus 4 years, close to traditional retirement age, bringing Pluto's powerful forces that confront our ability to resurrect our earlier goals we may have put on hold in order to make a living.

URANUS THROUGH THE SIGNS

Uranus represents our desire for that which is new, exciting, and different. It's the psychological equivalent of how excited we feel when we wake up in the morning and contemplate what we are going to be doing that day. If you want to stay in bed and pull the covers over your head, you can rest assured that you are not cooperating with Uranian energy, and when the planet contacts one of your personal planets by conjunction, square, or opposition, events will conspire to make life "interesting," as in the supposed Chinese curse, "May you live in interesting times." Suffice it to say, we are all better off bringing new and exciting things into our lives than we would be if we let Uranus do the choosing.

Uranus is all about daring to be different, shaking things up, for our sake and for the sake of future generations. Uranus is the planet that rules all technological matters and devices. It is the planet of invention and innovation—especially through disruptive discoveries that change the course of history in big and small ways. Remember that Uranus in a chart can show that a person is either comfortable or uncomfortable with Uranian energy. It is not easy to be different, to be willing to shake things up to make things better. Revolutionaries and inventors often face fierce opposition or fail and withdraw from the entrepreneurial or purely scientific pursuit of their dreams. Yet many will persevere and have an impact on humanity.

Since Uranus is all about freedom and rebellion, the following delineations of Uranus through the signs can also be read as, "Freedom from or rebellion against . . ." the various things Uranus is associated with. So while Uranus is usually associated with technology that advances the course of human existance, it can also, in a specific cosmic blueprint, represent a person who hates technology and wants to either escape it or rebel against it. Never forget my advice about the spectrum of meanings: It will keep you balanced and avoiding pat answers.

Uranus in Aries ♅ ♈

An unusual or revolutionary way of defining or experiencing revolution, honesty, dealing with lies and liars, being a pioneer, being alone, first, initiating, being bossy, being aggressive, and fighting for what you think is worth fighting for.

Uranus in Taurus ♅ ♉

An unusual or revolutionary way of defining or experiencing money, possessions, coping, giving up, adapting, sensuality, values, luxury, inertia, laziness, strength, weakness, stubbornness, anger, desire, wealth, singing, and music.

Uranus in Gemini ♅ ♊

An unusual or revolutionary way of defining or experiencing communicating, learning, paying attention, making connections, multitasking, boredom, understanding, superficiality, duality, sophistry, debating, and ultimate truths.

Uranus in Cancer ♅ ♋

An unusual or revolutionary way of defining or experiencing family, nurturing, the past, feeling supported, real estate, intuition, security, protection, one's birth mother or the caregiver(s) who fulfilled that role, and making a home.

Uranus in Leo ♅ ♌

An unusual or revolutionary way of defining or experiencing ego, pride, status, risk-taking, gambling, performing, leadership, politics, organization, embellishment, acting out, romance, creativity, the lion's share, and having a great time.

Uranus in Virgo ♅ ♍

An unusual or revolutionary way of defining or experiencing perfectionism, worry, tidiness, order, cleanliness, overthinking, analyzing, food, animals, health, service, details, thinking small, procrastination, and being a virgin.

Uranus in Libra ♅ ♎

An unusual or revolutionary way of defining or experiencing balance, harmony, contracts, agreements, commitment, public relations, judgment, compromise, partnerships, relationships, compromise, fairness, beauty, and peace.

Uranus in Scorpio ♅ ♏

An unusual or revolutionary way of defining or experiencing power, resurrection, change, sexuality, eliminations, other people's resources, deception, detecting, mysteries, magic, secrets, extremes, things metaphysical, and death.

Uranus in Sagittarius ♅ ♐

An unusual or revolutionary way of defining or experiencing truth, honesty, things foreign, laws, philosophy, higher education, good fortune, natural healing, mind-expanding travel, publishing, large animals, nature, and things religious.

Uranus in Capricorn ♅ ♑

An unusual or revolutionary way of defining or experiencing authority, career, discipline, limits, structure, time, timing, sensual needs versus business at hand, responsibility, teaching, learning, being serious, funny, older, and business.

Uranus in Aquarius (Ruler) ♅ ♒

An usual or revolutionary way of defining or experiencing revolution, disruption, freedom, being different, scientific advances, the future, being ahead of one's time, overreacting, distraction, extremism, emotions, friends, hopes, and wishes.

Uranus in Pisces ♅ ♓

An unusual or revolutionary way of defining or experiencing compassion, sensitivity, psychic matters, emotions, overwhelming things, idealism, personal needs versus humanity's, charity, large institutions, ego negation, solitude, and utopia.

A BRIEF LOOK AT PLANETS IN THE ELEVENTH HOUSE

The Sun ☉

You want to be an important part and maybe even the leader or founding organizer of a group of like-minded individuals banding together for a common purpose. The status quo does not interest you except in terms of understanding it so you can change it.

The Moon ☽

You are so concerned about the emotional state of your friends that you either act protectively to help them get through rough times or take their emotions on as your own. You are the center of your circle of friends. Their dependence on you is a major issue.

Mercury ☿

You are almost always thinking about what can be done to make your experience of the world better in some tangible way. You have a unique understanding of what is expected of a good friend and have the ability to motivate your friends for your common good.

Venus ♀

You truly love your friends and attract more of them than most. You experience more than your share of pleasurable and difficult experiences because you enmesh yourself so intimately with the lives of your friends, family, and others you care about.

Mars ♂

You are driven to discover and act with other people who share your desires and who are equally impatient to see these goals realized. You are not shy about your intentions and may have trouble with people who do not dedicate themselves at the same level as you do.

Jupiter ♃

You have successful, fulfilling associations with groups dedicated to a specific purpose or with supportive friends who can help you grow in some way. They may even benefit you financially, either directly or through their contacts with or influence on others.

Saturn ♄

You may have older or serious friends who may or may not help you financially as much as you might like but who can teach you valuable lessons that can ultimately help you accomplish your goals. You will do well allying yourself with unions or other business associations.

Uranus (Ruler) ♅

You want to be free of entanglements with groups, cliques, and even family or friends. You are not a joiner, though you find strength and comfort being part of a movement that is revolutionary in some way, even if you do not reveal your beliefs to all.

Neptune ♆

You care more about your friends and the movement to make the world a better place than you care about your own needs. You have a psychic connection with those you care about, but this becomes a problem if you mix it with any kind of escapist notions.

Pluto ♇

You likely have intense, charismatic, or powerful friends and associates who are as interested in changing you as they are in changing something about the world, just as you are interested in transforming them. Avoid obsessing about their odd actions and reactions.

RECAP: *The Eleventh House involves those you interact with due to your shared goals and aspirations. You can be more effective banding together to accomplish them and become the new authority (as symbolized by the Tenth House). This can be your circle of friends, clubs, trade unions, organizations, political parties, team sports, charities, and social movements. What you hope for is the essence of the Eleventh House.*

Taking action to make your dreams come true is as satisfying as having fun. In fact, one is essential for the other to happen. It is creativity with a purpose that will benefit other people as much if not more than it will benefit you. The Eleventh House also rules the unexpected, a factor that must be considered in all forecasts of the future. It denotes the native's attitude toward humanity—their harmony or disharmony with others.

The planet Uranus rules the Eleventh House. Wherever Uranus appears in a chart, freedom is an issue. The sign it is in also identifies areas of expression for Uranus's revolutionary ideas and actions. Uranus is the planet of eccentricity, the unusual, and the extreme. It is the planet of disruptive technology, like artificial intelligence, the internet, robotics, and technologies that have not even been invented yet. In psychological terms, Uranus represents the energy of our psyche that seeks to make life exciting. If that energy to create newness in our lives is consciously expressed then Uranus will help us. If it is not expressed, then Uranus will still try to help us but in ways that are disruptive and ill-timed.

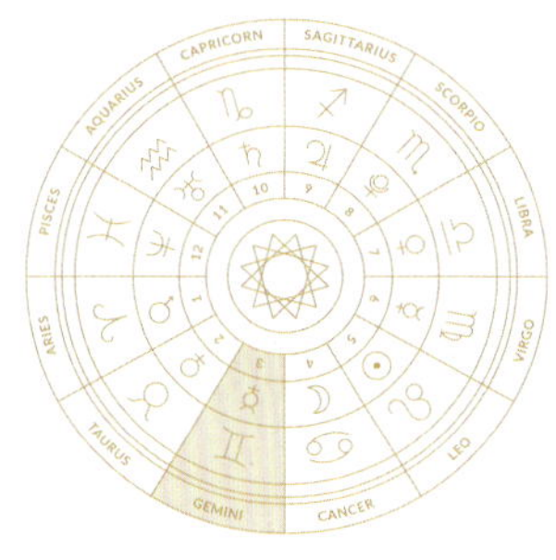

THE THIRD HOUSE

Whether we are young or old, Third House interactions teach us how other people and the world works, especially if we are paying attention and learn from our experiences so that we do not have to keep repeating the same ones until we do learn. For this reason, the Third House represents not only our potentially instructive social interactions but also our primary schooling up until college, when, ideally, the Ninth House, the house opposite the Third House, takes over for those who are willing to put their childish attitude toward learning behind them. Also, the Third House, ruled by the inquisitive sign of Gemini, ideally represents the kind of schooling that offers people a sampling of the various subjects available to be studied and teaches them how to think skillfully, while the Ninth House represents college and graduate studies that are more focused on a particular subject.

As we grow older, recalling our own stamina during our youth, most of us marvel at younger people and their ability to be constantly energized and on the move. During our younger years, the more we get around, the more we feel independent as we experience life without the watchful eye of our primary caregiver(s). For this reason, the Third House is associated with that kind of movement and short-distance or routine travel, where the object is to get from one place to another as quickly as possible so as to have more interactions, rather than travel to be savored for its own sake and learned from—Ninth House long-distance travel.

The Third House is the house of relating to and relations with who and what is around you, whether that is your close family (other than your parental figure[s]) or your neighborhood. It is connected with communications of all kinds, both the kind you make in person and through using all communications devices, speech, writing, sign language, body language, facial expressions, code, and every other method.

The Third House also rules the means for such communications, such as our mobile phones, writing implements, books, tablets, landline phones, computers, wireless devices, printers, printing presses, pagers, televisions, satellites, wire, radios, and everything you can imagine. It also rules gossip and puzzles and other mental work. Communicating often requires that you move yourself to a different location, so the Third House rules travel done with a practical purpose in mind—especially when you go to school to master the basics of a subject before you are able to use it in your own way. It is the house of busyness, taking care of the routine things that are the necessities of life. This is the house of short-distance, ordinary, and routine travel.

The Third House is ruled by Mercury, which we have already delineated on page 196. Mercury is the planet closest to the Sun. In fact, Mercury is never found more than about 28 degrees from the Sun, symbolizing our logical mind's close relationship with our sense of self, our ego, our purpose, and our vitality.

As the ruler of Virgo and the Sixth House, Mercury's association with our logical mind's ability to analyze and problem-solve gives it its association with work, manual dexterity, the design and use of tools, craftsmanship, and other skills used in figuring out the critical path of construction or otherwise accomplishing a task.

As the ruler too of Gemini, which is associated with the Third House, Mercury symbolizes our logical mind's ability to help us relate to and communicate with those to whom we wish to reach out. This gives the Third House rulership over all forms of communication, primary education, and travel that takes us to where there are people with whom we want to communicate.

A BRIEF LOOK AT PLANETS IN THE THIRD HOUSE

The general meaning of any planets found in the Third House of an astrology chart can, in addition to the following delineations, sometimes symbolize the way the person experiences a sibling, a close relative, or someone else they consider a member of their family at the time. In general, if this/these planet(s) does/do symbolize individuals, these people can also be important to this person throughout their life. I have found that when there is more than one planet in the Third House, this can often manifest as each planet symbolizing a different sibling or family member. So please apply these caveats to the following delineations of planets in the Third House.

The Sun ☉

You have to either always be on the go, always communicating with others, or both. You may work in communications. Your relationship with your sibling(s) or close relations is more important to you than to most people. You are a perpetual student.

The Moon ☽

You become restless and emotionally unsatisfied if you believe you have not thoroughly examined every feeling you have about anyone and anything you encounter. Journaling privately or writing professionally is the perfect outlet for your ability to relate.

Mercury (Ruler) ☿

You are almost always thinking about or traveling to nearby locations for work or social interactions so you can best interact with those you are interested in. You have a quick mind and a great sense of humor and are a born communicator. Boredom is your enemy.

Venus ♀

You love being busy, always on the go, and interacting with as many people as possible. You can see the good in people even if they do not see it in themselves. You can make an art of communicating and truly touch people's hearts with your words.

Mars ♂

You are driven to use your ability to communicate for the purpose of advancing your ideas and interests even if this goal conflicts with the ideas and interests of others. You are a forceful communicator, so be aware that others might react strongly to your words.

Jupiter ♃

You grow through your interactions with your sibling(s), relatives, and those you consider to be your family. Your ability to favorably impress others may find expression in politics, performing, or other endeavors where you bring out the best in those around you.

Saturn ♄

You act as a teacher in some way to your sibling(s), relatives, and those you consider to be your family. Your serious approach to life may be difficult for people to deal with, so avoid appearing critical, joyless, or dogmatic if and when you see this happening.

Uranus ♅

You use your words to habitually rebel against just about everyone and everything. You may have a very unusual sibling or one who is the person manifesting the rebelliousness. You may arrive and leave places abruptly, and do so for reasons that are not readily apparent.

Neptune ♆

You care for the people you interact with to an unusual degree. You may bend the truth or use your skill at fantasizing to inspire, impress, or convince them of something you believe strongly. A family member may require constant care and compassion from you.

Pluto ♇

You communicate only when you have something to say. Your words or silence can affect the lives of many. The deepness of your thought process is always on display. Your mind cannot be changed. You may have a serious power struggle with a family member.

RECAP: *The Third House is ruled by Mercury and relates to brothers, sisters, relatives, neighbors, education, short journeys, manuscripts, letters, and ability. It is strongly related to intellect and the nervous system.*

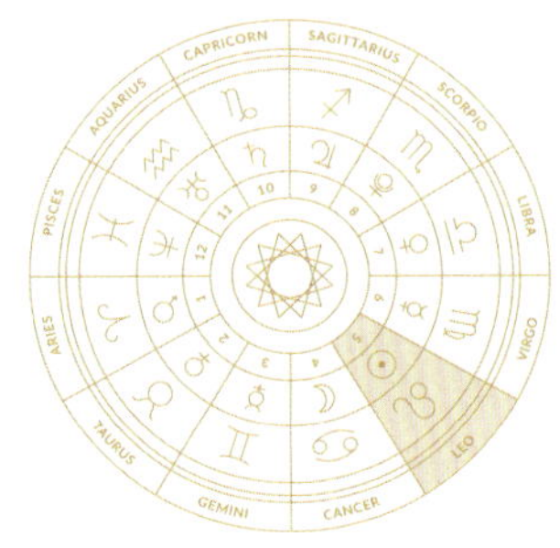

THE FIFTH HOUSE

The Fifth House, like the Third House, is strongly related to the Fourth House of an astrology chart. While the Fourth House represents the caregiver(s) who, ideally, protected you from the harshness of the world and showed you unconditional love, the Fifth House represents our attempt to find romantic love the way our parents or caregiver(s) did, ideally, so we can create a family of our own as we define *family*.

The family we create can be either children or some other creation(s) that have never existed before we brought them into our world. For this reason, the Fifth House rules creativity in general, as well as joy, having fun, being funny, games, sports, things done for their own sake without a specific goal, taking a chance, gambling, investing, and the thrill of romance, which I often suspect produces more children than Seventh House committed partnerships. A funny way to remember the meaning of the Fifth House is to remember that while the Eleventh House, the house opposite the Fifth House, is the house of friends, the Fifth House is the house of friends with benefits.

The Fifth House is not "just" related to your ability to be creative. I have seen it many times tied to a person's interaction with what it means to appear to be lucky and to enjoy life. The ability to approach life's challenges creatively exists in everyone, but not everyone is willing to take a chance on herself or himself.

The Fifth House is the house of being an artist and living the artist's life. Though making one's living from approaching life as an artist can be a lot of fun, creating something that has never existed before requires hard work, giving up control, and exposing yourself to criticism, misunderstanding, and ridicule. This may certainly come from one's stern Tenth House caregiver(s) and may even come from one's Fourth House unconditionally loving caregiver(s) because they do not want you to suffer the rejections and other vicissitudes that are part and parcel of the artist's way of making a living.

That is why the Fifth House is also related to making art of all kinds, acting, dance, sculpture, performance art, design, music, architecture, and creative endeavors of all kinds—especially the crafting of new art forms—as well as children and romance. Once "given birth to," these creations all take on a life of their own that is beyond one's control.

Gambling, investments, sports, and risk-taking in every way are also Fifth House matters. The purpose of life is to be happy, and the Fifth House is the house of what makes us happy. It is the thrill of life as the ultimate amusement park ride and the scariest of movies all rolled into one.

RECAP: *The Fifth House is related to pleasures, love affairs, entertainments, speculations, games, and children. It is opposed to the Eleventh House and, as it were, the fulfillment of it (hopes and wishes). The Fifth House is ruled by the Sun, which we have delineated through the signs of the zodiac starting on page 31.*

A BRIEF LOOK AT PLANETS IN THE FIFTH HOUSE

The Sun (Ruler) 

You are a very creative person in one or more ways. You are a romantic in every sense of the word. You are funny, a good sport, and willing to take a chance on things, including how you make your living. Your creations are your children—literally, figuratively, or both.

The Moon ☽

You seek an emotional connection to anyone and everything to which you become attracted, limiting your friendships and romantic involvements to those who are similarly inclined. You are a lover, gifted in one or more artistic pursuits, and a born gambler.

Mercury ☿

You seek to understand and creatively improve everything and everyone to which you become attracted, limiting your friendships and romantic involvement to those who enjoy your ways. You see the beauty, flaws, contradictions, hypocrisy, and humor in every person and situation.

Venus ♀

You are a fun-loving person, in love with love and taking a chance on the people you are attracted to. You are gifted creatively and can see beauty where others cannot. You enjoy and understand children well because you never lose your childlike joy in all things.

Mars ♂
You are driven to creatively impact whomever and whatever aspect of existence you are drawn to. You enjoy games and sports, as you define them, especially those requiring skill and risk-taking. You are both a lover and a fighter. Balancing the two will be a lifelong challenge.

Jupiter ♃
Your personal growth is tied to your attitude toward creativity. You are naturally gifted in all things creative and lucky in love and maybe even gambling too but must guard against it coming so easily to you that you do not value your good fortune in these and other areas.

Saturn ♄
You may be inclined to not value your creative abilities. Your serious attitude can help you help others identifying as creatives to interface with the world as an agent or manager or in some other advisory role, though you are as creative as they are. Romance does not come easily.

Uranus ♅
You are inclined to creatively disrupt any area of life you are drawn to. Your romantic relationships arise suddenly and disappear just as quickly if you start to feel your freedom limited. Your brave inventiveness impels you to redefine what it means to be an artist.

Neptune ♆
You use your creative ability to inspire reverence and the hope for a better life in the people you hold dear and in everything you do. You have a seemingly psychic connection to gambling, investing, and bringing new life into the world. Avoid escapism.

Pluto ♇
You are inclined to creatively change your world or the world at large in some major way. You may stand in your own way if you cannot give yourself the time to develop your talents until they can have the level of impact you expect. The issue of children will be extremely important.

RECAP: *The Third House and the Fifth House are strongly related to the Fourth House. The Fourth House of an astrology chart can indicate how you experienced your physical home and the primary caregiver, who was, ideally, supposed to love you unconditionally and help you to feel safe, secure, and loved just for being yourself. This caregiver—or, if you were extremely fortunate, these caregivers—was/were supposed to make you know beyond doubt that you could always count on them, no matter what transpired in the outside world.*

The Third House represents a person's interactions with the world outside their home and with people who may be family, such as siblings, cousins, aunts, uncles, grandparents, personal friends, friends of the family, neighbors, and other people who may be positively disposed to you but do not necessarily love you the way your Fourth House caregiver(s) love(d) you and, even if they do love you in their way, almost certainly do not love you unconditionally.

The Fifth House represents our attempt to find love the way our parents or caregiver(s) did, ideally, so we can create a family of our own, as we define family. That can be either children or some other creation(s) that have never existed before we brought them into our world. For this reason, the Fifth House rules creativity, fun, sports, things done for their own sake without a specific goal, taking a chance, gambling, investing, and passionate romance, which probably produces more children than Seventh House committed partnerships. While the Eleventh House, the house opposite the Fifth House, is the house of friends, the Fifth House is the house of friends with benefits.

REVIEW: THE TWELVE HOUSES

As I said when we started your astrological education, your astrology chart looks like a round pizza pie with twelve slices. These slices represent slices of life, which we astrologers call the houses. The houses of an astrological horoscope chart wheel are where the planets dwell. Knowing where they are in a person's chart can tell you a lot about their personality and the cycles of their life and can even describe and predict tendencies in their past, present, and future that can result in various events and actions. (Remember Heraclitus's saying, "Your character is your destiny.")

WHAT EACH HOUSE REPRESENTS

- First House = You
- Second House = Your resources, your values
- Third House = Those close to you, bros and sestras, grade school
- Fourth House = Mother and home, what makes you feel secure
- Fifth House = Intimate, creative fun and romance, kids
- Sixth House = Work and service, health
- Seventh House = Your partner(s), contracts, the public, public relations
- Eighth House = Your partner's (or partners') resources, sex, death, inheritances
- Ninth House = Those far from you, philosophy, college
- Tenth House = Father and career, respect
- Eleventh House = Groups of like-minded friends and associates
- Twelfth House = Your place in the big picture

What Each Planet Represents

Each planet in our cosmic blueprint reveals insights into various parts of our lives, how we deal with certain things, or how we avoid dealing with them. Here's a list that may help you lock in your understanding of the planets:

- The Sun: Our individual identity
- The Moon: Our emotional intelligence
- Mercury: Energy for understanding
- Venus: Energy for attraction and love
- Mars: Energy for working our will
- Jupiter: Energy for personal growth
- Saturn: Energy for personal advancement
- Uranus: Energy to keep our life exciting

- Neptune: Energy to create a better world
- Pluto: Energy for transforming ourselves

General Actions of the Planets in the Houses

In judging placements, one should always consider that the general action of the different planets in the houses are as follows:

- The Sun brings honor, glory, dignities, favors from others and, with what the ancients called affliction, hard or challenging aspects, the angles between the planets, the opposite.
- The Moon brings changes and publicity that is favorable or unfavorable, according to the aspects.
- Mercury brings adaptability, movability, memory, and, with affliction, disturbances.
- Venus brings happiness, harmony, and, with affliction, disharmony.
- Mars brings impulse, power of work, and, with affliction, intemperance and quarrels.
- Jupiter brings abundance, increase, philosophy, and, with affliction, adversities and insincerity.
- Saturn brings frugality, concentration, depth, and, with affliction, limitation, hindrance, and difficulties.
- Uranus brings originality, excitement and, with affliction, chaos and eccentric behavior in undeveloped individuals.
- Neptune brings idealization, compassion, fantasy, oneness, intuition, and, with affliction, escapism and ego-negating behavior.
- Pluto brings transformation, profound change, endings, and, with affliction, power struggles and overwhelming forces.

THE ASPECTS: THE ANGLES BETWEEN THE PLANETS TELL A STORY

At this point, you have read about all the planets, the signs of the zodiac, and the houses of an astrological chart and I hope you are excited by your new understanding of astrology and you want to learn more. Be proud of yourself and confident that the astrological knowledge you have accumulated by reading to this point is firmly inside your brain and heart and ready to be put to use. You don't have to be able to recall every meaning and concept—that's what the table of contents is for. What you have retained from reading the previous pages is enough to enable you to make use of the one aspect of astrology that otherwise confounds, confuses, and frustrates almost every student of astrology: the study of the aspects of astrology.

Aspect is another name for *angle*. In astrology, the angles/aspects tell the stories to us astrologers about how two planets relate to each other. We can gain deep insights into our charts and ourselves by adding the meaning of the aspects/angles of an astrology chart—the angular relationship between the planets.

The aspects of astrology are the angles that can be calculated between planets. There are harmonious angles and there are challenging aspects. Each angle imparts its basic meaning to the relationship between two planets in a chart, and that meaning qualifies the meaning of the individual planets in their signs and houses. This, in turn, helps us interpret the story of an astrology chart.

It may sound complicated and daunting, but once you get the concept of the various angles and add that to the story told by the two planets that are in aspect to each other, you will realize that knowing the aspects is not difficult, and, more importantly, that the additional insights offered make reading a chart easier and more enlightening.

Aspects are the glue that holds together the interpretation of the planets, signs, and house of a chart. There is no better time in your astrological education and no better way to learn, understand, and put to use my keyword concept the way it is meant to be used. I hope you have been using the basics of my keyword technique up to this point to prime your intuitive pump all along. If not, now is the time to start.

There are a lot of keyword meanings possible for each planet, sign, house, and aspect in astrology. How do you know which one is the right one? Using my keyword technique to interpret any planet in any sign in any house is the beginning of the journey to understanding which one (or more than one) is correct. One of the greatest benefits of astrology and my keyword technique is that it asks you to practice free association and to learn to use and trust your intuition.

With the technological revolution of the Aquarian Age on us, the explosion in use of artificial intelligence and machine learning makes it exceedingly difficult to know what is true and what is false. A developed intuition is just as important as one's logical mind and vision in the discernment of who and what can be trusted and used to guide our actions. I am very pleased to share my keyword technique with you because it will improve your intuition.

It never fails to intrigue me and my students how we can use one or more of these many keyword meanings to tell ourselves a little story and then let our experience as astrologers and human beings, our logical mind, and our intuition take over to help us build on this story, whether or not we have the benefit of being in conversation with the person whose chart we are looking at. Our astrology birth charts speak to us and our fellow astrologers. Let's learn how to better listen to what our charts are telling us.

STARRY TELLING: CREATING AND USING KEYWORD STORIES

Let's start with Mars, the god of war, traditional ruler of the First House and the zodiac sign of Aries. Aries is the sign that starts on the first day of spring and so rules starting, in general.

For this example, let's say that in our chart, Mars is in Libra, as it is in my chart, the sign opposite to Aries. As I have explained, Mars is the energy available to our ego, whose basic story is symbolized by the sign and house position of our Sun, to transform from idea into reality that which we desire, what we want, what we feel we need but that we believe we lack in sufficient quantity. Our personal Mars energy describes our ability to act, to overcome our inertia and fears to get the job done.

In the past, I described our Mars energy as our ability to act aggressively, to overcome our self-imposed limits in the sense of the famous saying by the legendary Chinese general Sun Tzu, author of the enduring classic *The Art of War*, who wrote, "One who overcomes others is great. One who overcomes themselves is greatest."

It may sound implausible, but for all my years studying astrology, I did not understand when people had a problem with my use of the word *aggressive* to describe these energies until I was writing this book and looked up the meaning ascribed to the word by the various dictionaries. I was surprised to see that the meanings ascribed to the word are all negative and based on the concept of the attacking of another being, place, or thing. How could I be so naive? Being a student of astrology, I did as I always do and turned to my keyword technique for an answer to my puzzlingly oblivious behavior. I have Mars in Libra, and the simple pertinent keywords tell us the following story: Aggressive energies (Mars) used to obtain peace, harmony, balance, or fairness (Libra).

This is the perfect description of my Mars DNA! I have always sought fairness and avoided violence whenever possible. I have devoted my life to using my aggressive energies to activate my artistic talents, first in writing and performing my music and then in my successful writing career. I have also used these energies in support of my incredibly talented artist/fashion designer wife, Amy Zerner.

The truly naive person is anyone who believes that two people like Amy and me, from humble beginnings, can make a living from the use of their artistic gifts, getting their work seen, heard, and financially supported by major publishers and other corporations taking on and selling our work, and ultimately by people around the world spending their hard-earned money to buy our creative work without us using our natural-born aggressive energies to rise above the challenges all freelance artists face.

Proving my point, here I am using my Mars/Libra energies (this planet/sign format is my shorthand for a planet in a sign or house) to push back against all the dictionaries because I believe that they are unfairly defining the word *aggressive*! We all have Mars energies, and I am sure you are using yours in the unique way you have come to define them. If one is using their Mars energy to obtain the beautifully balanced, fair, and desirable outcome sought and promised by Libra, how can that be negative?

Of course, you do not have to look far to see that some people use their Mars energies differently than for peace, love, and understanding. Mars energies can easily be used negatively, obviously, if one has the goal of attacking, overwhelming, or otherwise denying the rights of another being. And it is obvious that not everyone with Mars/Libra is as committed to using their aggressive energies for peace, justice, and harmony as I am. (I have actually been a professional close-protection bodyguard for famous movie stars, such as Michael J. Fox, who needed to be able to walk around without being mobbed by his legions of adoring fans—yet another definition of Mars/Libra.)

I am spending a lot of time doing a deep dive on this for two reasons:

- If I take you through the step-by-step free-associating of my thought process with Mars/Libra in aspect to another planet in a different sign, then you will have a detailed example you can use as a guide to interpreting any planet in any sign and in any house—and in relation to any other planet in any sign and house—using any of the aspects/angles I will soon be teaching you.

- I want you to do your own deep dive not just into your Mars energy but also into every planet, sign, and house position of your astrology chart. Do it slowly, and take as much time as you need. Students in the practice of psychiatry and psychology must themselves undergo analysis before being allowed to practice on other people, and astrology is a psychological language. The old saying "Physician, heal thyself!" is both powerful and practical.

Use my keyword technique to help you thoroughly understand your cosmic blueprint before you attempt the interpretation of another person's astrology chart. Resist the temptation to read for someone else before you feel in your heart of hearts that you understand astrology and have enough love and compassion for your client to the point that you are the living embodiment of the principle of the oath every physician must swear and live by: "First, do no harm."

Remember, also, Sun Tzu's advice: "One who overcomes others is great. One who overcomes themselves is greatest." Looking at your chart and yourself as objectively as you can is both a humbling experience and one of the most valuable things you can do to grow as a person and as an astrologer. Once you have done that to a reasonable degree, you can read for another person.

I speak from personal experience when I say you need to exercise great caution when you read for another person. Words you say to them casually or while thinking out loud when you are trying to understand their chart can have a tremendous impact, both positively and negatively.

When I read someone's chart, I usually start by asking them what they want to get from the reading. What about their life is the reason that has caused them to come? Many people do not know what they want or have a problem with accessing and harnessing the energies of their chart and using their strengths to compensate for their weaknesses. (We all have both.) Using keywords can help you understand this and help you in ways you might not suspect are possible.

Back to Mars in Libra and the redefining of our concept of aggression. Despite the dictionaries, I still maintain that we all need to stop dreaming, get off our butts, and act. All actions are to some degree aggressive when their purpose is to work our will on the world in some way and change it so that it is more to our liking.

A problem with taking action can stop someone from obtaining the life they want. But that prompts the question "What does anyone really want?" Answering that question is one of the most powerful and important skills anyone—not just astrologers with Mars/Libra—can possess.

So, I have Mars in Libra. Let's look at the keywords:

Mars keywords: *willpower, drive, desire, nature, "animal passions," "ability to marshal our energies on physical, mental, and spiritual levels so we can work our will on our world and the world at large," "aggression in the pure sense of the word."* Importantly, *aggression*, in the dictionaries' sense of trespassing on the rights of other beings, is also in the mix, as is every other positive and negative meaning you can see now that you know the meanings of all of the planets, signs, and houses of an astrology chart, not just Mars.

Here are some Libra keywords: *union, partnership, refinement, sophistication, "good taste," law, balance, cooperation, fairness, artistic, aesthetic, harmonious, romantic, ideas, opinions, politics, diplomacy, "good manners," in addition to indecisiveness, "perfectionism based on the desire to act in the most fair, balanced, and beautiful manner," and "failure to see and appreciate the inelegant, lawless, and downright ugly side of life and of people, places, and things."*

Our use of keywords should include as much of the spectrum of meanings of the various planets, signs, houses, and aspects as we are capable of using. Don't worry—I haven't forgotten. We'll get to the meaning of the aspects when I feel that you are ready to incorporate them into your astro–short story.

There is the aforementioned keyword story "Aggressive energies (Mars) used to obtain peace, harmony, balance, or fairness (Libra)."

We can also interpret Mars/Libra as balanced or harmonized aggressive energies. You can put the keyword meanings you assign to the planet and sign in any order you choose. The purpose of my technique is to help us get a jumping-off point for y/our interpretation of the astrological energies we are trying to understand.

While it is true that aggression used to obtain peace and balance is the goal of every martial artist, military person, and every person who wants to defend themselves and those they care about, Mars/Libra also contains a concept that is the mortal enemy of that harmonious aggression (i.e., indecisive aggression). To be indecisive in the face of aggression almost guarantees you will not be able to successfully overcome it or any obstacle, be that a person or persons or any forces pitted against you.

Yet there is also a spectrum of meanings for keyword stories that are on the surface negative or usually undesirable. How has indecisive aggression manifested in my life having Mars/Libra? So far, so good. Over the years, especially in my twenties in 1970s New York City, when men driven to misuse their Mars energy to override their basic humanity and become truly aggressive in the worst sense of the word as armed robbers pointed guns at my face, my Mars/Libra energy has enabled me to resist acting aggressively in self-defense. In several situations where someone else might have knee-jerk reacted in a mindless default mode when confronted with the threat of a gun or knife in their face and thereby escalated an already violent situation into a deadly one, I acted calmly and rationally and lived to tell the tale.

I used my Mars/Libra desire for balance, harmony, and peace to help me remember that the other people, the evildoers in the equation, were frightened too and maybe also wanted to deescalate the situation and avoid serious consequences. Lucky for me, my Pisces Moon helps amplify my intuitive abilities, and so if I were dealing with people who were beyond reason, I would hope I would know that in that case, fighting for peace, not talk therapy, was the prudent Mars/Libra action.

Some more Mars/Libra keyword stories:

- Desire (Mars) fairness (Libra)
- Fight for peace
- Aggressive diplomacy or diplomatic use of aggression
- Defending the law—my family business (both my father and my stepbrother were New York Police Department sergeants)

You can see how Mars/Libra was helpful when I was a bodyguard. You would also be correct in thinking Mars/Libra would be helpful if I were a lawyer. In fact, I have functioned as my own lawyer negotiating almost all publishing and licensing agreements and other contracts involving Amy and me.

Mars/Libra would also be helpful to someone not working in the security industry or law enforcement, though those are the obvious choices. There are as many unique definitions of Mars/Libra as there are people who have that combination in their astrology chart. I'm sure you can see many more possible keyword combinations for Mars in Libra, and yours are just as valid as mine, as long as you are using the accurate meanings of the planet and the sign.

We get significantly more information about a planet in a sign when we add the keywords for the astrological house to the mix. In my case, Mars is in my Second House but close enough to the cusp, the line that divides my Second House from my Third House.

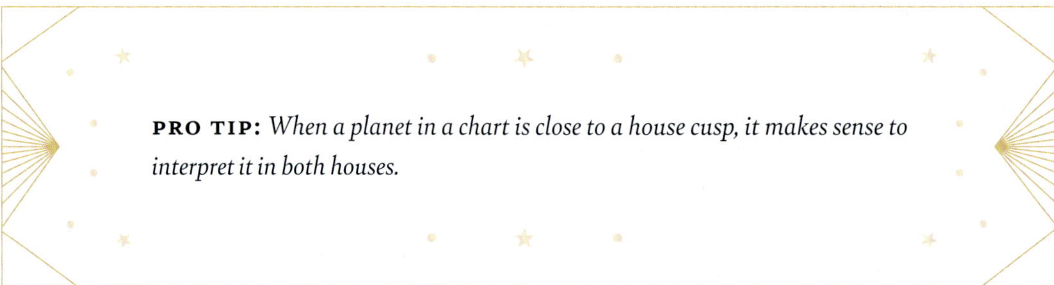

PRO TIP: *When a planet in a chart is close to a house cusp, it makes sense to interpret it in both houses.*

You might think that this is a cop-out or gives us so many meanings as to render useless our interpretation of the astro energies. In practice, however, reading a planet near a cusp as being in both houses gives your reading added nuance. You will usually find that interpreting that planet in both houses explains the unique take on those planetary energies the native displays. Just thinking about how that dual house meaning could affect the planet in question will help expand your understanding of both houses and the planet(s) close to the cusp.

Back to my Mars/Libra/Second House interpretation: Our Second House is the slice of life that has to do with our values—what we believe and affirm is valuable and necessary for us to properly exist in the world. Not everyone is in touch with their core beliefs and values. If they were, they would understand themselves better and have fewer problems. This is why the Second House planets exist in a person's astrology chart. They show us our value system on the spiritual level and our attitude toward obtaining, maintaining, and parting with what we value on the mental level and on the material level as well.

Here are some keywords for the Second House: *"financial circumstances," "movable possessions (not real estate)," values, possessiveness, wealth, "the lack or worry about wealth,"* and *"the benefits of and/or problems with having, not having, or being overly concerned about money or other resources."*

Sample keyword stories for Mars in Libra in the Second House:

- Driven or passionate about (Mars) the accumulating of beautiful or elegant (Libra) values and/or possessions (the Second House).
- Aggressive, possessive, or miserly (Mars) about whatever the native believes they own or need to own (the Second House), including people with whom the native is in relationship (Libra).
- Imbalance or disharmony (Libra) caused by fighting (Mars) with or about one's possessions (Second House). (This can be a person who has had to overcome a reluctance to share what they have. This keyword story can also be another way of saying that trouble can arise when one's possessions come to own their possessor.)

I'm sure you see other meanings, and that is precisely what I want you to be doing: making your own keyword stories. If you're doing it, congratulations. If not, give it a try.

How about reading my Mars/Libra in the Third House?

Third House keywords: *brothers, sisters, relatives, neighbors, education, "short journeys," study, manuscripts, letters,* and *"everything connected to our ability to communicate."*

A sample keyword story for Mars in Libra in the Third House: Driven or passionate about (Mars) communicating in a beautiful, elegant, or balanced fashion (Libra) with everyone with whom you interact (Third House). (This has certainly been my goal as a writer.)

Let's see whether a keyword story from Mars/Libra/Second House might work for Third House too, since it is so close (within 5 degrees) of the cusp between the two houses:

- Aggressive, possessive, or willing to fight (Mars) about whatever the native believes they own or need to own (Second House) can manifest as a propensity to share or even a difficulty sharing possessions with relatives, neighbors, or friends or difficulties sharing relatives, neighbors, or friends (the Third House) with other friends, or connections with people who might benefit from knowing people known to the native.
- A passion (Mars) for driving around a lot (Third House) for artistic or contractual reasons (Libra).

The second story was certainly true when I was in my thirties and was a location scout for feature films, TV shows, and commercials. I was rarely out of my car, either searching for the perfect locations or showing them to directors, producers, and art directors, and then driving from location to location when filming started, checking on the location where filming was taking place, going on ahead preparing the next one, and cleaning up the previous ones.

This is also certainly true for me today. As I wrote these words, Amy was going to have an art opening the next day, and we had made the twenty-mile trip to her gallery, the much missed MM Fine Art, in Southampton, New York, several times over a period of two weeks, including twice in one day! We are literally driven because of our passion for her amazing art.

So now you have seen my keyword technique in action for a planet in a sign and a house. Before we add another planet, sign, and house to the mix so you can see the meaning of their angular interaction and see also that you are ready to be able to interpret the aspect between two planets, it's time for me to explain to you exactly what the aspects are and are not.

THE ASPECTS

The word *aspect* is derived from the concept "to view" and pertains to the appearance of something. In astrology, it is used to describe the angles between two or more planets. It is the way in which the planets interact with each other because there are aspects that indicate a harmonious relationship and other angles (the words *aspect* and *angle* can be used interchangeably) that indicate that the energetic relationship between two or more planets is not conducive to them providing harmonious energies to the native without some deep thought and behavioral changes—hard work that can improve a person's life as much as or more than a "good" or harmonious aspect (the ease, flow, and benefits of which are often taken for granted).

I regard the aspects as being astrology's diagnostic X-rays that shine through us and bring the strong or weak places of our characters temporarily to light. Aspects can illuminate both our strengths and our weaknesses, a confirmation of our abilities to enjoy a life of quality and meaning. They can sometime be a warning that something we are inclined to do needs to be given more forethought.

The most important aspects or angles between two planets that astrologers use are found by dividing a circle by 1, 2, 3, 4, and 6. Most astrologers avoid dividing the circle by 5 or 7 until they turn pro, so we will do the same and leave that for my next astrology book.

These are the major aspects.

The Conjunction ☌

The conjunction has 0 degrees because in the case of an exact conjunction, the two conjunct planets are exactly on the same degree of the zodiac, and so there are no degrees between them. This is the mathematical equivalent of dividing the 360 degrees of a circle by 1.

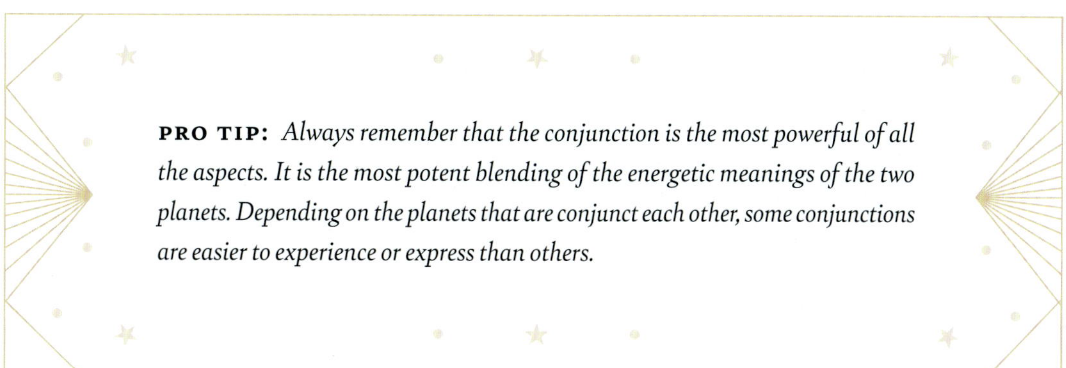

PRO TIP: *Always remember that the conjunction is the most powerful of all the aspects. It is the most potent blending of the energetic meanings of the two planets. Depending on the planets that are conjunct each other, some conjunctions are easier to experience or express than others.*

Most conjunctions amplify the energies of the planets involved. Some combinations of planets amplify the power of one planet and cancel out a lot of the energies of the other. A few confuse or even cancel the energies of both planets. Some aspects are very difficult for a child or even a young adult to deal with, yet another reason I believe it is imperative that parents learn about their child's astrology chart.

You will soon see that by adding the aspect keywords to the planetary interaction story, you can greatly affect the clarity and precision of the meaning of the keywords when strung together. They will either make sense, seem unclear in their meaning, or sometimes seem to contradict each other once the keywords of the aspect are added to the story. However, even when the sentence formed seems unclear, it is giving you a picture of why this aspect of a person's chart and of their personality is nebulous and not easy to understand, even for them.

When this happens, you are being challenged to think more deeply about it and try to get some semblance of a coherent meaning and message from this apparently confused energetic interaction. If you rise to the challenge, you can often get remarkable insights into this person's personality that may be more helpful to them than anything else you can ascertain from their chart.

How is it that a certain aspect—let's use a conjunction of the Moon and Saturn as an example—causes a heavy feeling of depression in one person, whereas with another, it manifests as difficulties expressing emotions, and with a third person it manifests as difficulties relating to women, those who identify as women, and/or femininity? And, in keeping with my often-stated admonition to never forget the spectrum of possible meanings and manifestations of astrological energies, many people with the same aspect become quite successful in manifesting their aspirations. How can we know precisely how an aspect is manifesting in a particular person?

When beginning to read an aspect between two planets, or with a planet in that person's astrology chart and that person's Rising Sign or Midheaven (yes, they count too!), it is best practice to first look at the keyword story told by just the planets or the planet and Rising Sign or Midheaven *without* adding the keyword stories told by the zodiac signs or, in the case of the planets, the house(s) of the astrology chart.

In our example, we start with Moon conjunct Saturn.

PRO TIP: *In astrological shorthand, we always list the faster-moving planet first, so the Moon, which moves about 14 degrees a day, is always first. Then comes the Sun, Mercury, Venus, Mars, Jupiter, Saturn, Uranus, and Neptune, with Pluto always being last in these equations.*

Sample keywords for the Moon include the following: *"emotional intelligence," "emotional reactions," habits, sensitivity, "intuition about a person one cares for," "the bestowing of the gift of unconditional love upon someone as an aid to their growing emotionally," "the ability to receive," "what has for centuries been called women or the feminine"* (though the definition of these words seems to be evolving here at the dawning of the Age of Aquarius).

Sample keywords for Saturn include the following: *discipline, "the authority of dedication and experience," "the harsh truths of reality," limits, time, timing, restriction, "hard work," difficulties, serious, mirthless, dark,* or *"sarcastic humor"*

Some keyword stories for Moon conjunct Saturn follow:

- Mirthless because of difficulties with or a lack of (all Saturn) unconditional love (the Moon).
- Mirthless because one of the harsh truths of reality was the lack of (all Saturn) a mother or someone who modeled emotional intelligence.
- Limits (Saturn) with women or the feminine (the Moon).
- Restrictions and/or limits imposed by (Saturn) one's dealing (or not dealing well) with emotional reactions (the Moon).
- The authority of experience attained through hard work and dedication to (all Saturn) attaining emotional intelligence (the Moon).

I think you can see why it is best to start with the basic keyword meanings of the planets or the Rising Sign or Midheaven stripped of the qualifiers that will be added to the stories once the sign(s) and house(s) are incorporated. It is always better to start off with a solid foundational understanding of the basic astrological story to be told and build from there, either through your personal knowledge of the person whose astrology chart you are reading or from interacting with the person.

This prompts an answer to my question, "How can we know precisely how an aspect is manifesting in a particular person?"

The simple answer is, we cannot. We cannot tell precisely how an aspect is manifesting in a particular person—certainly not to the exclusion of other interpretations. We human beings are quite complex, to put it mildly. We astrologers can have our basic idea of the energies at work and build from there, but astrology is a practice, like law, medicine, or any of the healing professions. We do our best to do our best. Who can do more?

Even when you look at the planetary stories told in your own chart, you will see that multiple keyword combinations will work perfectly for different events, different times of your life, and even different aspects of your personality. Some will be relevant throughout all your days, and some will make sense only in particular times of your life.

Most but not all conjunctions take place in the same sign of the zodiac. All aspects have an allowable orb, the distance between the planets involved that is close enough to be considered as that aspect, in this case a conjunction.

PRO TIP: *Sometimes, the planets are in different signs but close enough to be considered conjunct. When this is the case, your knowledge of the two planets and the two signs will be put to the test. Take your time mentally crafting a keyword story that makes sense to you, especially if you are reading the chart of another person and can communicate with them. Wait until you have a coherent blending of the energies that makes sense to you before asking the other person about the keyword story you have crafted.*

Orbs of Influence: How Close Is Close Enough?

Orbs of influence are yet another astrological subject in which there are strong differences of opinion, so once again, I recommend that you do not discuss the subject with other astrologers unless and until you have finished this book and looked at your chart and a few others so you can form an opinion based on your own research. Even the definition of the orbs has a spectrum of meanings. Some astrologers treat all planets in the same sign as conjunct, while on the other end of the spectrum are the astrologers who use a tight orb of 1 or 2 degrees, especially when the outer planets are involved.

Here are the orbs I would suggest you use for all the major aspects at this stage of your astrological education—once you have more experience, you will have formulated your own preferences for orbits of influence:

- When the Sun, the Moon, or the Rising Sign is involved in any major aspect, with any other planet(s), an orb of 10 degrees can be used.
- When the Midheaven of the chart or the planet that is the ruler of the astrology chart's Sun, Moon, or Rising Sign is involved in any major aspect with any other planet, an orb of 8 degrees can be used.
- For all the other planets involved in a major aspect, an orb of 5 degrees can be used.

Of course, if you are reading your chart or the chart of someone you know well and you see that the keyword story for a planet in aspect to another planet in the chart is out of my suggested orb range yet perfectly describes some personality trait, tendency, or experience, by all means, count this aspect as if it were within the above given orbs of influence.

Rather than continuing the delineation of the conjunction of the Moon to Saturn in the same sign, I will now delineate the opposition of the Moon in Pisces to Saturn in Virgo, an opposition I possess in my own astrology chart, so you can see the difference between the conjunction and the opposition.

THE OPPOSITION ☍

Dividing the 360 degrees of an astrology chart by 2 gives us 180 degrees, placing two planets or a planet and a Rising Sign or Midheaven point at opposite ends of the zodiac. This aspect, appropriately referred to as an opposition, is considered a difficult aspect because the energies of the two astrological entities are at odds with each other, and so the story told using my keyword technique is going to include the challenge of that conceptual face-off, competition, or struggle.

Remember that the aspects of your cosmic blueprint are alive and active throughout your life. The keyword stories you can create may symbolize energies that help you or another person you are reading for add to your enjoyment of life. They can also be a warning to be aware of self-defeating tendencies you may possess too. We are all a mixture of both. It is up to you to know, and to share this knowledge for any person you read for, that the potential for any or all of these stories is always going to be active in your life and theirs. It is up to each of us to make our best keyword stories our stories in real life.

Delineating the Moon in Pisces opposite Saturn in Virgo (or, abbreviated, Moon/Pisces opp Saturn/Virgo) will be the first time my keyword story technique actually creates enough words to qualify as a story.

As always, we start with the planetary keywords stripped of the qualifying keywords the sign and house they are in can add.

Moon Opposition Saturn (in Any Signs)

The development and use of emotional intelligence to experience your emotions, nurture others, and explore your emotional life (the Moon) cannot exist freely, purely, and independently, but must always be activated and blended with an opposing force (opposition) and, in this case, be further limited by the harsh realities of life (Saturn).

You can see that using my keyword story technique can enable you to create and build concepts based on what you see in a chart that are equivalent to the advice contained in astrology books and natal-chart reports.

Of course, sometimes, you are better off with using the fewest keywords, such as in the case of Moon/Pisces opposite Saturn/Virgo: Trouble (opposition) with a woman (the Moon) who cannot escape the self-destructive (Pisces) worrying about the details (Virgo) of a harsh experience (Saturn).

That's a keyword story that accurately describes my experience. In my youth, my Moon/Pisces opposite my Saturn/Virgo manifested as my having to deal with my mother's deteriorating mental state that put her in and out of mental hospitals starting from the time I was seven years old. As I've grown older, I've realized that while I was gestating in the womb, my embryonic fluid was literally mixed with the worry my mother had that there would be something mentally wrong with me, a concern caused by her having discovered her own mother having hung herself when my mother was only seventeen, an event that shattered her to her core. It's not hard for me to give in to worry, even though I am usually exceedingly grateful for my blessed life. My childhood, however, was not enjoyable, nor was the rest of my life until I met and fell in love with Amy in 1974.

I had a lot to overcome, but I was determined to do so. Given the secrecy so common back in mid-century America, my mother had kept this secret about her mother from my father. It was the unspoken cause of their constant fighting, although he had a secret of his own: His father had been a falling-down-in-the-street drunk who had died from a Demerol overdose. Despite him having his own sad family history, once he learned of my mother's background, my father hated my mother from that day on and expected me and my sister to follow my mother into a disastrous mental state, which we did not do. They divorced when I was twelve. Were it not for my truly unconditionally loving aunt, Rosie Harth, my mother's sister, and my brilliant, man-of-the-world uncle, Morris Harth, her brother, I would not be the person I am today.

I didn't penetrate the wall of secrecy and find out my parents' backstory until I was an adult and an astrologer. Living our no-drama life of love and light with Amy and her incredible, truly spiritual mother, Jessie Spicer Zerner, nicknamed Ma (the Moon!), was just what I needed to give me the structure and security (Saturn is structure and security) to work on myself (Saturn and Virgo are all about working) and affirm and support my childhood Aquarian rebellious decision that I would never be a cliché like the people I saw on our tiny black-and-white television screen blaming their parents and others for their various failures rather than taking responsibility for, and working to take control of, their lives.

Oppositions exist to challenge us to become more aware of the power of seemingly difficult or conflicting energies when we use our awareness to grow. In this case, astrology truly saved my life. I will always have Moon/Pisces opposite Saturn/Virgo, but I have avoided the trouble-with-women definition and, instead, do my best every day to manifest the more enjoyable and useful disciplined analysis of intuitive emotional intelligence, also known as being a professional intuitive or, if you prefer, a psychic who uses my gift in everything I do to help Amy and me help ourselves and others.

As it is with all oppositions, we must be prepared to spend our whole lives working on finding a way to make these opposing planetary energies work together. The key to leading a successful life is to align yourself with keyword stories that work for you and help you understand and become empowered by your astrology chart, thereby allowing your life to function smoothly and successfully, however you define success.

THE TRINE △

Dividing the 360 degrees of an astrology chart by 3 gives us the 120-degree aspect called a trine. While the conjunction blends the energies into a new, unique, unified expression of the two astrological entities that are conjunct and the opposition sets them up as polar opposites that must somehow be reconciled if we are to function well, the trine aspect says, "Let it flow" and the entities involved will always work to our benefit in some way, even when we cannot see that this is what is going on.

The trine aspect is closely tied to the elements of astrology—Fire, Air, Water, and Earth, which we discussed in depth starting on page 63. When you think of the trine aspect, think about it being harmonious, because the planets making a trine aspect to each other are usually, but not always, in the same element:

Fire: Aries, Leo, Sagittarius
Earth: Taurus, Virgo, Capricorn
Air: Gemini, Libra, Aquarius
Water: Cancer, Scorpio, Pisces

This is also true because the three zodiac signs that comprise each element are 120 degrees from each other. So if you have a planet or planets, a Rising Sign, or Midheaven in all three signs of a particular element, you may have what is known as a Grand Trine, a phenomenon in which these astrological entities are 120 degrees apart.

Be aware, however, that a Grand Trine can be formed by two planets, or one planet and either the Rising Sign or the Midheaven, in the first or last degrees of an element and the third placement comprising the Grand Trine located in the first or last degrees of a different element.

For example, if you have Mars on the 1st degree of Aries (Fire), the Sun on the 5th degree of Leo (Fire), and Pluto at 29 degrees of Scorpio (Water), you have a Grand Trine (and you are a pretty intense person!) because they are each within a trine orb, approximately 120 degrees from each other. This would also be true of a chart where two astrological entities were in the late degrees of two out of three signs of an element but were both within the orb of a trine to a third astrological entity located on the early degrees of a different sign.

The Grand Trine is often found in the charts of people who have what other people consider easy, lucky, or charmed lives. They have problems just like the rest of us do, but to others, it seems no matter what befalls these lucky people, somehow, they are always saved in some way or miraculously come through situations that would overwhelm other, less-fortunate people.

For most of us, however, we should consider ourselves fortunate to have even one trine, though many people, including very successful people, don't have even one. Why? Because trines can make a person indolent, overly content to the point of taking for granted their good fortune, talents, or opportunities. Their good fortune may mean that their material needs are taken care of and so they do not have the fear of poverty as a motivating force. Therefore, they may avoid the risk of trying and failing, come up with some other excuse for not pursuing their dreams and cultivating their talents, or otherwise avoid the experiences that help us grow in wisdom and understanding.

The difficult aspects, the conjunction with the planets Saturn, Uranus, Neptune, or Pluto, the opposition, or the 90-degree angular relationship, known as a square, can produce experiences and energies within our psyches that must be faced, understood, and managed to the best of our abilities. Confronting and successfully dealing with these admittedly challenging aspects of an astrology chart can produce strong character. Meanwhile, failing to do the work of personal growth can lead to failures of all kinds.

People with trines have character too, of course—even those with Grand Trines. This is true because their charts often have one or more of the harder aspects in them too, confronting, opposing, and motivating them to deal with difficulties and challenges and so become more fully their authentic self.

Having a Grand Trine is like having a fancy, fast, and expensive sports car: It's great to own, but unless you use the key of your intention to develop as a person to start the engine and fuel it with your willpower, you will never use it to its full potential.

Trine keywords: *"flows easily (into or with),"* *benefit, grace (all meanings of the word), "brings out the strongest example of," "brings out the best in," blesses, supports, helps, protects, ordains, "has great potential to bring about," harmonizes, "blends well with."*

I don't have a Grand Trine, but I do have some trine aspects, so let's take a look at one that involves two planets we have not used in our prior delineation of the aspects: Jupiter/Aquarius/Sixth House trine Neptune/Libra/Third House. In my chart, this aspect has a 6-degree orb. That would normally cause us to refer to this as a weak trine, if we considered it a trine at all, since we would normally assign a 5-degree orb to these two planets.

However, as you may recall, I have Moon/Pisces in my astrology chart and Pisces is ruled by Neptune, named after mythology's god of the sea. Since the keyword story involves one of the rulers of my Celestial Trilogy (Sun, Moon, Rising Sign), a 10-degree orb is indicated.

The story told by this aspect reveals a significant part of my personality, thereby lending credence to my suggested orb definitions. It is important to note that many astrologers would not have counted this aspect because of its wide orb, missing crucial information about me. I am not faulting the astrologers who would have done this. When you are reading a chart, there is limited time for the reading, so it is logical that an astrologer would turn their attention to the most exact aspects. This is yet another reason I have written this book, giving everyone the opportunity to spend as much time as they want investigating the truly empowering stories about them told by the planets, signs, houses, and aspects of their astrology chart.

Stripped of the keywords for the sign, and house, the story told by Jupiter trine Neptune can be told:

- Optimism (Jupiter) supports and blesses (trines) idealism (Neptune).
- Idealism (Neptune) ordains the appearance of (trines) optimism (Jupiter).
- Positiveness about good fortune (Jupiter) has great potential to bring about (trines) fantasy (Neptune).

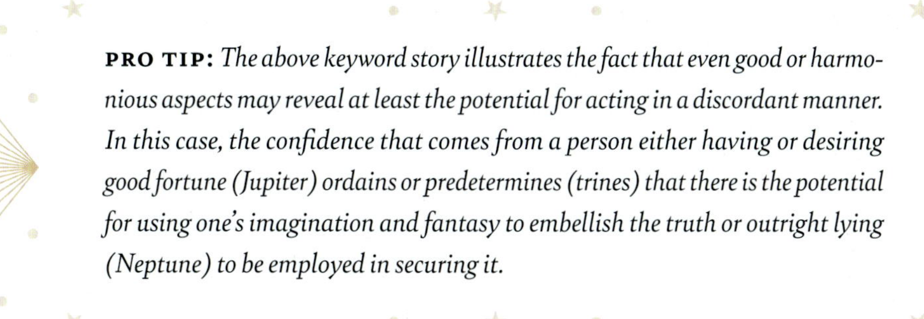

PRO TIP: *The above keyword story illustrates the fact that even good or harmonious aspects may reveal at least the potential for acting in a discordant manner. In this case, the confidence that comes from a person either having or desiring good fortune (Jupiter) ordains or predetermines (trines) that there is the potential for using one's imagination and fantasy to embellish the truth or outright lying (Neptune) to be employed in securing it.*

As usual, reversing the flow of this keyword story can help us understand it: Fantasy or the ability to inspire action to create a more ideal world or situation (Neptune) has great potential to bring about (trine) good fortune and increased prosperity (Jupiter).

The above keyword story brings us to my particular trine aspect between Jupiter/Aquarius/Sixth House and Neptune/Libra/Third House. My work (Sixth House) is my ability to understand astrology and write books about it (Third House), separating its timeless truths and beneficial wisdom (Jupiter) from the fantasies about it (Neptune) that are equally ancient, and inspire in you, dear reader, the reading of this book, which is, in my not-so-humble Leo Rising opinion, a decisive and positively determinative act on your part that benefits all of us and the world at large.

But let's lay out the keyword story and see where it takes us: Optimism and the desire to grow (Jupiter) and be part of a healthier situation that better supports and serves (Sixth House) the bringing into being of a better future (Aquarius) has great potential to bring about (trines) inspirational (Neptune) communications, associations, and all manner of travel, both virtual and physical (Third House), designed to bring about peace, justice, and harmony (Libra).

This is the story of both my singer-songwriter years and my eventual success as an author. The trine of Jupiter/Aquarius to Neptune/Libra, delineated above, existed in my cosmic blueprint from the day I was born and will be with me until the day I die.

THE SQUARE □

Dividing the circle by 4 gives us the 90-degree angle, an aspect we astrologers call the square. Squares are one of the stressful, difficult, or hard aspects because they represent the testing of your ability to live with the challenges and annoyances that are an integral part of daily life no matter whether you are rich or poor—though it's generally a lot easier to deal with most annoyances if you have the money to have skilled people take care of them for you.

Squares can be motivating in the sense that having a stone in your shoe motivates you to do something about it. Or, if you prefer, squares can be like a grain of sand in an oyster, irritating the mollusk and causing it to form a pearl. Squares motivate you to get things done so you don't have to deal with them anymore, at least in their present form.

Squares are similar in angular relationship to the planets of the Three Qualities, which we went into in detail starting on page 99. The signs of a particular quality are all square to each other. As a reminder, the Three Qualities include the following:

- The goal-oriented Cardinal signs, which coincide with the change of seasons—Aries (spring), Cancer (summer), Libra (fall), and Capricorn (winter)
- The stubborn, permanence-seeking Fixed signs—Taurus, Leo, Scorpio, and Aquarius
- The flexible Mutable signs—Gemini, Virgo, Sagittarius, and Pisces

Square keywords: *testing, "testing the limits of something," "stress test," "stress of all kinds," motivation, aggravation, "reveals strengths and weaknesses," "asks for the endurance of something difficult."*

Let's examine yet another aspect of my chart, my Mars in Libra squaring my Uranus (the ruling planet of my Sun sign, Aquarius) in Cancer. It is a relatively weak square in the sense that it is 7 degrees away from being exactly 90 degrees. However, when an aspect involves the ruling planet of the native's Sun, Moon, or Rising Sign, we give it the usual 10-degree orb, but we also pay closer attention to the keyword story told than if the planets had not been rulers.

This aspect actually explains, astrologically, why I'm using my own planets and aspects and being as honest as I can with you about the way they have manifested in my life. Mars square Uranus in a person's chart is an indication that their mission in life is to bring new ideas and concepts into being. Uranus is the planet that rules astrology, being both ancient and futuristic in its ability to adapt to changing times and bring a more hopeful future into being.

Once again, we begin by examining the story told by the planets square to each other, stripped of the signs and houses that they are in:

- Willpower and persistence (Mars) tested by (square) out-of-the-blue events that bring sudden changes (Uranus).
- Eccentricity or the longing for unrestricted freedom (Uranus) stresses or is stressed by the limits of (square) desire (Mars).
- Desire and/or acting aggressively (Mars) tests the limits of (square) eccentricity or the longing for unrestricted freedom (Uranus).
- Being different (Uranus) aggravates (square) the aggressive energies (Mars) of either others or yourself.
- Seeking to instigate revolutionary changes (Uranus) reveals the strength and weakness (square) of one's willpower and that of those who must be confronted (Mars).
- The eccentricities of others and ourselves (Uranus) must be endured and used as motivation (square) to work our will on the world (Mars).
- Destabilization (Uranus) is instigated by (Mars) sudden aggressive movements (both Uranus and Mars) that test our weaknesses (square), especially our ability to stay focused in risk-prone situations. (This keyword story is also a warning to those with this aspect to be careful and deliberate in their actions if they want to avoid accidents, which in this case would be caused by a lack ofsituational awareness.)

In a way, Uranus can be viewed as being the higher octave of Mars. While Mars is our personal energetic potential, Uranus can be seen to be our ability to tap into the energy of our generation and any powerful ideas whose time has come. When you have Mars square Uranus, you are impatient about wanting to see the realization of the many blessings you see as possible, but only if people take action to bring in a wonderful future.

Adding the signs and the houses to a keyword story can make it both long and intricate. Sometimes, you may want to break it up into a couple of sentences to create a richer and more understandable story.

Let's see what story about me is told by my Mars/Libra/in both the Second and the Third Houses, square Uranus/Cancer/Eleventh House: My desire to work my will on the world (Mars) to achieve peace, harmony, and fairness (Libra) in the discovery and application of my personal value system (Second House) is stress-tested (squared) by my innate tendency to be explosively forceful or rebellious (Uranus) even against my desire to nurture and protect (Cancer) myself, as well as my friends, hopes, and wishes (Eleventh House).

Wow! That was a surprise. I love my friends and I love myself (when I am not rebelling against my own best interests). I am not comfortable thinking that I am this easily capable of being too forceful because most people cannot handle that. I must be more careful of that unproductive way of rebelling against doing things more gently in ways that might help my friends or even help myself. I have to use the possibility of being too Mars square Uranus as a warning to myself when deciding how to act.

As I have been trying to help you see and remember, Mars and Uranus are not planets associated with patient deliberation. Yet if I want to make my chart work to my advantage, I, and anyone who has Mars and Uranus in square or opposition or even conjunction, have to add the awareness of this potentially self-defeating weakness of character to the list of strengths we possess. I state this to show you how powerful astrology can be if we are honest with ourselves and our desire to improve. To me, this is the real meaning of Socrates's famous quote at his trial: "The unexamined life is not worth living." This kind of examination and revelation is exactly what we all need if we are committed to getting out of our own way and really becoming our best self.

You may find that some of or all the keyword stories you create evoke memories of events that relate to these stories. Whether you do or don't is not important. If you learn from the stories and modify your behavior when necessary, you are doing what you need to do to be your authentic self.

Fortunately for me, there are other keyword stories to be made from Mars/Libra/Second House square Uranus/Cancer/Eleventh House: The desire and drive to act (Mars) in a fair and balanced manner (Libra) in the acquisition, maintenance, and sharing of resources (Second House) is motivated by (squared) the desire to free myself (Uranus) from the need to give and receive unconditional love (Cancer) to or from anyone, including my friends and groups of people who might share some of or all my desires to change the world (Eleventh House).

Before you chastise me for desiring to attain a level of freedom from the need to be nurtured and loved, please realize that this aspect of my personality enabled me to endure my difficult childhood, to rear myself without the need to blame my parents for my deficiencies, to nurture myself and resist the numerous stupidities of my friends and those bad ideas that were presented to us as desirable by the media and the culture of each decade I've lived through, and the strength to stand on my own two feet and live on my own after being homeless for years.

This aspect also speaks to the fact that I have never been a joiner. The idea of having a guru or joining a commune or a cult never occurred to me, even though I explored the written works of various people, alive and dead, who had formed such organizations. My independence, my desire to be myself, fully uninfluenced by anyone but myself, and my ability to nurture myself proved attractive to Amy and was a significant boost to our love affair. The Kabbalah, the mystical book of the Jewish religion, says, "A man finds freedom in marriage," and that is precisely what I have experienced.

Let's look at the keyword story told if we read my Mars/Libra/Third Hose square Uranus/Cancer/Eleventh House: The strengths and weaknesses (square) of friends (Eleventh House), as well as of relatives and neighbors (Third House), fight the urge (Mars) to partner with (Libra) and nurture (Cancer) these same people. (Once again, not a joiner.)

THE GRAND CROSS 

Just as we can have three astrological entities (planets, Rising Sign, Midheaven) that are 120 degrees away from each other, forming a Grand Trine, we can have four of them 90 degrees away from each other and forming a Grand Cross. For some people, having a Grand Cross in their charts is like the having a cross to bear. Having these four squares in your chart can motivate you, to be sure, but you will also know that you can only do so much and will always be aware of the keyword stories of the other three squares clamoring for your attention and for you to actualize their energies at the same time—an impossibility.

Some people with Grand Crosses deal with this energy by concentrating on one of the four square keyword stories and ignoring the other three to a surprising degree, though the other three do have a way of making their insulted presence felt. Some people explore the four aspects of their Grand Cross one at a time in life epochs lasting years or even decades that can be seen only in retrospect. Some throw themselves into each square's story for a relatively short period of time until they have accomplished a goal that is reasonable to set, given the time allotted to it. In my experience, most people with Grand Crosses spend large chunks of their life on one of the four square's keyword stories before moving on to the next one.

Some people become overwhelmed by the stressful energies of having a Grand Cross in their charts and either give up or manifest unpleasant behavior to show the world how unpleasant is their experience of reality. If astrology were a part of people's early education, they could be made aware of the benefits to be derived from having difficult aspects and difficult charts. The late, great astrologer Al Morrison told me that I have a difficult chart, which I took as a compliment. Life is a challenge to us all to rise to the occasion of the blessings and difficulties in our lives and make the whole thing work to our benefit and the benefit of those we care about.

THE T SQUARE ▷

Like the Grand Trine, the Grand Cross is fairly uncommon. Much more common is the T-square, an aspect pattern formed by two astrological entities that are in opposition to each other while both are also in square aspect to a third astrological entity.

Both Amy and I have a T-square in our difficult charts. In fact, we have the same planets involved: Moon opposite Mars with both planets square Uranus! At this stage of your astrological education, I believe you are ready for me to delineate both of our T-squares for you so you can see how different the keyword stories for the same aspect with the same planets can be with the addition of the signs and houses.

I have my Moon on 28th degree of Pisces—27 degrees and 26 minutes, to be precise—and in my Eighth House. Some astrologers talk about a planet being on the 0 degree when they are talking about a planet that is on the 1st degree of a sign, but I read it as that planet being on the 1st degree of that sign, so, I see my Moon at 27 degrees and 26 minutes as being on the 28th degree of Pisces.

My Moon is opposite my Mars, which is on the 9th degree of Libra—8 degrees and 45 minutes, to be precise—and in my Second House. Though this opposition aspect has an orb of 11.3 degrees, I count it for a couple of reasons I am presenting here for your edification so you too will feel free to take each aspect as it comes and consider it in the context of the chart as a whole. (The orb guidelines I have given you previously, on page 263, are suggestions, not immutable rules etched in stone.)

My Pisces Moon is so different from my Aquarian Sun in terms of the two signs' relative comfort with strong emotions that I'm willing to bend the 10-degree orb rule, even though the signs Pisces and Libra are not opposite each other. Additionally, that they are in signs not opposite each other is intriguing to me, and I want to see whether the keyword story resonates with my understanding of who I am. I cannot miss an opportunity for potential self-growth—my Jupiter/Aquarius would not like that!

So let's give that keyword story a whirl. We start with the planets stripped of their signs and houses. With the Moon opposing Mars, the following is true:

- Emotional intelligence (the Moon) is challenged by (opposition) the desire to work one's will on the world (Mars).
- This configuration can present as overly (opposition) aggressive (Mars) when emotional (the Moon).
- It also has a habit of (the Moon) pushing back (Mars) when opposed.

- Trying to get their way (Mars) too strongly can work against (opposition) their being nurtured and cared for.
- Fight/flight/freeze anxiety (Mars) caused by too much feeling (the Moon) and not enough (opposition) goal-directed doing (Mars) can result in moodiness (the Moon).
- An independent, original, pioneering individual (Mars) rises to the challenge (opposition) of using these powerful energies in tandem with their emotional intelligence (the Moon).

There is a lot of truth in these keyword stories. I am fortunate that I have done the hard work to smooth out the rough edges this aspect can incline a person to manifest. Amy, on the other hand, has manifested only the last, most positive expression of this aspect. One thing both she and I have been feeling of late is a variation on the feeling of a racehorse kicking the stall when a bell is heard: We are so used to being in action on multiple fronts that we have twinges of anxiousness when we are between battles (Mars).

We are very aware of how lucky we are. We often feel like we are two of the luckiest people in the world, and we hope heaven is very similar to our daily routine. Even so, there is a longing for new mountains to climb and new, exciting stories to live and share—which brings us to our Moon/Mars opposition being squared by Uranus, the planet that symbolizes how we grow from new, exciting, and unexpected experiences.

I have Uranus (ruler of my Aquarian Sun) on the 2nd degree of Cancer—1 degree and 49 minutes, to be precise.

Moon square Uranus:

- This eccentric person (Uranus) has volatile (more Uranus) emotions (the Moon) that often work at cross-purposes (square) but if harnessed correctly produce a very intuitive person (the Moon).
- Emotional intelligence (the Moon) is tested or motivated by (square) the desire for new and exciting experiences (Uranus).
- The need for security (the Moon) is tested or motivated by (square) the urge for experimentation and freedom (Uranus).
- This person experienced a disrupted (Uranus and square) home life (the Moon).
- This person was tested or motivated by (square) having an unusual, eccentric, and/or genius (Uranus) mother or home life (the Moon).

There's truth in most of these stories for both Amy and me, especially the last one. I've told you about my life being negatively affected by my mother's troubles and mental illness and how my life was basically saved when I met Amy and her amazing, emotionally intelligent, and artistic genius of a mother.

Mars square Uranus:

- The drive to work one's will on the world (Mars) motivates or tests (squares) the desire (Mars) to rebel, revolutionize, disrupt, or shake up the status quo (Uranus).
- The energy of a pioneer (Mars) brings out (squares) the mind of a visionary (Uranus).
- Action (Mars) is brought to bear strongly (square) by humanitarian ideals (Uranus).
- The desire for change just for change's sake (Uranus) can disrupt or misdirect (square) the efforts to get what a person wants (Mars).

Both Amy and I are proud to have spent our lives together creatively bringing new ideas into being. She has pioneered a unique and award-winning style of collage. Our Mars/ Uranus squares have empowered us to manifest our dreams and deal with the inertia and resistance of people, often in power or gatekeeper roles, who are desirous of maintaining their power and prestige and less courageous, pioneering, and free-spirited than they should be about bringing excitement and advancement to their industries. Luckily for us, we have also encountered many brave and visionary people in the publishing, art, and fashion businesses. Having Mars square Uranus can give boundless energy that, when harnessed purposefully and in harmony with planetary alignments that are happening in the sky, can bring about the success of ideas whose time has come.

We have seen some similarities in how Amy and I manifest our Moon opposite Mars squared to Uranus T-squares. Let's add the sign and house keywords to the planets involved in our T-square story to see some of the differences. We will do Amy first because she is a pioneering Aries, the first sign of the zodiac, and Aries natives always want to go first and should go first—and, by the way, should go by their first thought or intuitive hunch and not second-guess themselves.

Amy has her Moon on the 12th degree of Libra in the Eleventh House of her cosmic blueprint. Her Libra Moon is opposite to her Mars (ruler of her Aries Sun) just barely over the line on the 16th degree of the sign Mars rules, Aries, and in her Fifth House. Amy's Uranus is on the 6th degree of Cancer and in the Eighth House of her cosmic blueprint.

Here's the complete keyword story from her Moon opposition Mars square Uranus T-square: Emotional intelligence (the Moon) dedicated to art, beauty, harmony, and balance (Libra) succeeds against the odds in finding that balance (opposition) by allowing her personal power to work her will on the (art) world (Mars) as a brave pioneer blazing a new trail (Aries) motivated and energized by (square) her desire to bring to life art that is (Mars in the Fifth House) unique and exciting, and revolutionary energies (Uranus) that are also mystical, magical, powerful, and surreal (Uranus in the Eighth House), as a way to nurture and support (Cancer) her friends and to all those who wish to join her in bringing in a new and exciting paradigm (Uranus and the Eleventh House), to the world (the Moon in the Eleventh House), especially a rebellion (Uranus) struggling with (squaring) the past habits (the Moon) of the art world (the Moon in Libra opposite Mars in the Fifth House).

This works for me and, I hope, for you. Do you see how I constructed this keyword story? I certainly hope so because that means you are a real astrologer, and I would be interested to see what other keyword stories you could make from the same aspect.

Now, on to my T-square keyword story involving the same planets: the Moon, Mars, and Uranus: A sensitive person who feels deeply (the Moon in Pisces) and has mystical, magical tendencies (Eighth House) is challenged to find (opposition) a way to balance (Libra) his desire to fight (Mars) for his strongly held values (Second House) of beauty, justice, and harmony (Libra again) motivated or tested by (squared) the desire (Mars) to shake things up and rebel (Uranus) and not only join like-minded people in this collective effort to bring into being a new paradigm (Eleventh House) of the definition and meaning of those values (Second House) but also to take on the role of someone who nurtures and protects (Cancer) his friends and fellow rebels (Eleventh House) by using metaphysical expertise and his psychic intuitive gift (the Moon in Pisces in the Eighth House) as his means of defending and protecting them (Mars in Libra).

Once again, I hope you were able to follow the logic of my keyword stories. I also hope that as an astrologer, you realize that this T-square is one of the most important components of my cosmic blueprint because Uranus is the ruling planet of not only astrology itself but also my Sun sign, Aquarius. My Uranus is in the Eleventh House, the house Uranus rules.

THE PART OF FORTUNE

In a cosmic blueprint, you will see that there is a circle symbol with an *x* in it. That is what is called the Part of Fortune, and it is an indication of one of the primary areas of life where you will succeed. Having my Part of Fortune in my Eleventh House, the house of Aquarius, and so close to my Uranus, the ruler of both Aquarius and the Eleventh House, is an indication that I will succeed by being an important part of the revolution to bring the new paradigm into being and thereby bring in the bright future we all know has been waiting in the wings for the old paradigm to whither or otherwise get out of the way.

Having my Part of Fortune in Gemini, the sign of communications, is a further indication of how I will succeed, i.e., as a writer and all-around communicator. Though you may have never heard of me until you picked up this book, I have been successful as a writer, with over three million copies of my published works in print around the world in eighteen languages. I have created several innovative products designed to empower this revolution. These include *Karma Cards*, my simplification of astrology; *Instant Tarot*, my book that makes everyone an instant tarot reader; *Quantum Affirmations*, my science-based manifestation technique that actually can change your life; *The Vision Board Oracle*, which combines that technique with Amy's ability to make anyone a vision-board artist; and now *Your Cosmic Blueprint*, which is going to make thousands of new astrologers who are so desperately needed for this sacred time we have entered. So you see, knowing your cosmic blueprint is a vital part of finding your place in the world and making the impact on it you were born to create.

THE SEXTILE ✳

The astrological aspect known as a sextile is an angle of 60 degrees, a figure arrived at by dividing the 360 degrees of a circle by 6. It is also half a trine, though that does not mean a sextile is only half as wonderful as a trine. In fact, a sextile is like a self-motivated, dynamic trine. Not only does it reveal the potential for the good fortune the native may enjoy from the harmonious blending of the energies of two or more planets, but the sextile also means that the native will not just be sitting around enjoying nature's bounty and the raining down on them of the best the world has to offer, which the trine can sometimes indicate. The sextile shows that the good fortune portended by these planets in sextile aspect will be seen, appreciated, explored, usefully used, and built on—sometimes even shared.

Sextile keywords: *"explores the best expression of," "seeks to learn best practice(s)," "gently penetrates the secrets of," "takes others into account"* (sometimes, too much so), *"creatively deals with," "is strongly aware of," "approaches the situation like an artist," "is self-effacing regarding"* (sometimes too much so), *"causes a beneficial action and/or result."*

Most of us have Neptune sextile Pluto! Everyone born between 1941 and 2034 shares or will share the same *very important* astrological aspect: Neptune making a 60-degree angle sextile to Pluto.

So if it's so important, why don't many astrologers speak to this aspect that unites the generations in transformative idealism? As you have learned, Neptune and Pluto are transpersonal planets; they're slow moving and so stamp out generations with the same planetary position. But that's not why people don't talk about this aspect. They don't talk about it because they either don't really understand astrology or don't think the symbolism for this aspect works, because it is a powerfully important goal of humanity that most people think has not been attained and, therefore, some astrologers seem to be afraid that talking about it can make people think that astrology doesn't work.

Astrology works. The basic keywords of Neptune/Pluto, the idealization of transformation, is the water we modern fish have been swimming in for so long that we don't see it. But people in the past didn't idealize transformation the way we all do now and have done since around 1941. Neptune sextile Pluto has produced generations of people who have been part of the efforts to put the pedal to the metal and achieve a truly equitable society for everyone, a totally utopian and Neptunian concept.

Those of us with Neptune sextile Pluto have also tried and are still trying to put the brakes on senseless wars, corruption, and the worshipful idealization of rich, powerful people, aka plutocrats, and outright dictators. And it just looks like so much is happening now, but it's not happening fast enough for us Neptune sextile Pluto peeps. And everyone's got something to say about everything!

Like Andy Warhol predicted, now, everyone's famous for fifteen minutes, and social media marks the spot where people now dissipate the warlike energy that used to take to the streets to protest and effect transformation. Neptune injects idealization and compassion into Pluto's cut-them-off-or-cut-them-down attitude. Neptune's recent passage through its home/rulership sign of Pisces may soon be viewed as the good old days. Things will likely get a lot more kinetic, aggressive, and action oriented now that Neptune has gone into Aries and will stay there for fourteen years. Neptune/Aries, the idealization of aggressive action, will become the norm. Let's hope that action will be used for good purposes.

I would also like to use Pluto sextile the Rising Sign as an example because we have not used Pluto in my aspect delineations, nor have we used the Rising Sign. I am not going to add zodiac signs to the keyword story, because I want you to do some work—your first homework assignment! Craft a couple of keyword stories using your own Pluto sign, figuring out which two of the Rising Signs 60 degrees on either side of your Pluto position would be sextile to it, and then create a couple more keyword stories for your Rising Sign, figuring out which two signs Pluto would have to be in to be sextile to your Rising Sign.

This is a challenging test for your astrological knowledge, and it will highlight whether you have to reread any parts of this book. But note that there is no shame in having to reread anything. Astrology is a complex system—even the way I teach it. This assignment will show you how much you have actually learned and prepare you for the last chapter of this book, where I will show you how to read a full chart.

Pluto sextile the Rising Sign keyword stories:

- The ability to transform one's self or a situation (Pluto) causes a beneficial action and/or result (sextile) that affects how others see you (the Rising Sign).
- Judgment (Pluto) appears (Rising Sign) to penetrate (sextile) the way we look at other people (Rising Sign).
- Presenting ourselves (Rising Sign) as powerful (Pluto) is a best practice (sextile) that causes a beneficial action or result (the sextile again).
- Eliminating (Pluto) self-effacing behavior beneficially (sextile) affects the way others see us (Rising Sign).

As you have seen, the sextile softens and makes more palatable even Pluto, the most powerful and impersonal planet in astrology. If it can do this for Pluto, it can do it for the other planets.

RECAP: THE ASPECTS

The conjunction challenges us to live with a powerful blending of two or more characteristics of our personality that people unlike us do not usually experience. We go through life quite differently from those without those astrological entities in conjunction, challenging us to formulate a technique for dealing with this unique blending and somehow understanding what makes us different in this area. This is somewhat true of the following aspects as well, though less so.

The opposition challenges us to be able to not just see two opposite ways of understanding and acting about something—possibly in two opposing but related areas of our life—but to also act to somehow combine these opposing forces into a two-pronged attack to solve a problem.

The trine symbolizes the harmonizing or otherwise working together successfully of two or more aspects of our personality, talents, and beliefs to better our lives in one or more ways. Especially when Jupiter or Venus is part of a trine, we are challenged to successfully deal with the blessings of good fortune. This is not as easy as it sounds. As someone who has counseled many wealthy, successful, and even famous people, I must tell you that it is imperative you know they too have problems that plague them. Their problems may be different, but they are problems that challenge them nonetheless.

The square challenges us to reconcile two or more aspects of our personality, talents, and beliefs that are apparently at cross-purposes with one another so they will complement, reinforce, or otherwise help us in our efforts and not cancel out each other's strengths.

The sextile allows us to best take advantage of the energies of two or more astrological entities without the inertia that can sometimes cause those with powerful trines to sit out life in some way. Sextiles are more apt to bring us into interaction with everyday situations and people we are comfortable with.

BRIEF DISCUSSIONS OF THE MAJOR ASPECTS OF AN ASTROLOGY CHART

As a reward for your having come this far on our journey through the stars, I have taken the necessarily long and laborious task of delineating for your edification and convenience all the major aspects between the Sun and the Moon to the various planets. I have arranged them in the same order as I taught them to you, an order I derived from dividing the 360 degrees of a circle by 1 (the conjunction), 2 (the opposition), 3 (the trine), 4 (the square), and 6 (the sextile).

I will also give you the meanings of being a cosmic agent for each of the ten planets, by which I mean if you have a planet conjunct your Rising Sign. I am sharing these with you because I want you to really understand your Celestial Trilogy and have these powerful interpretations at your fingertips. I want *Your Cosmic Blueprint* to truly be all you need to read an astrology chart like a pro.

What I have not done is delineate the meanings of all the angles between all the rest of the planets, because it would make this book way too long and, more importantly, because at this point in your astrological education, you do not need me to do this for you.

By now, you know the art of starry telling. You know how to string together a keyword sentence describing the planet in the sign in the house, add the keyword for that aspect, and add the keyword sentence for the aspected planet. When you do this after finishing this book, think of it as your postgraduate work!

Please remember that reading a cosmic blueprint means that you are going to encounter both the supportive and the weakening aspects that exist in everyone's chart. Some of the following aspects between the Sun and the Moon and the rest of the planets are going to sound better to you than others. You can check how close in degrees are the angles, closer orbs being indicators of more intense energies, and then add to your mix how important one or both planets in the aspect are to that specific cosmic blueprint.

For example, an aspect between Mercury and Venus becomes more noteworthy in a chart with either or both planets being the ruler of the native's Sun and Rising Sign, like a Virgo or Gemini Sun or Rising Sign, all ruled by Mercury, with a Taurus or Libra Sun or Rising Sign—all combinations ruled by Venus—or if you had aspects between the Moon and other planets in a chart with a Cancer Sun or Rising Sign.

Do not worry about getting it perfectly. Do your best, go back to review the relevant page(s) until you do not feel like you have to anymore, and read a chart with the intention to help, with compassion for the human condition, and with an awareness that astrology is a practice, like medicine, or an art, if you will. Practice makes . . . well, if not perfect, it makes for a fun experience that can change for the better your life and the lives of everyone fortunate enough to have you for an astrologer. Helping yourself and others understand themselves better is the key to wisdom and a better life. Know thyself, and to thine own self be true. Now you know how to do it!

ASPECTS OF THE SUN

Aspects of the Sun to the Moon

Sun Conjunct Moon: Purpose Aligns with Emotional Intelligence

Individuality and emotional intelligence work as one force in those with the moral courage to accept and not fight themselves. Trauma can incline you to be one-sided, careless, and indifferent.

Sun Opposition Moon: Vitality Is Opposed by Emotions

It's difficult but important and possible to find a partner who fulfills your needs—especially your need to resolve the conflict you have with your feelings determining how your energy level functions. Let go of the past, and prosper.

Sun Trine Moon: Ego Is Helped by Emotional Intelligence

This aspect is favorable to reputation, health, acknowledgment, success, and harmony in general; personality and emotional intelligence are in harmony. It gives success wherever feelings and intuition are concerned and can balance out emotional problems.

Sun Square Moon: Ego and Emotional Intelligence Work at Cross-Purposes
This aspect offers the challenge of dealing with changeable, irresolute, meddling people and to fight those tendencies in yourself and their projection onto others. It can manifest an excess of self-confidence or self-overestimation if your early home life was traumatic.

Sun Sextile Moon: Purpose Is Activated by Emotional Intelligence
This is a very harmonious aspect indicating the free flow of positive experiences that enable you to accomplish your goals. If you experienced a harmonious home life early on or can create one now, you can achieve success.

Aspect of the Sun to Mercury (only possible aspect)
Sun Conjunct Mercury: Purpose Is Affected by Communication Skills
An orb of 7 degrees is optimal for intelligence, sense of humor, memory, and concentration, but can also result in your being nervous and high-strung. If the orb is closer than 7 degrees, the result is combustion—being burned by the Sun—which causes difficulties listening and/or communicating.

Aspect of the Sun to Venus (only possible aspect)
Sun Conjunct Venus: Purpose Is Love and Beauty
You are inclined to be amiable, courteous, and sympathetic. This aspect softens any harshness that may be indicated by the position and aspects to either planet and can indicate a tendency to run after pleasures and be very fond of luxury and an easy life.

Aspects of the Sun to Mars
Sun Conjunct Mars: Ego Is Aggressive
You get the job done and work best when allowed to either work alone or unsupervised. You have a strong, energetic will and are inclined to be ruled by self-interest and passion, not by forethought. You must avoid exaggeration and being too impulsive.

Sun Opposition Mars: Purpose Is Opposed by Aggression
You are a fighter who will not back down. Relentless combativeness or selfishness can cause others to push back openly or secretly. Using your abundant energies and abilities appropriately is a challenge that can pay off hugely if you can do it.

Sun Trine Mars: Ego Energies Flow Strongly
You have great vitality, with mental as well as physical strength, and are usually courageous, active, enterprising, faithful, and generous. You have organizing talent and feel attracted to vocations with a large responsibility.

Sun Square Mars: Ego Is Tested or Irritated by Aggressive Tendencies
You have strength and energy but also a propensity to fight against limitations, perceived or real. You can be impulsive and jump to conclusions and can be troublesome or irritable. This aspect can indicate discord

with authority figures. Your passions are stronger than your will.

Sun Sextile Mars: Vitality Is Strongly Energized
You possess an incredible amount of energy that can be successfully channeled into just about any activity. You are surprisingly open to the ideas of others. Others admire rather than are threatened by such obvious strength and your wisdom using it.

Aspects of the Sun to Jupiter

Sun Conjunct Jupiter: Ego Is Jovial
You are honest, generous, and sympathetic. This aspect brings many opportunities. You can progress morally and socially—people will help—and achieve success through loyalty and superiors while seeming to be blessed by good luck. This aspect offers pride and confidence and often honors material success.

Sun Opposition Jupiter: Ego Is Too Big
You are a charming, talented, and creative person, but you may have problems with competitors if an inflated ego and self-importance produce overconfident risk-taking. You may bend the truth to advance ambitions and should avoid selfishness at all costs.

Sun Trine Jupiter: Purpose Is Realized
This aspect is very favorable for everything—for vitality as well as success in business, love, legal affairs, and travel. It refines the character, gives hope and faith, and makes a person philanthropic, honest, generous, and ingenious. Good things happen to you.

Sun Square Jupiter: Ego Is Tested by Big Ideas
This aspect motivates you to learn and grow. It can symbolize difficulties in your ability to manage social interactions. You may find it hard to reconcile strongly held beliefs with what is taught as true and should avoid being superstitious, mistrustful, and arrogant at all costs.

Sun Sextile Jupiter: Purpose Is Expanded
You are a fortunate and enthusiastic person who shares the blessings that flow to them and are confident of your knowledge, wisdom, and brilliance—and are given, by circumstances, many opportunities to put it to use—but are not good dealing with routine or boredom.

Aspects of the Sun to Saturn

Sun Conjunct Saturn: Ego Is Serious
You are a disciplined person who may become an authority through hard work and perseverance. This aspect gives organizing talent. You are usually stern but surprisingly timid during bouts of depression caused by realizations of limits and imminent difficulties.

Sun Opposition Saturn: Ego Is Opposed by Limiting Forces
You will learn a lot from having to cope with difficult people and situations. You need to love yourself more, or others will feel the lack and mirror it. When self-confidence is attained, success soon follows. Do not be too sedentary.

Sun Trine Saturn: Ego Benefits from Structure
Perseverance, tact, and self-control inform success. You are methodical, conservative, and

active. You will find success through important jobs plus helping and having sympathy of and for elders. You have a strong character and organizing talent and are fit for positions of responsibility.

Sun Square Saturn: Ego Is Tested by Limits
You have exemplary discipline but a great need for self-love and confidence. You will find success from being your authentic self under pressures brought on by others and yourself. Avoid spite and jealousy inspiring malicious intent, especially with authority figures.

Sun Sextile Saturn: Ego Deals Well with Discipline
Your in-depth understanding of whatever you put your mind to enables you to teach it. Great organization and planning skills support your successful ambitions. You are an admirer of what lasts, and conservative. You are a respected role model who is always learning.

Aspects of the Sun to Uranus

Sun Conjunct Uranus: Ego Is Unusual
Intuitive genius? You are extraordinarily original and eccentric and have disruptive or revolutionary tendencies. You need freedom to explore, innovate, and err. Friends and partners must deal with your many ups and downs, strong will, and idiopathic mood swings.

Sun Opposition Uranus: Ego Is Challenged by Disruptive Forces
You are an uncompromising, high-strung individual who needs to make time each day to relax and regroup from the pressures imposed by others and yourself. Your enjoyment of life is directly proportional to your ability to allow others the freedoms you desire.

Sun Trine Uranus: Purpose Is Aided by Unorthodoxy
You are independent and have originality, often to the point of genius, and accurate intuition and find new solutions to old problems. You are fond of antiquities and strongly attracted to public life, and you incline to astrology and other metaphysical studies or pursuits.

Sun Square Uranus: Purpose Is Tested by Disruptive Forces
You are extremely quick and perceptive but nervous. Your personal growth is tied to lessons learned from unexpected and unforeseen obstacles, opposition, separations, estrangements—sudden difficulties that can be overcome just as suddenly.

Sun Sextile Uranus: Purpose Creates the Future
You are a freethinker, never bored or boring, and you often seem like you have arrived from the future to tell us what is really going on now. You are a loyal friend and partner to someone who is honest and communicative and you view life as an exciting classroom.

Aspects of the Sun to Neptune

Sun Conjunct Neptune: Ego Is Idealistic
You are dreamy and unusual, overwhelmed by harshness, and your high ideals inspire action or confusion, depending on life experiences. You must avoid intoxication or other addictions.

You are highly intuitive, often clairvoyant, clairaudient, and strongly mystical.

Sun Opposition Neptune: Purpose Is Challenged by Confusion
Your stellar intuition is accurate when your mind is calmed. You can feel threatened by competitive or hard-to-read people and situations. Avoid intoxication, addiction, and victimhood fantasies. Face reality. Know that you are as capable as anyone.

Sun Trine Neptune: Purpose Is Enhanced by Idealism
You are truly compassionate, with deeply felt emotions and feelings, and philanthropic, and have aesthetic taste and a love of fine arts and mysticism. You offer a wide vision and can see the overarching picture. You are inspired and inspiring and can be very successful.

Sun Square Neptune: Purpose Is Tested by Confusion
You have vivid dreams and a powerful ability to creatively imagine and visualize. You may be too idealistic and may not appreciate your talents as much as you should. Oversensitivity can be used against you by lying users, and you are in danger of succumbing to escapism and surrender.

Sun Sextile Neptune: Ego Is Energized by Imagination
You are creative, and you know it, and you are gifted with a rare intuition. You can inspire others to make positive changes and are inclined to use all your knowledge and resources in service to humanity. You have a deep understanding of all metaphysical subjects.

Aspects of the Sun to Pluto

Sun Conjunct Pluto: Ego Is Powerful
You are a forceful person with the drive to attain power and an almost mystical ability to change people's minds. You are extreme always and in all ways, and you must be constructive and avoid the inclination to ignore other people's desires when satisfying your own.

Sun Opposition Pluto: Purpose Is Threatened
You are capable of exemplary self-transformation, and powerful to the point of being perceived as threatening by others, but worried about threats real and imagined from more powerful forces. Avoid developing an all-or-nothing, win-at-all-costs attitude.

Sun Trine Pluto: Ego Enjoys Power
You are born to lead and can gain and use power wisely, and your personal magnetism attracts good people and good fortune. You know what is truly valuable and what success is. You achieve goals, even those that seem unrealistic. You are able to understand life at a deep level.

Sun Square Pluto: Ego Is Tested by Power
You are extremely competitive and have a potentially explosive temper that needs to be understood and professionally guided. You may have trouble handling power or addressing the needs of others, and you have a great need to learn moderation in all areas of life.

Sun Sextile Pluto: Purpose Is Enhanced by Power
You are powerful, and you know it. Once you visualize your goal, nothing will stop you from fully

realizing it in real life. You are strongly inclined to use all your gifts in service to fundamental transformation that benefits others as much as you.

ASPECTS OF THE MOON

Aspects of the Moon to Mercury

Moon Conjunct Mercury: Emotions Are Communicated

You express feelings easily, but you have to make a special effort to keep secrets. You have a quick and adaptable thought process, though your opinions can seem as changeable as your emotions. You are a voracious reader and constant communicator of ideas.

Moon Opposition Mercury: Emotions Challenge Mindfulness

You need to avoid letting your logical mind and your emotions interfere with each other. Confusion and distortion of facts can arise unless you make an effort to think before speaking. Your approach to communication can display a unique style or be too intellectual.

Moon Trine Mercury: Emotions Are Aided by Mindfulness

You communicate clearly and at a professional level. You are an intelligent intellectual with quick perception and accurate observation. This aspect is good for all kinds of study, amplifying alertness, quick-wittedness, and adaptability.

Moon Square Mercury: Emotions Are Tested by Logic

You have good mental faculties and are skilled, especially at researching and disseminating information, but you can avoid important subjects that do not interest you. Past trauma can make you inclined to be superficial or irresolute, or too independent.

Moon Sextile Mercury: Emotions Are Enhanced by Mindfulness

You are a kind and nurturing individual with a wide circle of friends, and you help others heal wounds both physical and emotional. You also learn, apply, and communicate habits that heal. You are a brilliant student who learns effortlessly and can teach too.

Aspects of the Moon to Venus

Moon Conjunct Venus: Emotions Are Married to Love

You are a lovely person comfortable with your emotions. You have an amorous nature but can be loyal once you establish a partnership. This aspect often grants the native a happy life of ease and pleasant surroundings where they are esteemed, loved, and prosperous.

Moon Opposition Venus: Emotions Are Challenged by Love

You are a good person and can be successful and well-known, but you may give or expect too much from family, friends, and romantic partners, and you can seem too good to be true when you try too hard around cynical, jaded, or dishonest people. You must avoid gossip.

Moon Trine Venus: Emotions Are Loving

You can gain prosperity and success, especially through women. You are favorable to marriage and family life, but indolence and boredom can undermine your gains. You are artistic, possess a pleasant, sympathetic, good-natured personality, and have an amorous nature.

Moon Square Venus: Emotions Are Tested by Love
You are sensuous and attractive but can be vain or indolent. If you do not cultivate the ability to focus and concentrate, you can become distracted and careless. You have a good memory but can get overly sentimental. Keeping up appearances can bring troubles in your marriage.

Moon Sextile Venus: Emotions Power Love
You are an esteemed and loved person, kind, understanding, and thoughtful, who will probably live a happy, prosperous life. You have a love of ease and comfort and are fond of pleasant surroundings. You are very caring and helpful to children and the deserving.

Aspects of the Moon to Mars

Moon Conjunct Mars: Emotions Are Aggressive
You have a tremendous passion and energy that needs an equal amount of emotional intelligence to contain it. Otherwise, you will be too brash, impulsive, and rash in action. Forceful displays of too much self-confidence can alienate others.

Moon Opposition Mars: Emotions Conflict with Action
You are analytical, and, beyond being one to think outside the box, you are original to the point of being rebellious. You are nervous when you lack an outlet for your abundant energy. You can appear selfish, and you must cultivate emotional self-control and avoid intolerance regarding the opinions of others.

Moon Trine Mars: Emotions Support Action
You are courageous and ready to defend family and the defenseless. You are also practical and enterprising, generous, energetic, adventurous, positive in speaking and acting, and capable but can be changeable and nervous if things stop moving forward.

Moon Square Mars: Emotions Stress Actions
Your emotional intelligence must be cultivated. Otherwise, your abundant energy, physical prowess, and adventurous spirit can result in impulsive, hasty actions that appear to be undertaken by an irritable, rude, and insensitive braggart.

Moon Sextile Mars: Emotions Energize Action
You are energetic, original, independent, and surprisingly thoughtful, with little of the rashness and self-aggrandizing seen in the other Moon/Mars aspects. You know how to have a placid home life but are willing to fight for peace. Avoid eating when upset.

Aspects of the Moon to Jupiter

Moon Conjunct Jupiter: Emotions Convey Blessings
You are esteemed and loved, as well as generous, charitable, and spiritual, and have a pleasant personality that is very favorable to success and prosperity. This aspect often brings powerful friends who help out and is good for body and spirit.

Moon Opposition Jupiter: Emotions Are Upset by Good Fortune
You are very evolved and philosophical in thought, with a rare creative ability. You are generous to a fault, and though you appreciate and value the opinions of the gifted, you can be overindulgent to those you admire. You need regular exercise and must avoid rich foods and drink.

Moon Trine Jupiter: Emotions Are Supported by Good Fortune
This is a very fortunate aspect that usually brings prosperity and success in seemingly every direction. You are an exemplary person, honest, religious, sympathetic, intuitive, and progressive. You can be very popular and may be consulted for philosophical wisdom.

Moon Square Jupiter: Emotions Are Stymied by Excess
For you, life experience with strife and disagreements leads to knowing how to fix things using applied spiritual practice. You have a rich emotional life but must avoid arrogance and carelessness and may have troubles and disappointments as a result of misplaced faith.

Moon Sextile Jupiter: Emotions Are Energized by Good Fortune
You are an exciting person to be around. You are lucky, and you have a unique openness and awareness that makes each moment an enjoyable learning experience. You are always growing, and that, and a strong ability to communicate, can lead to success in many areas of life.

Aspects of the Moon to Saturn

Moon Conjunct Saturn: Emotions Are Disciplined
You work best in positions where emotions play no part and are a good manager of projects but not people because your tendency to expect the worst and project mistrust causes problems and discontent. A difficult childhood causes melancholy and depression.

Moon Opposition Saturn: Emotions Emerge from the Past
You take life seriously and are wise beyond your years, and you will succeed in proportion to how optimistic you are. However, a difficult childhood leads to lingering distrust of authority and relationships, and fear can result in missteps that can cause anger, shame, and depression.

Moon Trine Saturn: Emotions Are Regulated
You have a calm, imposing manner and, economical in all things, a reserved and tactful character. Because you keep secrets and can be relied on, you have a fitness to occupy confidential posts. You have a pronounced talent for organization and are a model of perseverance, patience, and seriousness.

Moon Square Saturn: Emotions Are Troubled
You flourish if a trusted partner gives you nurturing and love daily. Otherwise, you are inclined to worry, anxiety, and indolence that might need care. You can be mistrustful, apathetic, despondent, shy, discontented, and insincere.

Moon Sextile Saturn: Emotions Are Understood

You are self-disciplined, dependable, and determined and can be trusted with authority. You are a wonderful student or teacher who is committed to lifelong learning, and you thrive in the company of wise, ambitious, or self-made people, especially older people.

Aspects of the Moon to Uranus

Moon Conjunct Uranus: Emotions Are Unpredictable

You have great intuition and a quick intellect, plus inventiveness and an inclination to become a disruptor or reformer—a pioneer in something new. You are progressive and hate all convention, and you are inclined to a wandering life. You are very eccentric, nervous, and changeable.

Moon Opposition Uranus: Emotions Are a Problem

You are extremely concerned with the lives of those perceived as family but can become emotionally attached to seemingly inappropriate people. You can be a surprisingly good teacher, but being different creates problem, and you need rest and serenity.

Moon Trine Uranus: Emotions Are Exciting

You have a love of learning—you are a historian at heart—and great mental activity, and you are a problem solver with an inspirational manner. This is a very favorable aspect for those who dance to the beat of a different drummer. You are refreshingly original and have occult inclinations, and yours is an unusual life, full of change.

Moon Square Uranus: Emotions Run Free

You are inclined to a romantic, self-willed life, and you do best in a profession that keeps you always on the move. Erratic conditions or caregivers in early life cause an inclination to eccentricity, strange conduct, and being irritable and very unpredictable.

Moon Sextile Uranus: Emotions Empower

You are intuitive and have a positive attitude about life, pleasantly excited by the beauty and goodness that can be found, ensuring a successful life. You are able to work well with others, but your scientific mind requires others to be equally logical and methodical.

Aspects of the Moon to Neptune

Moon Conjunct Neptune: Emotions Are Messages

You are artistic and sometimes ingenious, and you are a dreamy, psychic person, sensitive to the emotions of others and impressions from higher worlds. You are very sensitive and changeable and have vision and can interpret dreams. Avoid intoxication and disturbed people.

Moon Opposition Neptune: Emotions Are Obstacles

You are highly intuitive and creative but not always comfortable with this gift. Daydreaming, lack of focus, or not paying attention can allow innovative ideas but can also cause you problems. You must be careful to separate fact from fiction.

Moon Trine Neptune: Emotions Are Exalted
You have an attractive personality, and you are definitely sensitive, dreamy, and sometimes very artistic. Your spirit is very impressionable, and you possess a rich imagination, but you must not embellish the truth. You feel attracted to water.

Moon Square Neptune: Emotions Are Challenging
You possess a powerful psychic ability, but unless it is appreciated, trained, and used in service, it will be more trouble than gift. Your insecurities and lack of faith and trust in the universe can create peculiar adversities and disillusions. You have weird dreams.

Moon Sextile Neptune: Emotions Are Inspiring
You have innate psychic skills. You are very creative and will work hard to implement creative visions in service to a strong social conscience. Yours is an inspiring presence, and you are fair and tolerant of the failings of others and so a marvelous counselor or healer.

Aspects of the Moon to Pluto

Moon Conjunct Pluto: Emotions Are Powerful
You are a powerful person with definite passions—you are highly sexed—and ideas of what is good and bad, but you can be tyrannical and intolerant of the opinions of others, and vindictive and vengeful if betrayed. You are a great detective, and you are always evolving and reinventing yourself.

Moon Opposition Pluto: Emotions Are Dominant
You love powerfully—often overdramatically so—but respond vengefully if love is not returned in kind or is betrayed. Sex and desires of all kinds dominate your behaviors. You can see into the lives of others but fiercely resist others when they try to similarly pry.

Moon Trine Pluto: Emotions Are Controlled
In you, the desire to nurture and protect is taken to the next level, and you place a mystical level of protection on those you care for. Your financial acumen and organizational skills guarantee success or constant employment in the helping of others.

Moon Square Pluto: Emotions Are Protective
You feel deeply but are inclined to be a loner and do not want to open up or otherwise change your life for another person. You can sense trouble, and anticipatory fears instilled during your childhood make you a persistently vigilant protector.

Moon Sextile Pluto: Emotions Are Helpful
You care about others to the point where you may provide help anonymously. You love deeply and will usually find a satisfying partner. Your superior business sense is based on the search for understanding of all aspects of anything deemed worthy of interest.

PLANETARY AGENTS: HAVING A PLANET ON THE RISING SIGN

The following is an in-depth look at each planet when it conjuncts the Rising Sign of a cosmic blueprint and makes you a planetary agent for that planet or those planets. I mentioned this phenomenon very briefly when I delineated the First House, but your astrological knowledge is now vastly expanded and I can dive much deeper into this fascinating subject. I realize that not everyone has a planet near enough to their Rising Sign to make them a planetary agent, but I wanted to add this chapter to help you see how far your understanding of astrology has come. Also, if you do read the cosmic blueprints of other people, there is a good chance you will encounter planetary agents and this information will be very helpful to them and to you.

Before checking the meaning of having a planet on your Rising Sign or Ascendant, it is important that you closely examine your cosmic blueprint and reread the meaning of that particular Rising Sign. The reason for this should be clear to you by now in your astrological education.

For example, having a planet in Leo and a Leo Rising Ascendant would impart a much different flavor to having that planet in Scorpio and a Scorpio Ascendant. Even more nuanced would be having a Rising planet in the sign next to a Rising Sign. As I noted previously, the signs that are next to each other in the zodiac wheel are more different from each other than are the signs opposite each other.

Mixing and blending a single planet/sign meaning with the Rising Sign meaning is one of the areas where your level of astrological understanding becomes very important in being able to offer helpful guidance. Things get even more interesting if your cosmic blueprint has more than one planet Rising with the Rising Sign. As you know by now, we are all unique individuals, but having multiple planets close to your cosmic blueprint's Rising Sign is an indication of someone who has come into this life to deal with being perceived as more distinct than most other people in their social circles.

SUN CONJUNCT RISING SIGN: YOU APPEAR TO SHINE A LOT

If your Sun sign and Rising Sign are the same, you are a double whatever sign that is. What others see is what they get in terms of your ego, purpose, and vitality. You are an agent for both the Sun's zodiacal meanings and the meanings associated with that Rising Sign. If they are in adjacent signs, others see the traits associated with your Ascendant and may be surprised and confused when they get the traits associated with your Sun sign. In either case, you want people to pay attention to you, to be an important and respected go-to authority. You do not take kindly to being contradicted, ignored, or taken for granted. You may try to overwhelm anyone who seems to be trying to keep you from appearing your sunny and self-confident self. Having the Sun on your Rising Sign means you appear positive even when you might not feel that way about yourself inside, and very few people ever feel sorry for you. Life gets easier for you if you let other people shine their own light as much as you want them to let you shine yours.

MOON CONJUNCT RISING SIGN: YOU APPEAR TO REFLECT A LOT

If your Moon sign and Rising Sign are the same, you are a double whatever sign that is. What others see is what they get in terms of your emotions, emotional intelligence, and habits. You are an agent for both the Moon's zodiacal meanings and the meanings associated with that Rising Sign. If they are in adjacent signs, others see the traits associated with your Ascendant and may be surprised and confused when they see that you actually manifest the emotional traits associated with your Moon sign. In either case, when you are expressing the positive traits of the Moon conjunct your Rising Sign, you can be supportive and a great salesperson because you are able to react in a nurturing fashion, reflecting back to people you interact with their emotional traits, beliefs, and habits. They think you are one of them, and it sets up a rapport conducive to trusting you, unless you have other aspects to your Moon that might negatively affect this. In that case, you may appear moody or display a lack of emotional intelligence or habits that work against you. You may want emotional closeness, but not too close and not all the time, which confuses people. You can appear to misjudge people's motives for wanting to be part of your "family," with you failing to realize that others are reacting to what they see as clear signals you are putting out but that you seem surprisingly unaware of. Mutual support is the goal. Life gets easier for you if you drop your self-protective, defensive shields and compromise.

MERCURY CONJUNCT RISING SIGN: YOU APPEAR TO KNOW A LOT

Being an agent of Mercury makes communications a defining issue in how others see you, the basic function of the Rising Sign itself. Before you can show people the pure expression of your Mercury sign placement as an exemplary method of how to communicate, you are challenged to first get past the communication energy of Mercury focused through your Ascendant as appearing to be information almost exclusively related to you. You are challenged to develop discernment in listening closely and analyzing, another Mercurial pursuit. If you are overdoing the self-referenced too-much-information about what you think and not showing interest in the opinions of others, you are not fulfilling your cosmic mission as an agent of Mercury. Remember that Mercury rules two of the four Mutable signs, Gemini (Air) and Virgo (Earth). Gemini especially is all about two-way communications, and Virgo's attention to detail produces tangible results from applying dexterity and skill. With Mercury on your Ascendant, your communications have to incorporate both signs' attributes. Life gets easier for you if you shut up and listen sometimes.

VENUS CONJUNCT RISING SIGN: YOU APPEAR TO ATTRACT A LOT

This placement is often found in the charts of attractive people, as judged by the standards of their genetic forebears, or in people who as agents of Venus are involved in the beautification of their surroundings, the surroundings of others, and the beautification of the world in general. Venus is the ruler of Taurus, the Fixed Earth sign, and Libra, the Cardinal Air sign. Your lovely, charming, diplomatic Venus on your Ascendant enables you to appreciate, attract, and keep for your use and enjoyment a lot of beautiful and valuable possessions. If you have difficult aspects to your Venus, others may misinterpret your pleasant demeanor as being an act calculated to get you close to and enmeshed with people who can either give you what you want or introduce you to the people who can. And you may display the legendary Taurian temper if and when you are unjustly accused or misinterpreted and your desires are denied despite proving to your satisfaction (and not theirs) that you are sincere. Life gets easier if you want what you have right now.

MARS CONJUNCT RISING SIGN: YOU APPEAR TO ACT A LOT

It should come as no surprise that anyone with Mars, the planet that symbolizes the energy available to our ego to get what it wants, on their Rising Sign/Ascendant appears to have boundless energy, physical prowess, and courage as they constantly move forward to take on everything. The potentially relentlessly pugnacious quality of Mars is strongly dependent on what sign it is in and what is the Rising Sign if they are different from each other. Naturally, there is a big difference between Mars in Aries conjunct a person's Aries Ascendant and Mars in Pisces conjunct an Aries Ascendant. This person is driven to be aggressive projected out into the world versus driven to be sensitive and compassionate and create a utopian world. No matter the sign, the positive expression of this conjunction is enormous creative ability and success potential. It would be a shame to waste your energy fighting battle after battle with those who see you as aggressive and self-righteous. Life gets easier if you dial it down, delegate more, and flagellate less.

JUPITER CONJUNCT RISING SIGN: YOU APPEAR TO HOPE A LOT

The word *jovial* is derived from Jove, an alternate name for the mythological king of the Roman gods, Jupiter. You appear positive and optimistic to a large degree, and you do everything to a large degree—too large, sometimes. You like to do everything in a big way. Your motto is "If some is good, more is better." You have to watch your waistline if you are unable to be moderate with the good things in life, which you appear to attract. Jupiter is the bringer of good fortune, and you appear to be both lucky and a lucky charm for those you deem worthy of your attention. If Jupiter is adversely aspected, you may exaggerate your own importance by bragging and expanding on the truth. This can shock others because you are usually a spiritual philosopher interested in understanding the truth of everything, especially the wisdom of faith, which you have in great supply—faith not only in yourself but also in your future and the future of anyone with whom you share an interest. Life gets easier if you shut up about your great life and take part in some hard work.

SATURN CONJUNCT RISING SIGN: YOU APPEAR TO LIMIT A LOT

The word *saturnine* describes a person who appears somber or even gloomy to others. If you do not feel that way or want others to perceive you that way, you have to make a special effort to appear more grateful for your life and less sardonic or sarcastic. Saturn on one's Rising Sign is an indication of someone who is serious, disciplined, and responsible and knows what they are talking about before they speak. Saturn is the archetypal teacher, and I wish I could say that they are always good teachers, but a teacher has to make learning fun, at least sometimes, and this is not easy for you. If Saturn is adversely aspected, you may have problems loving and valuing yourself, stemming from the problems you had with being given too much responsibility by caregivers when you were young or with your less-thoughtful and more risk-taking friends, who considered you a drag on their good times. Life gets easier if you use your ability to bring order to chaos and put lightening up and enjoying life on your to-do list.

URANUS CONJUNCT RISING SIGN: YOU APPEAR TO BE DIFFERENT A LOT

Life is never dull for anyone who is an agent for Uranus, the planet whose meaning runs the gamut from displaying qualities of the helpful genius inventing new ways to improve society to being "different" and eccentric and all the way to the other end of the spectrum, a disruptive revolutionary instigator. You are an exciting person to be around, usually quite polite, and friendly to everyone you meet, affording them the same honoring of their uniqueness and freedom to be themselves that you demand from anyone who wants to be your friend. (I was going to say "from anyone who is close to you," but closeness is not easy for you.) You are future oriented, though interested in history and your past so you can learn from them to make tomorrow a better day. You have a very special relationship with technology, especially that on the cutting edge. Uranus rules astrology, so people with this placement may be a large cohort of this book's readers. Life gets easier for you when you cease expecting others to be as fearlessly themselves as you are.

NEPTUNE CONJUNCT RISING SIGN: YOU APPEAR TO DREAM A LOT

You're an agent for Neptune, the planet whose meaning runs the gamut from displaying qualities of the selfless, magnanimous, philanthropic helper of the needy to being seen as daydreaming, listening to your intuition, or picking up on the vibes of another and all the way to the other end of the spectrum: someone with an unclear self-image who has trouble withstanding the harshness of life. That being said, if you are not overly moody, feeling sorry for yourself, or just appearing so, you have the capability to inspire faith and hope in proportion to how much of each you do possess. Your psychic powers are quite strong, though if you are feeling vulnerable, you will have to make a special effort not to be overly influenced by your intuition or by the odd people who might be drawn to you because you have some of the qualities of an inspiring spiritual leader. You are living in a heightened emotional state and should avoid alcohol, drugs, or anything that interferes with your gifts. Life gets easier for you when you focus your intuition on navigating daily life.

PLUTO CONJUNCT RISING SIGN: YOU APPEAR TO CHANGE A LOT

Being an agent for Pluto means that your life is all about coming to understand all aspects of personal power—yours and that of others—and learning how to make changes in your life and the lives of others whenever possible. You are perceived as forceful, confident, and someone to be reckoned with, even when you do not believe that about yourself. You can appear judgmental, especially if Pluto is adversely aspected, and your ability to exert power over yourself can be challenged by deep-seated obsessions and compulsions. If these issues are successfully dealt with, your personal power is greatly enhanced, and you become able to transform aspects of your life and the life of those you care about in a seemingly magical way. You must be aware that your appearance might be threatening to those who are not comfortable with their own personal power or with authority. You will not hesitate to exert power over others who threaten you and yours or a project dear to you. Life gets easier when you make friends with your judgmental self.

CHIRON: THE WOUNDED HEALER

The comet or minor planet (depending on whom you ask) Chiron, named after Sagittarius's Centaur with a bow-and-arrow symbol—the teacher of the Greek hero Achilles of Achilles' heel fame—discovered in 1977, inspired the nickname *centaur*, which describes several large celestial bodies orbiting between the asteroid belt and the Kuiper belt.

I always include Chiron as one of the toppings I want my astrology software, AstroGraph, to display in any cosmic blueprint I examine. Why? Because I have seen too many times that the sign and house position of Chiron explains the experience of traumatic events in childhood or youth that may otherwise not be shown. This key to unlocking otherwise-hidden problems in one's chart and in one's life, Chiron, whose astrological symbol is, appropriately, an upright key, links us all to Achilles because his story reminds us that even the greatest hero has their vulnerable spot, no matter how much armor they put over it.

The astrological sign Chiron was in when we were born and the House of our horoscope Chiron occupies in our natal chart can give us astrologers a picture that tells a story of the theme of y/our childhood traumatic experience(s). And that leads us to the answer to the question most people have when I tell them about this astro-reveal of dealing with childhood trauma(s) indicated by Chiron: "How do I overcome it/them?"

Short answer: You don't.

Chiron is known as the Wounded Healer because we're talking about wounds that don't heal but that we carry through our life as a part of our being. It is to remind us that we are wounded and that we must be aware of our wounds and the wounds of others. To get well, you have to know you are sick. It is in the knowledge of our wounds that we find the key to living life, wounds and all.

Chiron is Big Medicine, in terms of the Native American meaning of medicine: that which helps us heal. You learn to deal with and live with them, and you learn that ignoring them only gives them an outsized importance in your daily life.

Chiron returns to the place it was on the day we were born when we are around fifty years old. If you are lucky enough to live to that age, you should not feel it's just you when you find yourself manifesting behavior that you haven't manifested in years, since you experienced significant childhood events: craving foods from that time, doing things you thought you'd never do again, revisiting issues and places and people you thought you'd never be visiting again, being very cognizant of how current events relate to your childhood traumas. It can also manifest as seeing the same thing in others, having their childhood traumatic memories come flooding back, and doing all in your power to either prevent that from happening to you or them or try to help them forget and put it past them. It's impossible, and though you're nice to try, it's all part of the story of your cosmic blueprint.

HOW TO READ YOUR COSMIC BLUEPRINT STEP-BY-STEP

Starry Telling: Creating Keyword Stories Enables It to Speak to Us

1. *Obtain an astrological birth chart—what we call your cosmic blueprint—from AstroGraph.com:*
    - First Things First: Download Your Cosmic Blueprint (page 21)
2. *How are the planetary toppings arranged?*
    - You Can Read a Bit About Your Astrology Chart Right Now (page 24)
3. *In which zodiac sign is the Sun in this cosmic blueprint?* *(page 31)*
    - Make a keyword story about *Sun/sign.*
        - Example: *Sun/Gemini* = Purpose (Sun) is communication (Gemini).
4. *In which house of this cosmic blueprint is the Sun dwelling?*
    - Make a keyword story about *Sun/sign/house*:
        - Example: *Sun/Gemini/Seventh House* = Ego (Sun) is inclined to think, speak, and/or act two ways about (Gemini) committed partnerships (Seventh House).

- *Remember that you can and should arrange the keyword concepts in any order to find as many stories as you can in every keyword story you create from this point forward in reading the cosmic blueprint:*
  - Example: Committed partnerships (Seventh House) incline this person to bring out the duality and/or conflicting ideas (Gemini) that are a part of their ego (Sun).

5. *In which of the Four Elements is the Sun in this cosmic blueprint? (page 63)*
   - Make a keyword story about *Sun/sign/element/house*:
     - Example: *Sun/Fire/Aries/Fifth House* = Purpose (Sun) is to manifest passion (Fire) about being or knowing about the first or only person to bravely act (Aries) to create or give birth to something that has never existed before (Fifth House).
6. *In which of the Three Qualities is the Sun in this cosmic blueprint? (page 99)*
   - Make a keyword story about *Sun/sign/quality/element/house*:
     - Example: *Sun/Taurus/Fixed/Earth/Tenth House* = This person's vitality and sense of self (Sun) are inextricably linked with their ability to prove to themselves and/or other people how strong they are (Taurus) and to keep going according to plan (Fixed) so they can reap the material rewards (Earth) that are the result of their career path (Tenth House).
7. *Which planet or planets are in aspect to the Sun in this astrological birth chart?*
8. *Which is/are the aspect(s) relating the Sun to the planet(s) in aspect in this horoscope?*
9. *Make a keyword story about the aspect or aspects and the planets involved in aspect to the Sun that are supportive of or detrimental to the keyword story or stories you created in step 6 above of the Sun/sign/quality/element/house:*

* Example: *Sun/Taurus/Fixed/Earth/Tenth House* is opposed by *Moon/Scorpio/Fixed/Water/Fourth House* = An internal conflict that must be dealt with by this person (opposition) is that although their vitality and sense of self are inextricably linked with their ability to prove to themselves and/or other people how strong they are and to keep going according to plan so they can reap the material rewards that are the result of their career path, their emotions (Moon) are so intense (Scorpio) and inflexible in what triggers them (Fixed) as to almost overwhelm (Water) their plan (the entire Sun/sign/quality/element/house keyword story) that it seems important that these emotions (Moon) and maybe even facts and events from this person's past (Fourth House) have to be kept secret (Scorpio), possibly buried so deep (Scorpio) along with their past (Fourth House), that the person cannot afford to be consciously aware of the conflict (opposition). But it is possible that these emotions (Moon) are being communicated to the person and to others on the intuitive or psychic-plane level of communication (Water).

NOTE: *Awareness of any astrological energy expression will usually bring with it the ability to successfully deal with any problem if the person is willing to maintain that awareness and do the work necessary to successfully blend the energies (always and all ways!). As the ancient oracles so wisely said, "If you really know your question, you know your answer."*

---

10. *In which zodiac sign is the Moon in this natal chart? (page 69)*
11. *Make a keyword story about Moon/sign.*
12. *In which house of the cosmic blueprint is the Moon dwelling?*
13. *Make a keyword story about Moon/sign/house.*
14. *In which of the Four Elements is the Moon in this nativity?*
15. *Make a keyword story about Moon/sign/element/house.*
16. *In which of the Three Qualities is the Moon in this horoscope? (page 69)*

17. *Make a keyword story about Moon/sign/quality/element/house.*
18. *Which planet or planets are in aspect to the Moon in this chart?*
19. *Which is/are the aspect(s) relating the Moon to the planet(s) in aspect in this birth chart?*
20. *Make a keyword story about the aspect(s) and the planets involved in that/those aspect(s) to the Moon that are either supportive of or detrimental to the keyword story or stories you created in step 14 above of the Moon/sign/quality/element/house.*
21. *What is the Rising Sign of this cosmic blueprint? (page 103)*
22. *Is this Rising Sign complementary or in conflict with the Sun sign of this chart?*
23. *Is this Rising Sign complementary or in conflict with the Moon sign of this horoscope?*
24. *If you are unsure about how the energies of this Rising Sign interact with the chart's Sun and/or Moon sign(s), make one or more keyword stories until you become surer.*
25. *Which planet(s) is/are in aspect to the Rising Sign in this cosmic blueprint?*
26. *Which is/are the aspect(s) relating the Rising Sign to the planet(s) in aspect in this chart?*
27. *Make a keyword story about the aspect(s) and the planets involved in that/those aspect(s) to the Rising Sign that are either supportive of or detrimental to the expression of this particular Rising Sign:*
    * Example: Rising Sign/is aspected by/planet/sign/quality/element/house.
28. *In which sign/quality/element/house is the ruling planet of the Sun's sign in this chart? (page 31)*
29. *Which planet(s) is/are in aspect to the ruling planet of the Sun's sign in this cosmic blueprint?*
30. *Which is/are the aspect(s) relating the ruling planet of the Sun's sign to the planet(s) in aspect in this astrological birth chart?*

31. *Make a keyword story about the aspect(s) and the planets involved in that/those aspect(s) to the ruling planet of the Sun's sign that are either supportive of or detrimental to the expression of this particular ruling planet/sign/quality/element/house:*

    * Example: Ruling planet/is aspected by/planet/sign/quality/element/house.

32. *In which sign/quality/element/house is the ruling planet of the Moon's sign in this chart? (page 69)*
33. *Which planet or planets are in aspect to the ruling planet of the Moon's sign in this horoscope?*
34. *Which is the aspect or aspects relating the ruling planet of the Moon's sign to the planet(s) in aspect in this cosmic blueprint?*
35. *Make a keyword story about the aspect or aspects and the planets involved in those aspects to the ruling planet of the Moon's sign that are either supportive of or detrimental to the expression of the Moon/sign/quality/element/house.*

    * Example: Moon/is aspected by/planet/sign/quality/element/house.

36. *In which sign/quality/element/house is the ruling planet of the Rising Sign of this chart? (page 103)*
37. *Which planet(s) is/are in aspect to the ruling planet of the Rising Sign in this nativity?*

    * Which is/are the aspect(s) relating the ruling planet of the Rising Sign to the planet(s) in aspect in this chart?

38. *Make a keyword story about the aspect(s) and the planets involved in those aspects to the ruling planet of the Rising Sign that are either supportive of or detrimental to the expression of the Rising Sign.*

    * Example: Rising Sign/is aspected by/planet/sign/quality/element/house.

39. *In which sign/quality/element/house are any planets in conjunction with each other?*

40. *Make a keyword story about these planets. Conjunctions and other aspects can sometimes involve more than two planets, so do not attempt to blend three or more planet/sign/quality/element/house keyword stories unless and until you feel you have become proficient with creating keyword stories from the interaction of two planets.*

41. *In which sign/quality/element/house are the two planets that are in the most exact aspect in the chart?*

    * Make a keyword story about these planets.

At this point, you should have a very good idea of the symbolic meanings of the cosmic blueprint in question and, therefore, be able to offer compassionate guidance based on your knowledge and understanding. It may sound obvious, but based on my years of experience reading for other readers, psychologists, and a few psychiatrists, I know beyond a doubt that it is as important that you be as compassionate toward yourself when reading for yourself as you are when reading for other people, if you are inclined to do so. Speaking of which, before you read any cosmic blueprint, pause for a nice, relaxing deep breath and remember the words of the great ancient astrologer, Ptolemy, who famously said, “The stars incline, they do not compel.” I always tell my clients, “There is no such thing as a good or a bad birth chart. This is your cosmic blueprint. Make it work for you.”

ABOUT THE AUTHOR AND THE ARTIST: MONTE FARBER & AMY ZERNER

Monte Farber is an internationally acclaimed author, astrologer, tarot scholar, psychic, and creator of spiritual guidance systems, with more than three million copies of his fifty-plus books and divination tools sold in eighteen languages.

Monte was born in Brooklyn, New York, but his mystical journey began in 1974 when he met his future wife and creative partner, Amy Zerner, whose extraordinary artistry and shared passion for metaphysics ignited a lifelong collaboration.

Together, they've crafted a legacy of accessible, transformative works, including best sellers like *Karma Cards*, *The Enchanted Tarot*, *Instant Tarot*, *The Creativity Oracle*, *The Intuition Oracle*, *The Vision Board Oracle*, and *Quantum Affirmations*, blending astrology, tarot, and mindfulness to empower readers worldwide.

Amy Zerner's visionary art brings a unique dimension to their work through her intricate tapestry collages, which grace the pages of this astrology book and their many other collaborative projects. Her vibrant, symbolic creations—often described as portals to the divine—draw from mythology and mysticism, inviting readers to connect deeply with their intuition and the cosmos. Her process, rooted in a meditative connection to the universe, transforms each piece into a sacred act of storytelling, complementing Monte's words with a visual language that speaks to the soul.

Before his metaphysical career, Monte worked as a location manager in the film industry and as a personal assistant to Michael J. Fox while honing his interactive creations. His childlike curiosity and belief that spirituality and creativity are intertwined infuse his work with playful wisdom and profound insight.

Monte is a former musician and countercultural figure, and his diverse experiences—from performing with his progressive spiritually oriented rock band the Flow, whose album, recorded in the late 1970s, is still sold, to writing astrology columns for popular papers—shape his unique approach to personal growth and self-discovery.

Amy has exhibited her art in many galleries worldwide, and her designs have adorned everything from celebrity clients to sacred spaces, earning her a devoted following among collectors and spiritual seekers alike.

Their one-hour documentary, *Amy & Monte: A Legacy of Love and Creativity*, chronicles their creative journey, showcasing their impact on spiritual self-discovery through their art, books, and divination systems.

Based in Amy's hometown of East Hampton, New York, Amy and Monte remain dedicated to their "Enchanted World," inspiring millions to find meaning and connection through their art and words.

For more, visit www.EnchantedWorld.com.

MANDALA
An Imprint of MandalaEarth
PO Box 3088
San Rafael, CA 94912
www.MandalaEarth.com

Publisher Raoul Goff
Associate Publisher Roger Shaw
Sponsoring Editor Amanda Nelson
Managing Editor Michelle Hope
Creative Director Ashley Quackenbush
Senior Designer Stephanie Odeh
VP Manufacturing Alix Nicholaeff
Senior Production Manager Joshua Smith
Strategic Production Planner Lina s Palma-Temena

MandalaEarth would also like to thank Mark Nichol and Karen Levy.

ISBN: 979-8-88762-178-4

Manufactured in China by Insight Editions

10 9 8 7 6 5 4 3 2 1

Insight Editions, in association with Roots of Peace, will plant two trees for each tree used in the manufacturing of this book. Roots of Peace is an internationally renowned humanitarian organization dedicated to eradicating land mines worldwide and converting war-torn lands into productive farms and wildlife habitats. Roots of Peace will plant two million fruit and nut trees in Afghanistan and provide farmers there with the skills and support necessary for sustainable land use.